The Death of
Joachim Murat

The Death of Joachim Murat

1815 and the Unfortunate Fate of One of Napoleon's Marshals

Jonathan North

Pen & Sword
MILITARY

First published in Great Britain in 2023 by
Pen & Sword Military
An imprint of Pen & Sword Books Limited
Yorkshire – Philadelphia

ISBN 978 1 39905 840 7

A CIP catalogue record for this book is
available from the British Library

Typeset by Mac Style
Printed in the UK by CPI Group (UK) Ltd, Croydon, CR0 4YY.

Pen & Sword Books Limited incorporates the imprints of After the
Battle, Atlas, Archaeology, Aviation, Discovery, Family History, Fiction,
History, Maritime, Military, Military Classics, Politics, Select, Transport,
True Crime, Air World, Frontline Publishing, Leo Cooper, Remember
When, Seaforth Publishing, The Praetorian Press, Wharncliffe
Local History, Wharncliffe Transport, Wharncliffe True Crime and
White Owl.

For a complete list of Pen & Sword titles please contact

PEN & SWORD BOOKS LIMITED
47 Church Street, Barnsley, South Yorkshire, S70 2AS, England
E-mail: enquiries@pen-and-sword.co.uk
Website: www.pen-and-sword.co.uk
or
PEN AND SWORD BOOKS
1950 Lawrence Rd, Havertown, PA 19083, USA
E-mail: Uspen-and-sword@casematepublishers.com
Website: www.penandswordbooks.com

For God's sake, let us sit upon the ground
And tell sad stories of the death of kings;
How some have been deposed; some slain in war,
Some haunted by the ghosts they have deposed;
Some poison'd by their wives: some sleeping kill'd;
All murder'd: for within the hollow crown
That rounds the mortal temples of a king
Keeps Death his court, and there the antic sits,
Scoffing his state and grinning at his pomp,
Allowing him a breath, a little scene,
To monarchize, be fear'd, and kill with looks;
Infusing him with self and vain conceit
As if this flesh which walls about our life
Were brass impregnable; and, humour'd thus
Comes at the last, and with a little pin
Bores thorough his castle wall, and farewell king!

Shakespeare, Act 3, Scene 2 of *Richard II*

Contents

Illustrations

Mono plates

An equestrian portrait of Joachim Murat by Antoine-Jean Gros.

Murat's family by François Gérard.

Prince Achille Murat, Murat's son and heir.

A sketch of Princess Louise.

Queen Caroline, Murat's capable wife.

King Joachim Napoleon as commander-in-chief of the Neapolitan army.

The Austrians enter Naples in May 1815.

A contemporary print of Murat's flight from the coast near Naples.

One of Murat's loyal followers: General Dominique César Franceschetti.

Murat's followers landed at the little town of Pizzo.

Pizzo's castle and the San Giorgio church.

General Vito Nunziante.

Colour plates

Murat enters Ajaccio, Corsica. (*Reproduced by permission of Yves Martin*)

Murat lands on the beach below Pizzo. (*Reproduced by permission of Yves Martin*)

In this violent scene, Murat is captured by the shore. (*Reproduced by permission of Yves Martin*)

Another, more fanciful view, of the taking of Murat.

Murat and his companions in the prison in the castle of Pizzo. (*Reproduced by permission of Yves Martin*)

The most accurate representation we have of Murat's execution. (*Reproduced by permission of Yves Martin*)

An image of the execution, this time by Friedrich Campe.

A proposed memorial to Murat. (*Reproduced by permission of Yves Martin*)

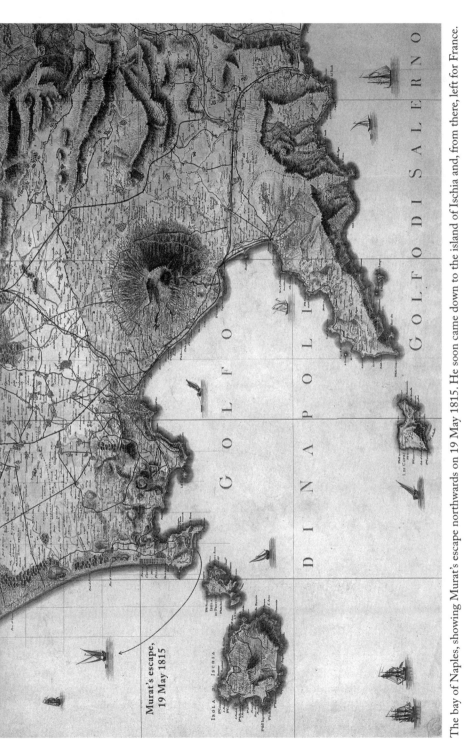

Murat's escape,
19 May 1815

GOLFO DI NAPOLI

GOLFO DI SALERNO

ISOLA ISCHIA

I. DI CAPRI

The bay of Naples, showing Murat's escape northwards on 19 May 1815. He soon came down to the island of Ischia and, from there, left for France.

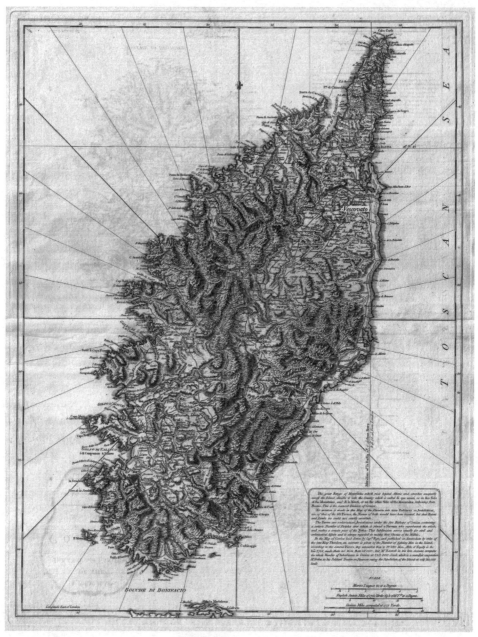

Corsica. Murat was welcomed at Vescovato before heading to Ajaccio from where he took ship to Calabria on 28 September 1815.

Southern Italy. Murat appeared before San Lucido on the evening of 6 October (point 1), then came down before Amantea (point 2) before coming ashore at Pizzo (point 3) on 8 October. From there he hoped to march to Monteleone (point 4) but was captured and confined in the fort at Pizzo.

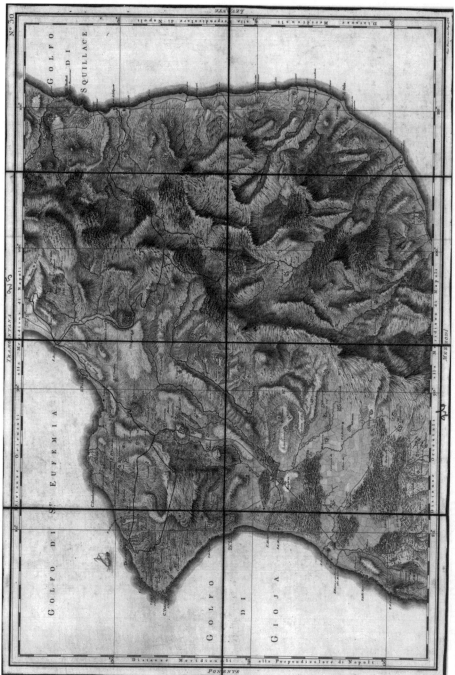

Calabria. This map shows Pizzo and the road to Monteleone, the regional centre a little inland.

Acknowledgements

I could not have achieved this task on my own. I would like to thank Jonathan Abel, Jacqueline Besse (of the Amis du Musée Murat), Giulio Brevetti, Massimo Fiorentino, Vincent Haegele, Sarah Hammell, Marek Tadeusz Lalowski, Vincenzina Logoteta, Renata de Lorenzo, Nicoletta Marini d'Armenia, Jonas De Neef, Antonella Orefice (of the Nuovo Monitore Napoletano), Cinzia Recca, Rick Schneid, Ornella Scognamiglio and Lorenzo Terzi.

Thanks must also go to Barbara Orciuoli and staff at the Archivio di Stato di Napoli; staff at the Archivio di Stato di Cosenza; Verusca Gallai at the Biblioteca Nazionale Centrale di Firenze; Peter Harrington at the ASKB Military Collection at Brown University Library; staff at the British Library; the Warburg Institute; the London Library; and the Archives Nationales de France. The participants at the Napoleon Series and Napoleonic Wars forum – in particular Stephen H. Smith, Thomas Hemmann, Eman Vovsi, Susan Howard and Tom Holmberg – have also provided considerable assistance over the years, as did the anonymous people who make the Bibliothèque Nationale de France's Gallica digital repository of rare texts possible. Also, I should not forget Annamaria Cirillo and her lovely bookshop in Naples.

Those reviewers who commented on the manuscript and who provided advice also deserve gratitude, and particular thanks go to Sarah Hammell for her expertise and diligence and to Yves Martin for his support. Thanks, too, to Harriet Fielding and her professional team at Pen & Sword for producing such an attractive book. As for the contents, I remain responsible for any errors or lapses in continuity.

The process of research, translation and writing has been one that has lasted many years, so my greatest debt is to a constant, and constantly bemused, Evgenia.

Preface

Napoleon famously declared that history is a set of lies that have been agreed upon. He was right in that history often resembles a museum of untruths. But he was also wrong, for there is very little agreement when it comes to many of them. The history of Napoleon and his age bears this out. Even today, the merits and achievements of the central figures of the Napoleonic era are subject to ongoing wars in scholarship in which heroes are constantly being made and unmade, and in which narratives are carefully constructed in one quarter while being hastily pulled down in another.

All the participants who approached greatness, or sought to, in that great age have unavoidably been fed into this seemingly endless battle between fabricating stories and telling the truth. After all, impartial biographies have always been collateral damage whenever writing is carried out to persuade. Napoleon himself has seen his legacy exulted or trashed in equal measure, and lesser personalities such as Metternich, Wellington, Czar Alexander, Josephine or a thousand others have not been spared either, finding themselves appointed to roles in a confected drama and assigned qualities they never had – or never pretended to have – all to win a point, prove a moral or sell a book.

This constant refashioning of reputations, however monumental they might appear, means that they are never really set in stone. They are too subject to the dictates of caprice, prejudice and moralizing to be fixed and constant. Of the reputations we still remember from the Napoleonic era, that of Joachim Murat – Napoleon's brother-in-law and, for a time, favourite lieutenant – stands out. But it is one that, more than most, has been the plaything of those who wish to cast the famous as either hero or rogue. The truth is, however, that Murat was sometimes one, sometimes the other ... and sometimes both.

Joachim Murat was famous as a soldier, but overlooked as a king. And while this dashing figure led a heroic and adventurous life, he was not always the hero in his own adventure. This complicates him as a person, and complicates his legacy too, but such complexity has not prevented successive waves of historians from simplifying his biography into that of a vain soldier, addicted to glory. He was vain, and fought, in part, for glory, but he was also much more than that. He was, for example, an important piece in Napoleon's new ordering of Europe, and also went on to play an unfortunate and controversial role in the French emperor's downfall.

Murat, son of an innkeeper, had won his spurs as Napoleon's finest cavalry general, and then won his throne when, in 1808, Napoleon appointed him King of Naples. He loyally ran this strategically important Italian kingdom with his wife, Caroline Bonaparte, for six years until, in 1814 – with Napoleon beaten and in retreat – the royal couple chose to betray their imperial relation and dramatically switched sides to save their crowns. This won them respite for just one year, but it earned them the undying hostility of those who had once idolized Murat as Napoleon's dutiful general.

Just one year after this dramatic betrayal, an act that still has the power to make one wince, came Murat's equally dramatic but perhaps inevitable fall. A series of miscalculations took the cavalier king from thinking he had secured his dynasty to fleeing his kingdom. After a brief period as a fugitive and exile in a France wracked by political turmoil, Murat then gambled everything in a rash bid to reverse his fortunes, only to lose everything in those final agonies on the Calabrian shore.

The idea behind this book was to chart that rapid and remarkable fall, one acted out in parallel to Napoleon's own disastrous 100 Days, and to try to make some sense of a drama that seemed as sublime as it was ridiculous.

I have tried to present this story as impartially as I can, but with some sympathy for all its victims. As I studied this particular decline and fall, I realized that this episode helps reveal some of the problems inherent in trying to understand how a defeat gets to be presented by those who experienced it, or those who subsequently try to excuse it. This makes Murat's failure worthy of study in its own right, but it is, of course, also an important event given that Murat lost his throne in one of the first attempts to unite Italy. Although contemporaries did not perhaps realize it, the circumstances surrounding Murat's death thus came at a critical juncture between two great historical movements. It brought an abrupt end to the first act in Italy's quest for independence, while also marking the finale of two decades of revolution, war and tumult in Europe.

Still, it is Murat's fate that is central to this story, and failure always lends events a poignancy to which victory can never really aspire. It seems that failure is also more complex; after all, history tends to ensure that charting the rise of any historical figure is much easier than understanding their mistakes. This is just as true of the final months in the life of Joachim Murat. The missteps and miscalculations that brought him from presiding over his flamboyant court in the spring of 1815 to being condemned to death by a court at Pizzo in Calabria just six months later are hard to explain. And that is largely because, unlike success, failure requires a much more careful examination of both the potential causes and the available sources.

However, regarding Murat's precipitous fall in 1815, it is the sources that prove the most problematic. All of those who participated in these events, and who recorded them for posterity or sought to explain them, had axes to grind and sabres to sharpen. Many of those who had taken part or witnessed key events in the fall of Murat, his brief exile and his unsuccessful landing in Calabria to retake his kingdom, were given to obscuring the truth even if they did not quite succumb to telling outright lies. Although some of them did go as far as that. Francis Maceroni has left at least three differing accounts of what he said to Murat the day before the king launched his attempt to retake his throne, while Ignazio Carabelli wrote an entire book to cover up what he was doing in Ajaccio that same evening. Of Murat's loyal followers, General Franceschetti, who accompanied Murat to Pizzo, wrote an account that borders on hagiography and omits anything which might make the writer or his hero look bad. Of the others who sailed with Murat, many would play the same trick, and while they were forced to distance themselves in the depositions taken during their own captivity, they eventually emerged as faithful partisans of Murat's cause (I'm thinking of you, Matthieu Galvani). As for official published records, little reliance can be placed on them when it comes to impartiality. The Minister of Police in Naples even went so far as to claim that they had lured Murat to Calabria to capture him, while a captain of gendarmes in Pizzo claimed the credit for seizing Murat when he landed, a claim loudly imitated by the entire population of that town when they realized that financial rewards were in the offing. We are at least on firmer ground when it comes to unpublished letters and accounts in the archives, yet these too can be drafted to make the writer look good in the eyes of the recipient and, equally, of posterity.

In this story, actions and behaviours have been countlessly reinvented, but so too has what was said and why. It was the style of nineteenth-century histories that every goodbye takes on the character of a rousing speech, while every harangue becomes a fine example of heroic rhetoric. Everyone is putting on an act for the history books, playing to their own gallery, creating a legend, and this is especially the case when it comes to the final moment. Murat's most memorable comment, bravely uttered before that firing squad, a phrase that summed up his bravery as well as his vanity, was 'shoot at my heart, but spare the face'. Well, that turns out not to be true, either.

Such legends, neat little parables of love or hate, do not sit well with writing a history, but they are often imposed by the cultural or political imperatives of the age. Murat's fall is just as subject to those imperatives as the decline and fall of Napoleon's empire, or that of the Romans, even if acted out on a comparatively smaller scale. That process of retelling began at once. No observer writing in 1815 could be neutral on the fate of a Bonaparte, and Joachim Murat was king by right of force of arms and for being married to Napoleon's sister. The restoration of the Old Order in 1815 saw to it that entire cultures were turned against anyone associated with the Bonaparte clan, and Murat, even if he had betrayed his brother-in-law, would be denigrated by court historians because they needed to see him as just another of Napoleon's troublesome revolutionaries. For most people in 1816, it stood to reason that Murat was a fool or knave, or both, and a criminal for having tried to unseat the re-established, and rather divine, order that had restored calm across Europe. Then, in the 1820s and 1830s, when that calm seems to have stagnated, and revolutionary glories seemed preferable to regal ineptitude, Murat began to find himself rehabilitated along with those who had served him. Indeed, such a revival in Murat's post-mortem fortunes was soon to take on even greater import when the dynasty that had killed him, the reviled Bourbons of Naples and Sicily, fell foul of the forces of destiny. For in 1860, the Bourbons were overthrown by an equally rash but rather more successful set of usurpers, Garibaldi's Red Shirts, and shortly afterwards that useless clan found themselves condemned to the same historical oblivion they had consigned Murat to in October 1815. Murat was now lifted out from obscurity and appointed as an early and prescient advocate of that spirit of unity that had seized all of Italy. He became a hero and his failure a tragedy; and because no hero is ever responsible for his own folly or his own fall, the events leading to his execution at Pizzo also now had to be re-examined and excused.

Murat's sudden and surprising elevation into Italy's pantheon of heroes was, no doubt, deserved, but it doomed to failure subsequent attempts to impartially establish his motives and behaviour in the final months of his life. Even if judgement on Murat later gained a little nuance when history began to pretend it was a science, the sober telling of Murat's ruination was always going to be compromised by accumulated stories that were so partisan and so intoxicated with passion.

Despite the distortions and the lies that complicate a task such as this, I have tried to understand what happened in these last, exciting months in the life of a man raised to greatness but ruined by folly, and to present my version of that story. I am sure I must have introduced my own mistakes and misconceptions. I am also certain that this cannot be the final word. Finding more evidence is possible; it may even now be lying on the shelves of some dusty archive. I have done what I can with the sources I have seen. I therefore close this gentle introduction with the admission that the real truth, the absolute truth, concerning these events lies buried with Murat himself. This admission leads me to one more: the body of that regal hero has yet to be found.

Chapter 1

Escape

History may lie, but it can also remind us of some important truths. And one of those, one that must still dog the powerful and the ambitious, is that power is much easier to lose than to win. Kings, princelings and presidents beware; status earned or unearned, handed down across generations, or taken in one, can be lost in a moment.

For Joachim Murat, made king of Naples by Napoleon Bonaparte, that moment came in May 1815. After a rash and unsuccessful attempt at conquering Italy in the spring of that year, he quit his disintegrating army and fled back to his capital, from where he resolved to abandon his kingdom before it could abandon him. As his soldiers quit their colours, and his officials cleared their desks, Joachim Murat, who had ridden at the head of a thousand cavalry charges, prepared to steal away like a thief in the night.

It was the evening of 19 May 1815. Clad in a grey riding coat of the kind Napoleon had worn in happier times, and with his distinctive curly hair cropped short, Joachim Murat watched as a trunk of clothes and another with 400,000 Francs in cash were loaded onto the Marquis di Giuliano's coach. He then bade farewell to his queen – Napoleon's sister, Caroline – stuffed his sash with diamonds and quit the royal palace in Naples. Clambering on board the coach, he ordered his faithful groom, Narcisse Pouleur, to drive them off to the nearby coast and an uncertain future. A month beforehand he had been surrounded by an impressive army and a resplendent staff, but now, in defeat, his entourage was nervous and modest. He was accompanied by his loyal valets Charles Thillier, Armand-Victor Blanchard (known as Armand) and Leblanc. The soldiers serving as escort were General Eugene Bonafous and Colonel Pierre Bonafous,[1] as well as Murat's aides de camp, the Marquis de Giuliano and the 38-year-old General Joseph Marie Thomas Rossetti. Fortunately for us, Rossetti, a

---

1. There were three Bonafous brothers in Murat's service: two soldiers, Pierre (born in 1786) and Eugene (born in 1792), and a naval officer, Joseph (born in 1788). They were the sons of Murat's sister, Antoinette Murat.

normally taciturn man from Turin, was an inveterate diarist and his entry for that night describes Murat's escape:

'At eight the king climbed into the carriage of the Marquis de Giuliano, his aide de camp, and we set off for the caves of Posilippo where fresh horses awaited us, and we reached Pozzuoli at dusk. The officer in charge of the town gate asked us who goes there and I went forward and made myself known to this officer without giving too much away. However, as we passed through the town the king was recognised. The governor sent an officer over to warn us to be careful because some armed peasants had been seen hereabouts sporting red [Bourbon] cockades and it was thought they had been sent from Sicily. The officer added that he would send out a patrol of the Civic Guard to clear the way. The king paid no attention to this and we continued on our way and at eleven that evening we were at Miniscola [*sic*; Miliscola] where Major Malceswki [*sic*; Colonel Malczewski] waited for us with two boats. We waited half an hour more for Monsieur Decoussy [August de Coussy], the king's secretary, and for my brother, who was also coming with us, and no sooner had they arrived than we embarked from a headland and set sail for Gaeta.'[2]

The boats on the beach at Miliscola near Bacoli had been commandeered by Colonel Jan Adam Malczewski and General Armand Millet de Villeneuve. Upon arrival, Murat's party had handed over the coach and their horses to Millet, who returned to Naples, and then made their way on foot towards Torrefumo, before clambering down the sandy cliffs to the waiting boats.

The king was fleeing his kingdom. He had ruled for seven years over his corner of Napoleon's empire. He had tried his best and Naples had nearly flourished under him. Generous to his enemies, endlessly forgiving to his friends, his panache and vanity were more obvious than his intellect. Yet he had earned his crown, or at least done more for it than the stuffed robes of the *Ancien Régime* ever had, although Murat acknowledged that he was only king because of his brother-in-law's generosity. Well, perhaps not generosity, for it was Napoleon's preferred system to place family on

2. Archives nationales (AN), fonds Murat, 31AP/10: 42 (Le Journal du Général Rossetti).

the thrones of conquered Europe, and so, while he reserved the choicest parts for himself and France, he established the Bonaparte clan on thrones vacated by those pretending to divine, rather than imperial, right. In Italy, Napoleon made himself king in the north but needed a lieutenant he could trust for the more unstable south, where the throne of Naples had been vacated, albeit unwillingly, by the congenitally depraved Bourbons. The latter had fled to Sicily, nursing resentment at British expense, so Napoleon selected his lawyerly elder brother, Joseph, for king. Joseph was, however, promoted to Spain in 1808, in a troubling example of dynastic overreach; as Naples could not be left vacant in case the Bourbons attempted a return, so Napoleon was glad to gift it to Joachim Murat and his wife, Maria Annunciata Carolina, the emperor's youngest sister and, by all accounts, the second most capable Bonaparte.

Naples was, for all its faults – poverty, stagnation and a lust for violent revolt – quite a gift. Murat's first kingdom was, at least geographically, impressive, forming the entire south of the Italian peninsula and dominating much of the central Mediterranean, boasting a capital that even some Frenchmen considered second only to Paris. The land itself sustained its people, and had the resources and potential to be even richer and more prosperous were it not for the fact that, hitherto, it had been cruelly mismanaged. And were it not for the fact that, throughout this period, Murat's kingdom laboured under the dead hand of war.

Joachim Murat would not shield Naples from the wars consuming Europe; after all, he was, first and foremost, a soldier. Son of an innkeeper from near Cahors, he had joined the French Army in 1787, but it had been the Revolution that had been his making; promotion and advancement had been especially rapid after he had caught the eye of Napoleon. The Corsican, the Revolution's best general, and soon to be the general in charge of the Revolution, conquered Italy and brought the empires of central Europe to their knees. In every successful battle, Murat had always been to the fore, breaking squares and sabring squadrons, bolstering Napoleon's reputation and aiding his consolidation of power. As the Revolution was forgotten in this lust for glory, the rewards of lands and titles were showered upon the humble Frenchman. Murat found himself marshal, grand duke, Admiral of France and then, finally, king.

Murat assumed the throne as King Joachim Napoleon in July 1808, when, sword in one hand and sceptre in the other, the Cardinal Archbishop of Naples positioned the crown among his curly locks. King Joachim and Queen Caroline began their rule energetically enough, introducing modernizing reforms in the French style, battling stagnation by rationalizing laws and finances, and – no doubt to the considerable regret of the Cardinal Archbishop – breaking the power of the Church through land reform and the adoption of the *Code Napoleon*. They were popular enough,[3] but would have earned more affection from their modernized subjects had they been able to end that other blight on the land: the incessant demand for blood and money to fuel Napoleon's constant conquests. The Neapolitans were not willing to die, or fight much either, for a cause that was clearly not their cause; and when, after 1809, conscription was expanded and Napoleon's demands for troops for his invasions of Spain and Russia increased, Naples bridled at the cost. War closer to home was just as ruinous, and conscription for Napoleon – just as much as Bourbon money and arms – fed an insurgency that ravaged Calabria, Murat's most impoverished province, for much of his reign.

Murat would eventually triumph over that insurgency, but disasters in northern Europe proved a more existential threat. Napoleon had been routed in Russia in 1812, then driven from Germany, and soon he retained control of just France and Italy. As the coalition facing Napoleon closed in on Italy's rich resources, it was increasingly plain to Murat and Caroline that only some dramatic change in fortune might save them. They certainly opted for the dramatic, surprising everyone, and most especially Napoleon, by changing sides. This was an act of betrayal in which Murat lost his honour to keep his throne, but it delighted the Austrians, who promptly seized northern Italy. While the British were less taken with 'the person who currently exercises power in Naples' – after all, they had been hosting the Bourbon King Ferdinand and his queen in exile in Sicily – they were pragmatic enough to see that Murat's treason hastened Napoleon's inevitable end.

---

3. Sir Henry Holland, visiting in 1815, noted: 'The French are extremely unpopular. It does not seem to me that the king is personally disliked, his character would appear to be that of a good soldier, somewhat too fond of personal finery, by no means cruel, generous to those around him, perhaps not very adroit in his personal capacity, but well served by his ministers who are themselves exceedingly well paid. Queen Caroline is obviously a woman of great cleverness and masculine intrepidity; to her it is said that much of the stateliness of the court is due.' Cited in Lady Seymour's *The Pope of Holland House, selections from the correspondence of John Wishaw and friends, 1813–1840* (London, 1906).

Although many of his French officers promptly resigned in protest, Murat mustered enough Neapolitans to make a bold foray into northern Italy in February 1814. There, deaf to Napoleon's curses, his troops took an active, although not *very* active, part in the coalition against the French Empire. They marched northwards accompanied by their king and the lingering stench of betrayal, and had entered Rome and pushed through Parma before Napoleon, beaten in France and ejected from Paris, ended the unhappy war that April and abdicated in favour of his son.

The Allies ignored this optimistic transfer of power to young Napoleon II, sending the first and most dangerous Napoleon into exile on Elba and bringing back the Bourbons so they could trample over all the glory of the empire and undo all the gains of the Revolution. Murat and Caroline therefore found themselves in the unenviable position of being the last of the Bonaparte clan left with a crown, and as the palaces of Europe again filled with those whose only claim to legitimacy sprang from acceptable levels of incest, their position in Naples seemed increasingly tenuous. Betraying Napoleon had not won them any friends, nor had Murat's indiscrete hints that he might like to see himself at the head of a united Italy, so it was not long before Europe's crowned heads were plotting a betrayal of their own. At the Congress of Vienna, convened in late 1814 to allow those mandated by God or Prince Metternich to settle the fate of peoples, Europe's diplomats agreed that Murat would have to go and that Ferdinand of Bourbon, evicted by the French in February 1806, should be brought back from Sicily and restored to his Kingdom of the Two Sicilies.[4] Soon, amid all the polite talk of divine right and the noise of turning back clocks, the delegates were all making barbed jokes that 'Murat will be soon keeping his brother-in-law company' on Elba. On 25 February 1815, Cardinal Ercole Consalvi was even telling a concerned Pope: 'Murat's fall is decided.'

Then everything changed: Napoleon escaped from his island prison. With just a few hundred loyal men, the Corsican adventurer landed in the south of France and marched on Paris to put back on his imperial robes and reclaim his empire. The Congress of Vienna, hesitating briefly between shock and disgust, declared Napoleon outside the law before the

---

4. Ferdinand was Ferdinand IV of Naples and Ferdinand III of Sicily, uniting the two crowns in his person much as the British royal family represented England and Scotland. In 1816, the two crowns were united, Ferdinand becoming Ferdinand I of the Two Sicilies.

diplomats scurried home just as the French, enthusiastic again for their empire, welcomed Napoleon back to Paris as their emperor and turned their backs on the Bourbons as they fled for Belgium and more sad days of exile.

Further south, another ruler was on the move. Murat, who had sensed that the Allies had been sharpening their knives while looking in his direction, sought to turn Allied confusion to his own advantage. He planned to quickly seize the rest of Italy for himself, uniting that tired peninsula under his banners, distracting the Allies at a critical moment and thus easing the pressure on Napoleon. This, or so the king calculated, would win him territory but also, perhaps, earn him imperial forgiveness for the treason of the previous year. Consequently, declaring that the hour of vengeance had come, Murat began to marshal his soldiers along the northern limits of his anxious kingdom while he lingered a little longer in Naples in an attempt to win over his wife to this eminently risky endeavour. Caroline was, however, against a war with the armed might of Austria. She was outspoken in her disdain, even telling one visitor: 'You would think it enough for a peasant from Le Quercy to sit on the fairest throne of Italy; but no, he needs to have the entire peninsula.'

Murat, having failed in a domestic campaign to win over his wife, clambered into an eight-horse carriage on 17 March to begin his military campaign against the vast and equally formidable Austrian Army. However, his plans were rather at odds with Napoleon's own ideas for the coming clash of empires. Napoleon did not then wish to antagonize the Austrians too much, hoping to keep them neutral and to encourage them to return his wife and son from Vienna. His most recent advice to Murat had therefore limited itself to asking the king to distract the Austrians rather than charge directly at them.[5] Murat, however, was in a bellicose mood, and on 26 March his messenger handed Napoleon a note declaring that he would advance to the Po 'to show you I have always been devoted to you and to justify to you and the whole of Europe that the opinion you had of me was right'.

---

5. Napoleon's brother, Joseph, did apparently urge Murat to march north to the rallying cry of 'no more Bourbons!'; Archives Nationales de France (AN), Dossier 335. Lettre du roi Joseph à Murat : transcription d'une lettre chiffrée pour l'engager à prendre les armes. Prangins, sur le lac de Genève, 16 mars 1815.

Napoleon's opinion of Murat was not what it had once been, but in any case, the emperor had no opportunity to give it. The day after Murat's messenger handed Napoleon that defiant declaration, Murat launched his rash war on Austria. With a surprising lack of self-awareness, he declared to his assembled soldiers that they were 'to fight an enemy with bad faith and perfidy emblazoned on their banners', and promptly sent his men forwards under his own standards that, rather appropriately, bore the symbol of a wild and rearing horse. It was an ill-judged gamble, but Murat shrugged away any doubts and did not so much pass the Rubicon as charge right through it, leading 35,000 men[6] against Pesaro and soon seizing Bologna. There, as Murat happily related, the Neapolitans were greeted as liberators and such initial success saw his enemies recoil before him, with the Pope fleeing Rome and the Austrians falling back. Unfortunately, it was a victory of the worst kind – a temporary one – and before long the forces of the concert of Europe composed themselves and returned to the fray, playing havoc across a front that was too broad. The Austrians sent forwards vast reinforcements of infantry, while the British embarked troops in Sicily and cleared their ships for battle. Before such juggernauts of land and sea, Italian support for their uncalled-for champion proved illusory. Even the proclamation Murat published in Rimini on 30 March, promising Italians liberty, independence and freedom from the yoke of foreign powers, failed to rally Italians to his colours. This may have been because this broadside against foreign rule was signed by two foreigners, Murat and General Millet de Villeneuve, but the fact that the Italians could now plainly see tens of thousands of well-armed strangers bearing down on Murat with the aim of driving him from his throne was probably more telling.

As this first, almost farcical, act in the drama of Italy's *Risorgimento* drew to a close, it was becoming clear that the second act would be a tragedy. Napoleon remained unmoved and unmoving, his attention absorbed by the state of France, and Murat's gamble that the British would remain neutral proved illusory too. Indeed, Britain's representative in Italy, Lord William Henry Cavendish Bentinck, Clerk of the Pipe and, less mysteriously, a man who viewed Murat as an irritating troublemaker, relished the opportunity to flush the Bonapartes from Italy and was soon confiding that: 'I think it

---

6. Sir John Dalrymple, a British envoy sent to Murat in late March, said the Neapolitan "infantry is very good, his artillery middling and his cavalry very bad."

may be decisive to the fate of Italy, that Murat should be destroyed. The Austrians must not give up the pursuit until they have killed and eaten him.[7] So it came as no surprise to anyone, apart from perhaps to Murat, when, on 11 April, the Royal Navy joined in the fight, beginning to seize Neapolitan ships and threatening to bombard their ports.

Faced by this Allied revival, and concerned the British would bring the Bourbons and their army over from Sicily and land in his rear, Murat wavered and fell back. Ferrara, Bologna and Florence were all abandoned, and on 21 April Murat's offer to the Allies to negotiate was brushed aside as easily as a Neapolitan division. The despondent king was back in Ancona on 29 April, just a month after he had opened his campaign. By this time, he was dramatically telling all within earshot that he preferred to reign with glory or cease to live. The chance to decide which one it would be came when the Austrians and Neapolitans faced each other at Tolentino on 2 May. There, on the banks of the River Chienti, King Joachim turned to face his less-numerous pursuers and, launching the opening charge in his usual style, nearly broke the Austrian line. Then, however, Murat found that bravery was no equal to skill, and before long his valiant soldiers were falling back before equally resolute, but better-directed, foes. Murat's army, repulsed and shaken, staggered, fell back and promptly began to dissolve, suffering some 4,000 casualties against Austrian losses of about 800.

The fortunes of war had now turned against Murat, and were quickly followed by its disasters. Murat, largely abandoned, fled through the panicking masses and, with just a small escort of light horse under Pierre Bonafous, found refuge in his baroque palace at Caserta. There, in a *palazzo* built by the Bourbons, the desperate king spent a week anticipating his dark future, imagining a thousand projects but without being able to decide on one. His aide, General Rossetti, saw that Murat knew he was defeated and all but damned:

'17 May, Caserta. The king told me that he had asked for an armistice as a prelude to negotiations but that the Austrians had refused to treat with him. He added that he preferred to die rather than abdicate and said that his plan was to go into Calabria where he would place

---

7. *Correspondence of Lord Burghersh*, p. 146.

himself at the head of what remained of his army and his Guards and there hold out for some time against the Austrians.'[8]

Murat did not retire to Calabria to continue the fight until Napoleon could rescue him, nor did he remain much longer among the gilt of Caserta. Instead, he fell back to his capital, sending out his foreign minister, the Duke of Gallo, to delay the Austrians and the British by warning them he still had the stomach for war. Even as Gallo was communicating this exaggeration to Allied generals who could plainly see the enemy making more use of their legs than their stomachs, Murat was resigning command of what remained of his army and was asking his two senior generals, Michele Carrascosa and Pietro Colletta, to get the best terms he could for a ceasefire. When these equally surprised gentlemen asked what terms they should settle for, Murat burst out emotionally that they might 'sacrifice everything save the honour of the army and the repose of the nation; fortune has betrayed me but I hope I am the only one brought down'.[9]

An armistice might win time in this lost war, but the truth was that Murat was a broken man and he had no clear idea what to do when he reached Naples on 18 May. He perhaps hoped his wife would know, and went directly to the palace to see her, bursting in on the surprised Caroline and declaring: 'Do not be surprised to find me alive, I have done all I can to find death.' Their discussion as to what to do next was equally emotional, and Caroline may even have broken the news that she was making arrangements with the British under Commodore Robert Campbell of the Royal Navy to surrender the port should the Allied advance trigger the expected disorder. The loyal Rossetti saw the end was very much nigh:

'When he reached the palace he went to see the queen at once and remained with her for two hours. There we waited impatiently for orders but when he came out and went to his apartments he seemed so overcome with emotion that nobody dared ask him for any.'

Murat's reign was coming to an end. To the north, at Casa Lanza, 4 miles from Capua, generals Carrascosa and Colletta had met the one-eyed

8. Le Journal du Général Rossetti. AN, 31AP/10.
9. Weil, vol. V, p. 200.

Neipperg and the observant Bianchi representing the Austrians, with Lord Burghersh there to see British interests represented. The Neapolitan generals were ushered in for an early breakfast on 20 May, but their hope for a simple armistice to keep the Allies from the capital evaporated as quickly as the morning dew. Burghersh informed his Austrian colleagues that the only agreeable terms to the British would be 'the abdication of Marshal Murat, his placing himself within our power, his releasing from its engagement to him both the Neapolitan nation and army, and engaging publicly not to touch any public money, and, as security of the sincerity of the act as well as for the tranquillity of the country, to cede to us at once all the fortresses of the kingdom'.[10] Thus, among the vines of the Lanza mansion, the Allies insisted on a complete capitulation and the end of the Murat dynasty, in return promising only that 'to Marshal Murat we offer a safe retreat', with the Austrians suggesting it could be in Austria, and everyone agreeing that it should never be Italy. The generals caved in to all the Allied demands, and by four o'clock that afternoon had agreed to sign the surrender with its thirteen unlucky (for Murat) articles.[11] The kingdom would submit, the Bourbons would return[12] and Murat, if he valued his life, would abdicate and hand himself in.

While Murat's kingdom was there for the taking, the king himself had disappeared. Determined not to fall into Bourbon hands or to surrender himself to hostile powers, after his tearful meeting with Caroline he began to prepare for an exit, gathering up family jewels and as much coin as he could find. Although he told some he was returning to the front at Capua, his initial idea seems to have been to leave by sea for Gaeta, an impregnable bastion on the coast between Naples and Rome, and there – surrounded by his children – to somehow prolong the war. However, as his aide Rossetti noted on 19 May, all plans and any arrangements to carry them out were by then clearly in a state of considerable confusion:

---

10. *Correspondence of Lord Burghersh*, p. 164.
11. Metternich, in charge of Austrian foreign policy, and much of Europe's, was disappointed and thought that the Austrians should never have included the British in the negotiations, as they had not done any of the actual fighting. The Austrian emperor agreed, saying he had 'doubts as to the competence of Neupperg [*sic*; Neipperg]'.
12. Prince Leopold was with the Allied army. His father, the ageing King Ferdinand IV, was keeping busy in Sicily with his young wife, the Princess of Partanna.

'At six that morning I was summoned to the palace where everything was as usual; not a piece of furniture was out of place and the king's valets were still waiting for instructions regarding the packing of the trunks. I was introduced and the king told me that he was planning to head for Gaeta today and that he would die a king in the ruins of that place. He ordered me to return to the palace at ten and [stated] that some other individuals had also been ordered to appear. At ten I found the following with the king: the Duke of Rocaromana, Grand Equerry; the Marquis of Giuliano, his aide-de-camp; General of Brigade Bonafoux and Colonel Bonafoux [*sic*], his nephews. The king told us that, reassured concerning the fate of the queen and his children following the capitulation that had been signed by her and Commodore Canspbelle [*sic*], he himself just wished to oppose as much as he could and for as long as he could, enemy progress. However, he felt obliged to quit the capital and, with his usual good humour, dismissed us saying "go, gentlemen, your time is precious but return here at six this evening." As I went out I asked the Grand Equerry whether any orders had been given so that the king might be able to take ship. He replied that no, none had been. As I knew the king was careless when it came to the details of such operations I could see that if no one had asked for orders regarding the means of getting away then we would find ourselves without any boats or oarsmen. This reflection made me turn back and I asked the king whether any order had been issued to secure a boat and he said that none had and, moreover, that no such orders were necessary, for one could always find fishing boats, which was all that was needed. I observed that, in circumstances such as these, it was better not to leave things to chance and particularly when the English controlled the port and the harbour. This made it imperative to embark some way from the town. I suggested the fort at Baja where he might embark in absolute security on one of the government launches that pass between Pozzuoli and Baja. He thought this too near to Naples and that he preferred to embark at Miniscola [*sic*]. I impressed upon him the need to send a trustworthy person to wait for us there and to secure a seaworthy vessel for the voyage to Gaeta. I suggested sending Major Malceswki, his ordnance officer (a young Pole of extraordinary bravery who was devoted to the king) on this mission and the king approved my choice and had me warn the officer to ready himself. That evening, at the appointed time, all those individuals listed above arrived at the palace in civilian attire.'

That evening, as Murat set off in the coach of the Marquis de Giuliano for the beach at Milliscola, still uncertain as to where the currents would take him, he saddled his regent and wife with the unenviable task of handing over the keys to their kingdom. Caroline had tried regally to keep Naples peaceful, and had already sent her children to Gaeta just in case the capital and its revolting inhabitants got out of hand. However, she was soon telling the city's governor, General Manhès, that 'things are desperate, look out for your own safety; the king has just now gone, he is heading to Gaeta or to France. God knows if he shall manage.' She herself had made what she thought were reliable arrangements with the British for her own evacuation, agreeing with Commodore Campbell that she and her suite would find refuge on Royal Navy ships should the situation on land turn dangerous. Campbell's superior, Admiral Exmouth, had been kept informed of this and also felt able to make a guess at Murat's whereabouts:

> 'You will learn that Murat went off last night. He tried to obtain a passport from Campbell, but, failing, is supposed to have gone to the coast and embarked for Corsica in an open boat.'[13]

Murat was indeed all at sea, but, as General Rossetti related, he was just as unsure of his destination as the British admiral. Gaeta, alas, was soon ruled out as a possible option:

> 'At ten that morning [20 May] we caught sight of a large vessel sailing from Gaeta to Ischia. The king bade us approach it and we learned that it was the daily ferry that passed between Gaeta and Ischia. The king climbed on board and ordered the captain to turn back and take us to Gaeta but the man told him that it would be impossible to enter there as they were conducting thorough searches of all vessels and, since yesterday, the place was being blockaded from the sea by a British brig and corvette. Some of the passengers confirmed these

---

13. *Correspondence of Lord Burghersh*, p. 166.

details and added that, yesterday evening, additional British craft had been sighted heading towards that port. Nevertheless, the king wished to ascertain for himself whether there was a way of getting in and so we continued on towards Gaeta towing our two boats behind. At dawn we came within sight of Gaeta and, seeing that it was indeed impossible to slip through the British vessels then cruising before the port, the king had us turn around and land at Ischia which we did at two that afternoon.

'His Majesty was much affected by not having been able to enter Gaeta as he very much wished to embrace his children and he was most concerned as to Prince Achille, whose health had been in doubt for several days. Major Malceswki [sic; Colonel Malczewski], who, whenever there was a dangerous mission to fulfil was always the first to volunteer, asked the king if he could carry any orders to Gaeta and there learn if there was any word of his children. His Majesty was only too pleased to accept his offer and Monsieur Malceswki set off carrying orders for General Begani, the commander of the fort, using one of the boats we had brought from Naples. This brave officer was taken by the British who treated him most horribly.'[14]

While Colonel Jan Adam Malczewski was being subjected to British abuse, his royal master was hovering off the little island of Ischia. Rossetti noted that 'the king did not wish to disembark during the daytime so we waited off the coast and only came ashore at around six that evening, landing on the north-west of the island by the customs house'. Murat then spent the night at the Grande Sentinella inn, reviewing his limited options. It is not altogether clear why he had left Naples or what he had intended to do had he reached Gaeta, but now he was forced to contemplate going even further, perhaps 'to Corsica, Elba or even the coast of France'. The means to do so then put in an appearance, as Rossetti explained:

14. General Rossetti's unpublished diary, entry for 20 May, 31AP/10: 42 (*Le Journal du Général Rossetti*). Colonel Jan Adam Malczewski was sent off to Gaeta, only to be later held by the Austrians at Trieste. He escaped in time to bring Napoleon a letter from Caroline and to serve at Waterloo. Gaeta was commanded by General Begani, who had sworn 'to resist until he received formal notification from King Joachim to open the gates of the fort confined to me'. He would keep the gates closed until 8 August 1815.

'At dawn the Duchess of Coregliano, the king's niece, came before him. She had been taking the waters at Ischia and she threw herself into her uncle's arms and through her tears and inability to speak she conveyed to him just how overcome she was by his misfortune. The presence of the duchess calmed our own fears a little for we heard that she had chartered a Danish ship at Naples which was due to call at Ischia in order to take her to France. It was agreed that the king would embark with her.'[15]

Later that morning, the valet Leblanc shaved Murat and trimmed his copious moustache and whiskers, then, with breakfast digested, the refugees trooped down to Pozzillo to wait for the promised vessel. However, it was here that they heard some bad news from Murat's secretary, August de Coussy. He had been sent to Naples on an errand but now returned with a copy of the Casa Lanza capitulation, 'by which the kingdom of Naples was delivered up to Ferdinand IV'.[16] Murat was devastated that his crown had been handed over so easily and so quickly, but he also now began to worry that once the Bourbons were installed in Naples they would send some of their thugs to Ischia to kidnap him.[17]

Fortunately, escape was approaching from the capital too. Rossetti confirms that 'around two that afternoon we spied a ship heading out from Naples and which was manoeuvring to pass around the island in such a way as to indicate that it was probably carrying individuals attempting to make their way to France'. It was not the Danish ship everyone had anticipated but rather a swift little xebec, the *Santa Catarina* of Elba, hired from a Genoese banker, captained by a Maltese officer and – even more confusingly – flying a British flag. Murat commanded Eugene Bonafous

15. General Rossetti's unpublished diary, entry for 21 May.
16. As reported in General Rossetti's unpublished diary, entry for 21 May.
17. Rossetti was aware of the dangers, writing: 'Although we were reassured by the attachment the islanders showed to His Majesty, nevertheless we knew that a prolonged stay here would risk compromising the king's safety either because our enemies, learning of his presence, would come to seize him or, from the other side of a narrow channel, the people of Procida, for the most parts smugglers who would do anything for gain, and assured of impunity for whatever atrocity they may care to commit, might also descend on the island (and the king had brought a dozen sacks each containing 25 or 30,000 Francs in gold with him). Such reflections therefore plunged us into great melancholy and only the king retained his accustomed attitude, seeming to have forgotten his tribulations and ignoring the danger.' The Bourbons did indeed send some troops and they landed on 27 May.

and August de Coussy to row out to this mysterious vessel to find out what it was. Waving a white handkerchief, they managed to attract the attention of the passengers. These turned out to be friends. There was Eugene's brother Joseph Bonafous, the Duke of Roccaromana (Lucio Caracciolo), who had lost his fingers in the snows of Russia, and the former governor of the capital, General Charles-Antoine Manhès, who had lost his soul putting down the rebellion in Calabria.[18] Manhès was heading for France with his 15-year-old wife and a group of Murat's officers and families keen to escape Naples, as the Allies were declaring any French or Italian soldier a prisoner of war.[19] The request to take on another passenger came as no surprise, but the revelation that it would be King Joachim Murat certainly did. Recovering from the shock, Manhès told De Coussy:

'Go, hurry, tell the king I can't accommodate all of his current entourage but that if he comes now with four or five others, then I await him this evening.'[20]

Murat hurried over, his valet Charles Thillier relating that 'He only took his nephew Eugene, his secretary and one of his valets [Leblanc] but urged the others to follow him and to join him as soon as possible in Toulon.'[21] However, there was room for his luggage, which seems to have consisted

---

18. Madame Cavaignac recites an anecdote about Manhès in which the general told her: 'If Napoleon ordered me to kill my own father, I would obey; Madame, I would then kill myself.' To which Cavaignac tartly replied that 'it would be better to do things the other way around'.

19. The ship had left Naples on the night of the 20th. On board were Manhès' young wife, Laura Pignatelli, and her father and uncle, Manhès' brother, Louis, the judge Pietro Vollaro, two secretaries, five servants and twelve Italian officers. There was also Francesco Pinto (Prince d'Ischitella) and Adjutant Garnier of the gendarmes.

20. *Notizia Storica del Conte Carlo Antonio Manhès*, p. 227

21. The valet Charles has left an account in AN 31AP/21, Dossier 362. The rest of the party did indeed follow on shortly afterwards. Armand had been sent up to keep watch from Madame Rocqueman's cliff-top house and spied a ship. Rossetti adds: 'At seven that morning a vessel from Naples en route for France arrived in the port to collect Madame Vanchelles, wife of the intendent general of the army, there were several eminent French persons on board and they suggested we continue our journey with them. We accepted and, an hour later, we were all on board with the exception of General Bonafoux, the king's nephew, who was to embark on the vessel his cousin, the Duchess of Coregliano, had chartered at her expense.' Francesco Pinto, a former colonel of Murat's Guard Hussars, relates that he, and the rest of Murat's suite, had to wait behind, but that 'A little later another boat appeared and that took all of us on board and we left.'

of a large cloth bag full of sausages, some English cheese and some bread, along with a portfolio, emblazoned with a crowned 'J', some shirts and a few sacks containing 3,000 gold Francs. The passengers lined up on deck to greet him and Manhès welcomed him with a little homily that was sure to go down well, declaring that while danger was all around – the Austrians on land, the British at sea – at least 'we are 40 armed men, brave and resolute; so if destiny smiles on us we shall reach our France in an English brig'.

Murat was moved into the cabin with the family of Manhès and soon reverted to habit, issuing instructions and dreaming up schemes. Gaeta was out of bounds, as was Calabria, for Manhès had a difficult history with the province, having hanged many of its youth, so the general sought to turn Murat's gaze from Italy: 'Tunisia, Algeria, Morocco, England, perhaps, but why return to Naples now?' The winds were even driving them south, but Murat seems to have come round to the idea that his most sensible option lay to the west. He thus directed Joseph Bonafous to set course for Napoleon's France.

Back in Naples, among the debris of Murat's army, Captain Giuseppe Mallardi, formerly of Murat's Guard cavalry, chanced across General Guglielmo Pepe. Following the capitulation at Casa Lanza, Murat's army had been sent off to Salerno to be disbanded and its officers faced an uncertain future. However, the topic of immediate concern for these officers was their departed king. Mallardi asked: 'General, do you think King Joachim will ever return?' 'I don't believe so,' replied the general, 'and even if Napoleon wins the war against the Allies he will never give the throne of Naples back to him.'

Murat was at sea and midway between Naples, where he was unwelcome, and France, where – as he was soon to find out – he remained unforgiven.

Chapter 2

France

On the morning of 25 May 1815, Murat set foot in France. He came ashore at Cannes, close to the point where Napoleon had landed following his escape from Elba. There any similarities ended. Napoleon had quickly marched on Paris and, amid popular acclaim, had restored his empire. Now, some sixty days into his Hundred Days, the Emperor was busy in his capital preparing for war by rallying his people who, with the exception of royalist Provence and the west, responded with considerable enthusiasm. Despite everything that had happened, Napoleon could still charm the French, even passing himself off as a liberator. Murat, however, could not expect the same kind of welcome. Not from the French, and certainly not from Napoleon. Murat had betrayed his compatriots the year before, so Napoleonic loyalists viewed him as a traitor, while the royalists, still an ominous presence in Provence, resented him as just another Bonaparte. As for Napoleon, news of Murat's landing may have caused imperial indignation at the events of 1814 to flair once again, while confirmation of Murat's absurd defeat, combined with him having declared Italian independence when Napoleon still evidently viewed himself as King of Italy, had only made things worse.

Murat's reception that summer would therefore be a little cool. Things got off to a bad start when Pignatelli and Garnier, sent ashore to deal with the port authorities, were told any passengers from Naples were subject to quarantine for ten days. Murat and his companions had to resort to pleading with the prefect at Grasse to be let ashore and for his secretary to be allowed to ride to Paris with despatches for the Emperor. Those despatches, written 'from the bay of Cannes' by a fugitive king to a busy emperor, also contained a rather pleading justification for his conduct:

'Sire, I have read all Your Majesty's letters. It is without doubt a great misfortune that a letter from Joseph, which I received at the time and that, speaking to me in your name, made me decide to commence the operations which were so important to combine with those of

Your Majesty.[1] But I was told to take myself rapidly to the Alps and believing the opening of hostilities useful, I set my army in motion. Your Majesty has since been carefully informed of everything. The Cardinal [Fesch] and Madame Mère must have told you that I was lost ... Yes, Sire, I had to abandon a kingdom that the desertion of 20,000 men in 24 hours placed at the mercy of my numerous enemies, in order to find asylum in some stronghold of the kingdom or in your states. I wanted to throw myself into Gaeta, but my efforts were in vain; twice, I had to renounce this enterprise even though I was on a fisherman's barque, in order not to fall into the power of the English who had tightly blocked this place. Forced to return to the island of Ischia, I had to resort to the first merchant vessel which passed through the channel, the queen having told me that the English did not want to hear of me, and that the Austrians only wanted to treat on the condition that I abdicate and go to Austria as a prisoner of war with all my family. In this dreadful situation, I saw a vessel from the island of Elba, and requested a place for a French officer and, in three days, I am brought to the very same bay which received you three months ago. I decided not to disembark [*sic*; he was told not to do so because of quarantine] and to await the orders of Your Majesty. It is not known in the country that I am here. If you are forced to make war, use me, I offer you my services. If you have hopes of maintaining the peace, and my presence in the empire might complicate your negotiations, I beg you to give asylum to my wife and children, and I am at your feet to beg you to reject me. I maintain all my courage, I feel capable of bearing anything, and the idea of being useful to you through this new misfortune will expand my soul and render it superior to that same misfortune. In this moment, consult only the interest of your subjects; I did so, one year ago, in the hope of better serving you one day. I will not love you less, and the wishes that I have for your happiness will be neither less sincere nor less ardent. I will still be happy by the thought that I have lost for you the throne that you have given me. It is very unfortunate that Prince Joseph wrote to me then. I would have been much more useful to you today, and I

---

1. The letter Joseph Bonaparte sent to Murat urging him to march on the Alps. However, Napoleon was in favour of a more cautious approach, and limited himself to telling General Belliard 'Murat has acted for me; I will support him', but without actually sending support.

would not have been so unfortunate. The queen and my children seek to be brought back to France, they believe me in Gaeta. The kingdom conducted itself marvellously, but the soldiers abandoned me!'

That Murat betrayed Napoleon in 1814 'in the hope of better serving' him one day was preposterous, and while the Emperor knew this, Murat seems to have persuaded himself it was true and sent a very similar letter to his only friend in Paris, the Minister of the Interior, Fouché. That, too, can't have gone down well, even if Fouché held a higher opinion of Murat than Napoleon.

Some of Murat's special pleading did bear fruit, however, and the Sanitary Commission of Cannes permitted Murat's party to spend their quarantine in the only slightly less unwholesome quarters of the Three Pigeons, 'a bad little inn near the town' according to the valet Armand. On the fourth day, the vice-prefect from Grasse arrived and granted permission for the visitors to end their quarantine. August de Coussy was sent off to find a carriage, as Murat expected he would need one when summoned by the Emperor, and then set off for Paris himself, while Murat welcomed the rest of his entourage who had just arrived.[2] Rossetti was surprised to find Murat lingering in Provence rather than gone with de Coussy to Paris:

'We reached Toulon at four in the afternoon. As the king had set off 24 hours before us, and had not called in at Elba, we thought he must have put in at Marseille and, from there, continued on to Paris in order to see the Emperor. Accordingly, we made our own preparations to follow on the following morning. However, General Belliard, who came in during the day, persuaded us to wait for the arrival of the queen who, according to the terms of the agreement

---

2. Murat would describe the key members of his entourage in France thus: 'The Marquis de Giuliani is a young man trained by me and who showed what he was made of during the Russian campaign. He is utterly devoted to me. The Duke de Roccaromana, as noted for his refined manners as he is for his stylish dress, is someone I hesitated to attach to my household but he proved me wrong by showing extraordinary devotion. From then on that good Roccaromana was always thus, he saw his only son killed at Tolentino and asked that he might accompany me into exile. I shall never forget such noble devotion. As for the brave General Rossetti, he was my friend but it took me some time to grow accustomed to his rather brusque character but one must judge the character of a man when being tested and the queen had good reason to call this man The Imperturbable. What is more, had I heeded his advice, I would have been spared many regrets.'

between her and Commodore Campsbell [*sic*], was soon expected at Toulon. We therefore prepared some lodgings and General Belliard, having made his carriage available to us, we were able to prepare for the arrival of the queen and her suite. The Duchess of Coregliano and General Bonafoux also arrived that day and they also chose to wait in Toulon for the queen.'[3]

Murat was lingering in the hope that Caroline would come to join him. But she was not coming. He had left her in Naples and her plan had been to trust to the British should the Neapolitans rise against her or the Bourbons seek to ensnare her. Her convention with Commodore Campbell even allowed her the hope that she might be evacuated to France. However, events – and British perfidy – would conspire against her and send her in a completely different direction.

When the capitulation at Casa Lanza was signed, the Allies were authorized to seize control of every strategic point in the kingdom on behalf of the soon-to-return Bourbons. There was some disorder when the news reached the capital; the customs house was burned down and some prisoners escaped from prison, and whatever remained of the troops loyal to Murat began to mutiny or desert. Caroline, acting as regent, had tried, on 19 May, to rally any loyal supporters, even proclaiming a constitution, something her friend Lord Holland had helped draft, but it was too late. Popular sentiment, combined with the imminent arrival of the Austrians and British, made it clear the game was up.

Caroline prepared to carry out her own plan for an exit. As early as 13 May, she had sent her children and their pet dog to Gaeta in the care of her mother and her uncle, Cardinal Fesch, along with their governesses, Mrs Pulsford and Miss Davies. Then she instructed Count Mosbourg to treat with the British flotilla hovering off the coast, requesting she be allowed asylum on their ships, with anyone else who might need to seek shelter, should Naples turn into a bloodbath as it had when the Neapolitan Republic had fallen in 1799. Commodore Campbell was pleased to comply and welcome her aboard HMS *Tremendous*, and, or so he said, he would be pleased to have her taken to France. In return, she would need to surrender the Neapolitan fleet, port and all military supplies. Caroline

---

3. General Rossetti's unpublished diary, entry for 29 May.

was in no position to haggle, so the British were handed the Neapolitan warships, and on 20 May, Caroline and her suite[4] duly came down to the Castel Uovo to claim their side of the bargain. The British felt obliged to accept them onto the *Tremendous* and kindly refused to impose a stringent baggage allowance, allowing her to bring on board such 'essentials' as busts of Pericles and Cicero, trunks of jewels and a one-horned cow named Caroline that would provide milk for the crew. The British then secured the Neapolitan forts, sending their marines through crowds shouting '*lo mariuolo e fuiuto*' (the scoundrel has gone), just as the Austrians also began to arrive, bringing a measure of order in their train along with young Prince Leopold of Bourbon, representative and sixteenth child of the libidinous King Ferdinand IV.[5]

Caroline's plan, and any residual faith in British honour, quickly came undone. The Austrian generals now occupying her palace insisted that she be taken to Austria with her children, more or less to act as hostages for Murat's future good behaviour, even though the British naval officers had already promised Caroline that she would be taken to Antibes. The Duchess of Bedford, Georgina Gordon, one of the Murats' new British friends, had even decided to accompany her to France and act as her interpreter for the voyage. Even more importantly, Admiral Pellew, Admiral Exmouth, Campbell's dour superior, arriving to take charge of the British contingent, was soon writing: 'Captain Campbell receives the Queen, and I shall have her landed about Antibes and I should think Ferdinand will rejoice to permit all her partisans to go away.'[6]

However, as Caroline watched the city illuminated from the deck of a British warship and listened to the crowds cheering the Allies just as they

---

4. She was accompanied by Count Mosbourg, Giuseppe Zurlo, David Winspeare, General Pierre Henry Gaston de Livron with his aides-de-camp Pfeil and Drouville, and General Francesco Macdonald, Murat's Neapolitan minister of war descended from Jacobite exiles. The rest of her household consisted of Mademoiselles Lavernette and Tarlet, Dr Lamparelli, secretaries Guibot, Soisson and Monsieur Mary, Madame Marie Charlotte de Courval and her daughters, Madame Soisson, fourteen servants, two cooks, two assistant cooks, a kitchen manager, seven chambermaids and six grooms.
5. Giuseppe Mallardi, a former soldier, said that on 21 May, 'at around four that afternoon, Prince Leopold the Bourbon swept down Via Toledo with a large entourage and he went to the Church of Spirito Santo to give thanks to God for the reconquest of the kingdom (done by the Austrians)'.
6. *Correspondence of Lord Burghersh*, p. 167.

had cheered her the week before,[7] Lord Burghersh and General Neipperg were agreeing to break the promised agreements. Tearing up principles and good faith, they sought to prevent Caroline and her children from joining her husband or her brother in France, and from there launching a bid to return to Italy with more than just a few dozen servants in tow. Old Pellew put up some flaccid resistance, mumbling something about taking Caroline to Malta or Corfu, or perhaps even London, but he was easily brushed aside. She was instead to be sent to Trieste, where she would be interned in Austrian lands in sufficient luxury to compensate for a life of considerable tedium. General Neipperg, who would later run off with Napoleon's wife, wrote triumphantly to Vienna boasting to Prince Metternich, that maker and breaker of nations – and a man who had tender feelings of his own towards Caroline – that 'this fine campaign of 28 days has now brilliantly ended by placing into our power as hostage a queen who was always more the king of this land than her mad husband'.[8] Caroline objected, strongly, to this reversal of fortune but, still on Campbell's *Tremendous*, she was taken off as a hostage to Gaeta to collect her children. Then with Achille, Laetizia, Lucien and Louise on board, and with Laetizia acting as interpreter for the captain, the Murat family sailed eastwards into exile.[9] They disembarked at Trieste on 8 June, settling in to the Casa Schneitzer, and Caroline assumed the fetching title Countess Lipona,[10] beginning a letter-writing campaign demanding that she be permitted to leave for France. As she waited, fruitlessly, for such permission from the Austrian emperor, she wrote to her imperial brother in Paris. In one such letter, intercepted by Baron Hager's discrete

---

7. The diarist Nicola recorded that 'boats carrying the populace surrounded the ship where the wife of Joachim could be found. They shouted out all kinds of insults under the eyes of the English who just laughed about it.'
8. Weil, vol. V. p. 249. Not everyone was delighted with the outcome. The consternation of some British friends then in the capital – not only the Bedfords but also Lord Sligo, Sir Henry Holland, Edward Harley, Earl of Oxford, and his wife and former lover of Byron, Jane Elizabeth – was palpable, and they told Exmouth they would raise complaints in the House of Lords. The year before, in November 1814, Oxford had been arrested in Paris carrying secret correspondence for Murat.
9. Exmouth warned Campbell 'be very careful to make sure that Murat does not creep on board; rejoin the squadron as soon as your mission is terminated.'
10. An anagram of Napoli. She had originally thought to be called the Comtesse de Bari, but her friends said it sounded too Bourbon.

secret police,[11] she expressed dismay that she was still ignorant of her husband's whereabouts:

> 'I am in the most dire uncertainty when it comes to the fate of the king. Has he managed to rejoin Your Majesty? I do not know. I have had no news of him since he left. Your Majesty can imagine how much I am suffering.'

She also sent out a letter to that lost husband, also intercepted, which she hoped would somehow reach him, wherever he was:

> 'I have had no word of you since you left. I am so very sad, so worried. The children, as well as I, hope our stay here will be a short one. We need to see you, to come and look after you. We talk of nothing else and all that we desire is you.'[12]

She still hoped she would be allowed to leave for France or he would escape to find her in Trieste and they might then settle around the Austrian court in Prague.[13] But neither would happen. She would be kept in her gilded cage, slowly worn down by mounting debt and kept under constant surveillance. Her husband the king had gone, and her kingdom now belonged to others. King Ferdinand, that anachronistic perversion swathed in lace and ermine, had made the crossing from Sicily to reclaim Naples as his own, entering his capital on 17 June after nine years of exile. Lord Burghersh, recently awarded the Order of St Ferdinand – which, ironically, would be stolen from him in Paris a month later – was there to lavish obsequious praise on this fine example of royalty:

---

11. Caroline was controlled quite closely. She was permitted French newspapers, but only if military events were redacted or crossed out. Baron Hager employed two agents, Spiegelfeld and Fortunati, to watch her, and they managed on 19 June to intercept two of her servants, the boy Tarlet and François Terlin, carrying thirty-three of her letters addressed to Napoleon, Joachim, her family and Fouché.

12. She went on to tell him: 'We get up at six in the morning and study until ten; we eat and then walk until noon. Once we have returned we work until six and then stroll a little or chat until seven. We dine then play a little after dinner and then we go to bed and do the same the following day. I am pleased with Achille and he is well, Count de Mosbourg pays close attention to him and better results could not be hoped for.'

13. The Austrians considered sending her to Ljubljana, Gratz, Brunn (where her sister, Elisa, was) or Prague. However, that September she rented Hainburg, a small but comfortable chateau.

'The king entered Naples at the head of his own troops together with the Austrians and British, who filed before him on his arrival at his palace. The constant attachment the Neapolitan people are known to have ever borne their legitimate sovereign makes it unnecessary to detail to your lordship their joy at his return. His Majesty reassumes the government of his country beloved and respected by all classes of his subjects, and looked to by them as their security for a reign of justice and tranquillity.'[14]

---

14. *Correspondence of Lord Burghersh*, p. 186.

Chapter 3

Exile

Murat, the fugitive king, was in Provence, where he would experience neither justice nor very much tranquillity, although the deafening silence from Paris, where Napoleon still nursed some resentment towards him, might be mistaken for such. Murat had lost his throne and was about to lose his family, but he had the optimism of a brawler and was resolved to rebuild something from the wreckage of his fall. He sought out some of his old comrades, perhaps hoping they would ease him back into Napoleon's good graces, and thus wrote to Marshal Guillaume Brune, a man who had shared many a campfire with Murat and who was glad to come over for a more luxurious dinner. Brune's aide-de-camp, Louis Bourgoin, saw them meet on the beach at Cannes:

'The marshal [Brune] had left Toulon at around eight or nine in the evening. He travelled through the night. The following morning, as he approached the village of Cannes, his aide-de-camp caught sight of a group of people coming towards the coach and amongst them one could distinguish the prince [Murat] dressed in rather fine civilian clothes, coloured boots and a round hat over his black, wavy hair. The aide-de-camp had to wake the marshal because the heat and fatigue had sent him to sleep. He climbed down from the coach and Murat hurried over and they embraced. After they had greeted one another they went towards the battery by the beach, situated to the right of the inn where the prince was staying, and they held a conversation which lasted for about an hour. After which General Merle arrived.'[1]

The three then had a cheerful evening, especially when some unexpected guests also reached the inn:

---

1. Bourgoin, Louis, *Esquisse historique sur le maréchal Brune, pub. D'après sa correspondance et les manuscrits originaux conservés dans sa famille* (Paris, 1840).

'His Majesty welcomed Marshal Brune there whilst the 14th Light Infantry Regiment and a squadron of the 14th Chasseurs came to shout "Long live the Emperor, long live Prince Murat!" below his windows.'[2]

More supporters were soon gathering. Some French officers who had remained in Neapolitan service sailed in from Genoa, and then on 9 June General Nicolas Philibert Desvernois arrived with an entire transport of exiles. He had held onto Calabria for a full week after Murat's flight, eventually surrendering the province to the courtly General Nunziante, and now he reached France with his wife, thirty-nine French officers and ninety-five soldiers. There were also a handful of Neapolitan refugees, including a certain Matthieu Galvani, and assorted Italians fearing Bourbon revenge. As proof of their undiminished loyalty, their ship was flying King Joachim's flag.

   This must have stirred Murat's blood, but he was soon fretting that his own family had still not arrived and that there had been no word from them. This upset and angered Murat, as Rossetti noted:

'One other circumstance contributed greatly to the king's anger and that was the delay in the arrival of the queen and his children. In fact, according to the terms of the agreement with Commodore Campbell, she should have embarked on a Neapolitan ship on the day following the Austrian entry into Naples in order to be transported to France. The Austrians had entered on 22 May but still the queen had not yet arrived.'

General Desvernois told Murat that he had seen Queen Caroline and Murat's children sailing through the straits of Messina and on to Trieste, which confirmed Murat's fears. Nevertheless, like any successful subordinate, the general also raised Murat's hopes. With Murat's imagination washed by wine during one of the nostalgic dinners that followed, Desvernois thought it opportune to speak of the loyalty of those who had been left behind. Indeed, as they sat on the veranda one evening, Desvernois went

---

2. Account by the valet Armand, AN, 31AP/21, Dossier 361, entitled 'Relation manuscrite d'Armand : sur la tentative de débarkment de Murat au Pizzo et sur sa mort'. His colleague, Charles, makes the same claim in Dossier 362.

as far as to promise that 20,000 Calabrians were just waiting for Murat's return and would eagerly take up arms to serve him. Soon he was boasting that they would both lead '150,000 intrepid and devoted patriots' and chase the last Austrian soldier from Italy. Murat responded to this exaggeration with a smile, as well he might, but added that, regarding the Austrians, he hoped 'those wretches eat lead', but only after Napoleon had appointed him to command in Italy.

Such flattery at least won Desvernois the title of count of the kingdom of Two Sicilies and, without any sense of irony, governor general of Calabria.[3] Rossetti, far less verbose, and hence enjoying fewer favours, may have had Desvernois or courtiers like him in mind when he confided to his diary that:

> 'Nearly every day we received news from Naples as it was brought in by French citizens landing at Toulon or Antibes. For the most part these were officers who left in order to avoid being held as prisoners of war by the Austrians. They knew the king was at Toulon and so they approached him for assistance. In order to flatter the ego of their benefactor they told a thousand absurd tales and made him believe that he had a large number of supporters at Naples, that Calabria, not wishing to accept the sovereignty of Ferdinand, had risen for him. All this was believed by a king too eager to hear such things and his imagination ran away with him, and he was soon believing that all he had to do was to land in his kingdom and the crown would be his.'

But it seems he also had another, and quite specific, example in mind:

> 'General Franceschetti had come over to Toulon a couple of days ago. He was a rather excitable fellow, with an imagination prone to exaggeration, and he was soon able to embroil the king in some of his schemes and he had such an effect on the king that when the king emerged from his meeting with the general he talked of nothing else but the revolt in Calabria and the effect that his presence there would have on it.'

---

3. Murat also promoted six of the French officers who had come with him, although rather less grandly, and the officers were given a month's pay; each non-commissioned officer was given 50 Francs and each soldier 30 Francs.

Such tales were pleasing to a monarch for whom support had evaporated so quickly a few weeks before, but what would really have delighted Murat was a hint from Napoleon that he had been forgiven. Napoleon had raised him up from subaltern to marshal, made him Grand Admiral of France, Grand Duke of Berg and Cleves and, of course, King of Naples (and, despite it being occupied by the British and the rival claimant, King of Sicily), and he certainly had the power to now rehabilitate his wayward subordinate if he so wished. This might have been in the form of a public gesture of forgiveness, perhaps by making Murat a general in the armies the Emperor was mustering to fight the powers that had declared Napoleon an outlaw, or at least by inviting him to Paris. For now, however, Napoleon showed no desire to see Murat, let alone employ him, even on one of the secondary fronts.[4] Indeed, at this critical time for the French military, Napoleon was still not done with his criticisms; these would soon be communicated to the former king through a seemingly friendly intermediary, Jean-Louis Amable de Baudus of the Foreign Office. Baudus had once tutored Murat's sons, the wayward Achille and the vain Lucien, but this new role of communicating Napoleon's ire to Murat would prove an even greater challenge.

Caulaincourt, Napoleon's Minister of Foreign Affairs, briefed Baudus that Napoleon wished him to convey 'in language of courteous restraint how greatly the Emperor regrets that the king took the offensive on his own initiative and before any steps had been taken to instruct the loyal subjects of Italy how they were to act'.[5] Having thus hinted that he, Napoleon, was King of Italy, the Emperor then advised Murat to retire to Sisteron, or to a country house at the spas of Greoux-les-Bains, and there wait for his wife. He was also told, with less courteous restraint, that when she arrived she would be permitted to come to Paris alone, 'so the public might first accustom themselves to his disgrace'.[6]

---

4. This was not just for personal reasons, although Napoleon was sometimes wary of family feuding and, after all, in this case, he had been betrayed by both his brother-in-law and his sister. It was also because some in the French Army also proved resentful. When Murat's companions had arrived in Provence, those French officers who had remained in Neapolitan service were viewed as traitors by soldiers loyal to Napoleon, all on account of Murat's betrayal of the cause the year before. There were duels between the new arrivals and officers of the garrison of the 9th Line. Consequently, Napoleon could not be sure that Murat would be welcome among his own marshals and staff officers.
5. Masson, Frédéric, *Napoleon et sa famille*, volume XII.
6. Napoleon thought that Caroline might be permitted to establish her household at Compiegne.

Baudus reached Cannes on 9 June and soon had his difficult interview with Murat. Rossetti heard, but wasn't surprised, that it had not gone well:

> 'Monsieur Peborde [Baron Jean de Peborde, the king's former doctor], who met us on his return from Cannes, told us that the Emperor had not replied to the letter from the king but that Monsieur Baudus, the governor of the king's children who had returned to France in 1814, had been sent by the Duke d'Otranto [Fouché] to see the king. Monsieur Peborde added that the king was much hurt by the silence of the Emperor and he openly complained to Monsieur Baudus and found that his justifications for the Emperor's silence were far from being satisfactory.'[7]

Baudus, however, earned the trust of those who sent him by managing to placate Murat with some promises of better times to come:

> 'Monsieur Baudus shared that, in the current circumstances, the Emperor dared not summon him as he was a sovereign who had borne arms against France in 1814, therefore his decision was to keep the king until military affairs were more settled, which would be relatively soon.'[8]

Napoleon's mind was elsewhere. He was, after all, about to launch his armies into Belgium, an offensive that would certainly settle military affairs, although not in the way Napoleon intended. So Murat decided he must be patient and wait. He determined to do so in a little more comfort, as Rossetti narrates:

---

7. General Rossetti's unpublished diary, entry for 9 June. Rossetti states that Murat suspected Baudus was being used by hostile factions to frustrate a return to Paris: 'I found the king most displeased with Monsieur Baudus who had followed him to Toulon but whose suspicious behaviour raised some suspicion in the mind of the king. I observed to the king that the frank and loyal character of Monsieur Baudus, and his attachment to the children of His Majesty, who had been his charges, and his marked zeal to serve His Majesty, should all place him above any suspicion. I added that, in any case, I did not see any possibility of him causing any harm unless he was acting on instructions or orders to oppose whatever resolutions the king might determine upon, and, even then, I felt that Monsieur Baudus was incapable of accepting such a commission. The king seemed satisfied with my observations although his doubts regarding Monsieur Baudus did not entirely disappear.'
8. General Rossetti's unpublished diary, entry for 14 June.

'His Majesty determined to come to Toulon in order to rent a country
house in the vicinity. To that effect we rented a pretty place a few miles
from Toulon and which belonged to General Lallemand [*sic*; Admiral
Zacharie Allemand]. This country house was known as Plaisance.'

Plaisance, a kilometre from Toulon, would constitute a pleasant enough
purgatory.[9] There was talking and eating among the orange groves and
figs, and Murat's 20-year-old niece, Duchess Jeanne de Coregliano, proved
a charming host for this impromptu court. But the absence of his family
grated, although it soon became clear to Murat that they would not be
joining him:

'A merchant ship which had left Naples on the 3rd, and carrying
Monsieur Serralonga, an official from the king's cabinet, along with
a few French passengers, came into port at noon [13 June]. Monsieur
Serralonga had obtained permission to leave in order to be with the king
but he informed him that Lord Exlemout [Exmouth] had refused to
ratify the agreement made by Commodore Campbell and that, instead
of having the queen sent to France, as the agreement stipulated, in a
Neapolitan vessel, she, with the children, was to be sent to Trieste on
board an English vessel. This sad news was like a bolt from the blue for
the king as he had been more affected by the separation from his wife
and children than he had been by the loss of his kingdom.'[10]

Murat had suspected as much, but even so, this was bad news and, given the
recent snub from Napoleon, he even went as far as blaming the Emperor
for his misfortune, telling Madame Récamier that 'I fought for the emperor
and it is for him that my wife and children are in captivity'. His resentment
was evidently festering that idle summer, and Desvernois also heard him
rant how:

'The Emperor has left me languishing here whilst I should be at his
side, and my sword would have brought such support to him against

9. Francesco Pinto recalled: 'When we reached Toulon we rejoined the king but he went to
stay in Lallemand's [*sic*] villa whilst we remained in a hotel in Toulon for a month. The king
had written to the Emperor asking that he might come to join him in Paris.'
10. Diary entry on 13 June by Rossetti.

his enemies. Separated from my wife and children, the Lord knows if I shall ever see them again.'

Napoleon was unmoved. The best that Fouché could do for his friend was to advise still more patience, but also to come a little further north. Fouché's advice reached Murat on 17 June, as Rossetti noted:

'Captain Gruchet, on the king's staff, arrived from Paris bearing despatches from the Duke D'Otranto in which he confirmed all Monsieur Baudus had said concerning the Emperor's position and begged him to be patient concerning the Emperor's silence. He advised him to leave Cannes (he thought he was still there) in order to come to Lyon and to there await the outcome of the great events then unfolding.'

Fouché, Minister of Police, had, like Murat, been destined for the Church, but the Revolution held out other possibilities for power over mortals and this arch-intriguer had subsequently wormed his way upwards through Republic, Empire and kingdom to high office. He was was loyal to his friends, if unforgiving to his enemies, and seemed to realize that Murat would only prosper if he had access to some resources. He therefore worked with Murat's secretary, August de Coussy, to untangle the legal knots preventing the restoration of Murat's property, most significantly the family estates of Neuilly and Villers, with a view to giving him not only somewhere to live – and in better style than the inns of Provence – but also the means to eventually reappear at Napoleon's court.

Murat's own attempts to ingratiate himself with the Emperor may have been counter-productive. On 19 June, as the French were fleeing the disaster at Waterloo, Murat sent yet another letter to Napoleon chiding him for keeping him waiting, sulkily telling him 'may your ministers make positively known to me the place of my exile; I will go there without a murmur'. He concluded: 'It is hard and not at all easy to explain to the French and to their enemies that Napoleon denied the honour of fighting for France when she was most in danger a prince who had just lost his throne and his family.'

The trouble was, France was in even more danger now. And Napoleon was also about to lose his own throne and family.

Chapter 4

The White Terror

Napoleon had travelled down the bitter roads from Waterloo, with his defeated army trailing behind him, but he still thought he could conjure up other armies and repel the advancing Allies. As he was busy making his arrangements from Paris, demanding more men and poring over his maps, an overlooked manoeuvre was taking place far to the south. There, Murat was advancing from Provence. Quite ignorant of what was unfolding in the north, he had decided to follow the advice of his friends and establish himself at Lyon. Rossetti says such a plan was agreed on a week after Fouché's friendly message had arrived:

> 'Monsieur De Coussy [back from Paris] and the members of the king's household (with the exception of Leblanc, the king's senior valet) left Toulon in order to rent a house in the environs of Lyon. Matters had been arranged such that the king would set off 48 hours later and that his groom, Narcisse, should wait for him at Lyon with fresh horses so that he could be conveyed to his new residence. Monsieur De Coussy should then set off for Paris and he would take the valet Armand with him in order to ensure that he had someone with him who could be used as a confidential person should the need arise.'

The plan was to settle near Lyon and there wait until Fouché could engineer the hoped-for reconciliation between king and emperor. So Murat's party set off on the evening of 25 June, but, as Rossetti narrates, early the following morning, history caught up with them on the road:

> 'At six in the morning, as we were changing horses at Aubagne, the last staging post before Marseille, the postmaster advised us not to continue along that route as he had heard that a revolt had broken out at Marseille and that the garrison had been obliged to withdraw into the forts and that the entire population had risen up against the

imperial government and raised the white [Bourbon] flag. However, as the king neither wished to halt nor retreat, we continued on but had scarcely gone another mile and a half when we encountered the garrison of Marseille marching for Toulon under the command of General Verdier. This general informed the king that when news reached Marseille that the battle of Waterloo had been lost the town had, at around one in the afternoon, risen in revolt and any isolated soldiers had been massacred in the streets.'

Defeat at Waterloo had proved fatal for Napoleon's cause, and it had not taken long for those royalists in sympathetic parts of the country, namely the western coast and much of Provence, to rise up and demand the re-restoration of the Bourbon royal family. At Marseille, which had always loathed the Emperor and the ruination his wars had brought to its commerce, the royalists had hastily formed a committee on the afternoon of Sunday 25 June, with the mayor, Raymond, and the governor, Colonel Borely, declaring fealty to Louis XVIII. This triggered a rising and a settling of scores that, on account of the widespread violence, would soon be dubbed the White Terror. The first to feel the effects were the unfortunate Egyptian and Syrian refugees of Marseille, many of whom had served in Napoleon's Mamelukes. A large number of them were killed and the mob easily overwhelmed resistance, such that even General Verdier and his garrison felt it prudent to evacuate the town.

The mob had turned against the army because the soldiers were still loyal to the man who had given them glory, but the royalists were also settling perceived scores with anyone guilty of Bonapartism, even by association, and this inevitably included Murat. He was now in grave danger, so it seemed that seeking shelter among the ranks might be a sensible course of action. Rossetti saw Napoleon's soldiers not only welcome him but beseech him to lead them:

'It is impossible to describe the joy the French soldiers showed when they encountered His Majesty; cries of "Long live the king of Naples" ran along the length of the column and a great number of officers gathered around him. The soldiers were furious with the people of Marseille who had massacred their comrades and many of the soldiers in the column had been wounded and were crying out for vengeance.

Indeed, they were most reluctant to follow the orders of General Verdier and so, when they learned that Murat was among them there was just one hope, one demand, namely that His Majesty would lead them against Marseille in order to exact revenge for their comrades who had been murdered in such a cowardly fashion.'

Murat, however, preferred not to be embroiled in what could soon be a civil war, so, as Rossetti noted, 'the king managed to calm them, and we returned to Plaisance' so he and Rossetti could consider their rather limited options:

'The situation the king found himself in was becoming critical, however. The defeat at Waterloo brought about the fall of the Emperor and this was a heavy blow to Murat. In addition the revolution in Marseille had sparked a general revolt across Provence, closing any potential escape routes into the French interior. I observed to the king that now was the time to take decisive measures in order to secure ourselves.'

Rossetti's advice was rather unhelpful, but he was right. Napoleon's government had fallen. The Emperor had attempted to abdicate in favour of his son on 22 June, but young Napoleon II was quickly deposed by a provisional government of slippery rogues who promptly invited the Allies in and the Bourbons back. Some in the south, including Marshal Brune, actually declared for Napoleon II, hoping to prolong their empire, and it seemed for a time as though the army would prefer a civil war to submitting to Louis XVIII. Amid such events and the likelihood of more bloodshed, Murat rightly assumed that Provence was not the best place to be stranded. So Rossetti was sent to see whether the military commander in the south, Brune, might be able to aid him in his decisive measure of escaping:

'The king ordered me to go to the headquarters of Marshal Brune at Antibes in order to find out what the marshal intended to do. I was to tell him that if he could not march through to the Var then it was the king's opinion that the marshal should quit Antibes and place a strong garrison in Toulon, thus securing that place from any insult, before, with the remainder of his men, striving to penetrate into the interior of the country. If the marshal were to adopt this plan then I was authorised to add that the king would offer to join him in this endeavour.'

On 1 July, Rossetti recorded:

'I reached Antibes at six that morning. The soldiers had still not heard
of the disaster at Waterloo, only the officers were aware. The corps
commanded by the marshal [Brune] had only 8,000 or 9,000 men
but the soldiers were in good spirits, turned out well and wanting for
nothing. I met with the marshal for some three hours and during this
time he told me that Marshal Suchet, after having won some success
against the Austro-Sardinian forces in the region of Maurienne, had
accepted a proposed armistice. Consequently, he could not rely on
the support of Marshal Suchet and therefore he found himself in a
most critical position, especially as the roads through the Dauphiné
were closed and that Arles had raised the white flag, meaning that
communication with the interior of the country was now interrupted.'[1]

The threat of being stranded in the hostile south was being discussed
openly in Murat's entourage and some of his followers even began floating
the idea of a return voyage to Italy, with Calabria again being mentioned as
a safe haven. Rossetti felt the need to speak up for common sense:

'The Duke de Roccaromana and I thought that it was time to put
an end to these fantasies and so we spoke to the king saying that he
should not rely on the mere mood of the Calabrians and that it would
be wrong to risk so bold an adventure on information as vague as his.
We observed that, since the fall of his brother in law, the only viable
course of action was to ask the Duke d'Otranto to open negotiations
with the Emperor of Austria with the aim of obtaining permission
for him to be allowed to reside with his wife and his children in
his territories. We added that no sooner had the duke received the
necessary authorisation than four days would suffice to resolve the
issue and that the king would then receive passports from Austria and
England at Toulon and thus be able to go and join his wife. We were
so animated and insistent in our proposal that the king was persuaded
and set down his instructions, and the granting of powers, to the

---

1. Nor was it easy to escape by sea, although Marshal Brune's suggestion was 'Gentlemen, we
should embark, seize an island, form a colony and live as free men.'

Duke of Otranto and allowing him to treat with Prince Metternich. Monsieur Serralonga, of the king's cabinet, was tasked with carrying the necessary despatches to the duke and set off that evening along the road through the mountains.'

In the meantime, and while Fouché negotiated for the passports in Paris, Rossetti recommended that they keep trying to break through to Lyon, ideally with a military escort, and so the persuadable and indecisive king 'wrote to General Perreimont [*sic*; André Thomas Perreimond], then commanding the royalist troops at Marseille, asking for his written authority so that he could cross Provence in greater security in order to reach Lyon'.[2]
Rossetti drafted the letter:

'The king of Naples, being obliged by the fortunes of war to quit his kingdom, sought refuge in a country house a short distance from Toulon and there lived simply and isolated from society, taking no part in political affairs. However, his presence was now required in Paris for he is required to sanction a treaty which his agents shall draw up between him and Prince Metternich and so he beseeches you to order and take those measures necessary so that His Majesty might traverse Provence in safety.'

Murat added that he hoped the general would furnish him with an escort from the 14th Chasseurs. But the royalist general sent back a firm refusal, saying that the political situation was too dangerous and Rossetti watched as 'the response from General Perremon [*sic*] extinguished all remaining hope of the king being able to extricate himself from the hole he found himself in'.
The hole was growing deeper and darker with each passing day. Louis XVIII had entered Paris on 8 July, or as Colonel Francis Maceroni put it, Louis, 'big as he was, had been by dint of Allied bayonets, crammed down the throat of France'. Those new royalist authorities sent emissaries and officials across France to impose royal rule. In Marseille, the Marquis de Rivière replaced the improvised royalist administration and assumed the role of governor on 10 July. One rumour had it that he had placed a price on Murat's head of 48,000 Francs, and another that he had been sent

---

2. General Rossetti's unpublished diary, entry for 2 July.

to seize the treasure Murat was supposedly hiding. General Rossetti, still open to pleading Murat's cause to anyone who might listen, was sent to treat with the marquis, and, surprisingly, he found the aristocrat disposed to assist:

'The Marquis de Rivière had recently arrived in Marseille to act as extraordinary representative of His Majesty Louis XVIII and he had assumed full control of the place. I came before his residence at six that morning and he was most surprised when I announced my name and my role as he had not been informed of my arrival. Having informed him as to the purpose of my visit, I then asked for his assistance in carrying out my mission, adding "the King of Naples hopes that in the circumstances you shall not overlook the services he once performed for you".[3] The marquis informed me that he would follow my negotiations with the keenest interest and that he would be happy, should the opportunity arise, to convey his gratitude to Marshal Murat. He added "Bonaparte would rid me of my life without having the right to do so, but it is no less true than I owe my life to the kindness of Monsieur Murat".'[4]

Across much of France, these new Bourbon authorities were being propped up by Allied bayonets, or sails. On 11 July, a British fleet came into view off the French coast with transports full of British, Neapolitan and Sardinian troops under Hudson Lowe. Admiral Exmouth stationed himself off Marseille, while Major General Richard Church, a former Quaker who had been wounded in the head fighting Murat's troops in 1808, was sent ashore four days later. He reported back: 'Murat is here, or at Toulon, and we are making great efforts to discover his hiding place and to arrest him.' Again, rumours circulated that the British were also offering a reward for Murat.[5]

---

3. Murat had helped commute De Rivière's death sentence in 1804 following the arrest of the marquis after the Cadoudal plot against Napoleon was foiled.
4. This concern is borne out by a later incident in which the marquis told Bonafous that he would offer Murat a safe conduct to a British ship or an Austrian army, providing written guarantees and also offering to escort him personally to safety. This stands in contrast with many accounts that depict the marquis bent on revenge.
5. Murat's friend Francis Maceroni later heard from Admiral Exmouth himself that he had offered £1,000 for information leading to Murat's discovery.

That proved unnecessary as Murat soon made himself known to the British. Their arrival had raised Murat's spirits, perhaps because he was unaware of Richard Church's personal grudge against him, and Exmouth seemed, in the absence of evidence to the contrary, like a man of honour. Murat apparently hoped to make use of him, much to Rossetti's surprise:

'His Majesty informed us that we could no longer count on the marshal [Brune] to release us from our mousetrap but added that he had the idea of turning to Admiral Exmouth who, a few days previously, had entered the harbour of Marseille, with the intention of asking to be permitted to board an English ship and transported to England! Some of those amongst us approved of this idea and insisted that it be carried out, adding that his lordship was sure to know of the warm reception he had always shown to distinguished English visitors to Naples and that his grace was therefore sure to do whatever was in his power for the king.'

On 12 July, Rossetti again found himself entrusted with conducting negotiations for Murat's escape, this time with the admiral who had so recently betrayed Caroline Murat:

'The king, persisting with his idea, had me prepare to go to Marseille and I was instructed to visit the English admiral and ask, firstly, if the king might come on board an English ship and be taken to England and, secondly, for a formal guarantee that he could then live freely in a town of his choice in one of the three kingdoms, London excepted. The king would do so as a private person with a small number of his friends. Also that he be permitted, when appropriate, to enter into negotiations between the Duke d'Otranto and Prince Metternich. I was provided with a letter from the king to the admiral in which His Majesty stated the object of this mission and the powers he was delegating to me.'

However, this time Exmouth was more cautious in making promises, replying:

'If he [Murat] so wished, he may come aboard one of the ships before Toulon and there find protection but that he could in no way guarantee anything in terms of his ultimate destination as this would be decided in England.'[6]

It is one of the ironies of history that, just then, Napoleon was surrendering himself to Captain Frederick Maitland on the *Bellerophon* off Rochefort, and his ultimate destination, also decided in England, would be the barren South Atlantic rock of Saint Helena. The glowering presence of Richard Church hinted that Murat might find himself similarly disposed of, so Rossetti made a bid for better terms:

'To the admiral I observed that I would not be able to accept any conditions without formal approval that he would be permitted to remain free and would not accept anything else, and I added that I had reason to believe that the Emperor of Austria was offering honourable terms. The admiral then seemed to hesitate before asking me to wait a few moments whilst he took some time to consult General Curch [*sic*; Church], commanding the land forces. A moment later and a general arrived and the admiral went with him and the marquis to confer in an office. After some 15 minutes they returned to the room and the admiral informed me that he could not alter the propositions made hitherto for anything else might see any promises made compromised later.'

This was honest enough, but this negotiation, and the one that would be held with Metternich in Paris, merely confirmed that it was the Allies who were not only deciding the fate of France, but also that of Murat. In his mousetrap, Murat could not afford to be too precious; he had already instructed De Coussy 'to find out which of them [the Allied sovereigns] is most disposed to granting me exile. If possible, I never want to go to Austria even though this is a difficult resolution as I don't wish to be separated from my queen and children for too long.'[7] De Coussy, a loyal

6. The valet Charles heard that 'The king sent General Rossetti to treat with the English admiral who was then in Marseille, requesting that he be permitted to come to England on the conditions the general was charged with conveying to the admiral; when General Rossetti returned to the king he told him that the admiral would willingly receive him on board his ship to take him to England, but as a prisoner of war.' AN, 31AP/21, Dossier 362.
7. Masson, Frédéric, *Napoleon et sa famille*, volume XII.

servant and avid violinist, got to work and reported back that of all the powers it was Russia that was most sympathetic, and its minister, Pozzo di Borgo, thought Murat might even be compensated for abdicating his crown, perhaps by returning the Grand Duchy of Berg to him. Murat, however, was fixated on a British exile and so, keeping Austria's offer as an insurance policy, he not only continued prodding Admiral Exmouth but also opened a new front in his campaign for preferential terms. He began pressuring British representatives then in Paris to grant him asylum. Unfortunately, this campaign would be entrusted to an amateur colonel keen to make a name for himself but bereft of tact, caution or any other useful quality for a diplomatic mission of some delicacy.

Colonel Francis Maceroni liked to surround himself with an air of mystery, one usually punctured by an excessive fondness for gossip, and he was especially keen to be at the centre of any intrigue. Born to a Roman family in London, Maceroni had spent a few years cheerfully interned in Italy, his Grand Tour having been cut short by war, during which he had founded a cricket club[8] in Naples and socialized with the city's elite. When Murat joined the Allies in early 1814, the king made him a colonel and sent this Anglo-Roman oddity to conduct negotiations with the British command in Italy. After this rather easy innings, the disaster of the 1815 campaign came as a shock and Maceroni also soon found himself exiled following the fall of his king. He made his way to Paris where, in due course, he found himself nicely placed to represent his master as Napoleon fell and the Duke of Wellington made his triumphal entry.

Maceroni appointed himself intermediary pleading Murat's case with Wellington and managed to secure interviews with the duke on 28 June and 4 July. The duke was initially encouraging, even expressing a wish to hear from Murat,[9] but, he too preferred Murat to surrender himself unconditionally before his fate could be determined. On 12 July, De Coussy also suggested to Maceroni that he request – through the British

---

8. Roccaromana was a keen cricketer.
9. Murat did indeed write to Wellington, opening his letter with the rather grand 'an unfortunate prince, a captain who is not without renown, confidently writes to a captain as generous as he is famous' before asking for his protection, and expressing his regret that he had not encountered the great captain on the battlefield, all while, once again, voicing his Waterloo regrets. Maceroni thought the letter unsuitable as, in the meantime, the British had made their position known, so he did not deliver it to the Iron Duke. BNF Fonds Charavay M a W 15 July 1815, also cited in Masson.

ambassador, Sir Charles Stuart – permission for Murat to be exiled in England, but at the end of that month, the ambassador informed him that the Prince Regent would not permit entry to Marshal Murat.[10]

Fouché had better success as a diplomat, and following the change of regime he even managed to preserve the sense he was both influential and useful to the Allied statesmen then arriving in Paris. Fouché knew about Maceroni and Wellington, and wasn't averse to asking the British himself. Nevertheless, he was sure the Austrians were the safest bet, and he had spontaneously approached Prince Metternich to see what might be on offer. Metternich had already indicated as early as 28 June that Murat would be welcome in Trieste, although for now some of the terms and conditions remained vague. Murat's servant Armand brought that initial offer to Murat. Rossetti saw the valet carrying Fouché's letter at Toulon on 12 July and heard that:

'In his despatches the Duke d'Otranto announced that His Imperial Highness the Emperor of Austria had granted permission for the king to live in his territories on condition that he abdicated and agreed to accept the title of count, adding that he also agreed to pay a stipend of 300,000 Florins. The duke added that he only needed the king's consent to have this agreement settled with Prince Metternich.'

Then on 15 July, Rossetti heard that Murat had accepted:

'The king replied to the duke saying that he agreed to the Austrian proposal on condition that he be reunited with his family and so he sent his authorisation to the duke so that this agreement could be signed with Monsieur Metternich and urged him to hurry so that this affair could be brought to a conclusion and to send back, as soon as possible, Captain Gruchet[11] and the necessary passports for the

10. This was possibly out of spite because Murat had entertained the Princess of Wales lavishly while she was in Naples in early 1815 (Princess Caroline left Naples on 12 March 1815). The prince and his princess had separated and were locked in a series of acrimonious disputes.
11. Captain Gruchet was Fouché's preferred courier, but around this time had been detained by the royalist police when an officer named Martelli searched him as he passed through Cuges-les-Pins and found him carrying a Bologna sausage inside of which had been inserted a metal tube containing letters.

voyage to Austria. The valet Armand set off that evening carrying the despatches from the king to the duke.'

However, on 17 July, just as things seemed more settled, diplomatic niceties collapsed before mortal peril. Word reached Murat that his life was in danger. Any exile would be preferable to being butchered by vengeful royalists, but before he could be whisked away to a place of safety, Murat was forced to put safety first and, as Rossetti explains, find a temporary refuge:

'Monsieur Joliclere [*sic*; Joliclerc], police commissioner, warned the king that he should quit Plaisance estate and come into town [Toulon] as he had been informed that a band of men from Marseille had, for the last few days, been out in the hinterlands of Toulon looking for him. The military authorities had sent patrols around Plaisance and the king went to stay in town.'[12]

Joliclerc explained his actions to Fouché:

'The military authorities are expending energy looking for Murat. Some houses in the town and environs have been searched. Some of the more active people from the rural community have also gone out looking and searching in a way that, should they find who they are looking for, I do not know what shall befall him.'[13]

Rossetti provides some additional detail on those trying to track Murat down:

'A messenger from Monsieur Joliclere [*sic*]. He had been removed from his post of commissioner of police three days ago but now he sent word that he had something vital to communicate to me. I went to see him and he informed me that the leader of one of Marseille's gangs had made an offer to a distinguished individual saying that he

---

12. This prompted Murat to write to the beleaguered Marshal Brune asking whether Admiral Duperré would grant him a ship to transport him and his officers.
13. 14 August 1815. Masson, volume XII, p. 168. Rivière wanted Joliclerc replaced by his own creature, Martelli.

would rid France of Murat for a specified sum and that this proposal had been accepted.'

Murat had any number of enemies, and while Charles François Marquis de Rivière may or may not have been the 'distinguished individual' in question, someone else was sure to try ridding France of this troublesome king. Royalist gangs were the most obvious threat to life, but a strange influx of foreigners of dubious credentials had also been noticed. Some Neapolitan agents were starting to appear in Provence, and rumour had it that spies from Spain had also been sent to find the Spanish diamonds that Murat had borrowed when, in 1808, he had been governor of Madrid and which he was now rumoured to have on his person. It was a question of who might find him first, foreign agents or a gang of ultras, the kind of loyal upholders of royal rule who made a sport of butchering Bonapartists, Protestants and, on 2 August, at Avignon, Murat's friend Marshal Brune.

It became clearer by the day that the King of Naples would need a secure hiding place. A modest one was quickly located for his majesty and Murat's little court was promptly dissolved, as Rossetti relates:

'Our preferred hiding place for the king was a small country house belonging to the lawyer Monsieur Maroin who was well known for his honesty, good character and attachment to constitutional principles. The house was four miles from Toulon between the road to Italy and the sea. It was agreed that the Duchess de Coregliano, then still at Toulon, would set off with Madame Soulaigre and General Bonafoux, her cousin, returning to her home at Quercy. That morning [21 July] the Duchess de Coregliano left the king, travelling down the road to Marseille.[14] That evening Colonel Bonafoux and I accompanied the king to his new abode.

'Only the following remained with the king: the Duke de Roccaromana, the Marquis de Giuliani [sic; Giuliano], the two Bonafoux brothers, Joseph and Eugene, and myself. Monsieur Peborde, his doctor, had left for Marseille a few days later. In order not to compromise His Majesty's security, it was agreed that only

---

14. Her coach was stopped and searched, with the police finding some money and some diamonds but nothing incriminating.

the valet Leblanc would remain with the king in the new house and that we would circulate the news that His Majesty had set off for the interior of France. It was also agreed that one of us would pay a visit to the king each evening either travelling by sea or by land using the back roads and all the while taking precautions so that His Majesty, who would not go out during the day, would not be discovered.'[15]

Murat was already impatient, but such a confinement doubled his anxiety, perhaps even more than the daily prospect of being butchered. He therefore gave up all dreams of Calabria or England and turned to his insurance policy, Austria's offer, the only one that had actually been proffered to him. Rossetti was therefore told he would be sent to Paris to hurry matters on:

'I was with the king that evening [25 July] and he was most affected by the news that the authorities of Toulon were hunting for him. He was naturally impatient and now he told me to ready myself for Paris where I would see the Duke D'Otranto and hasten the negotiations with Austria, his intention being that no sooner was that agreement signed than I would send on the passports with Monsieur De Coussy, his secretary, and that I would go to Trieste to the queen to warn her that the king was due to arrive and wait for him there.'

In the event, Rossetti did not leave, at least not just yet, for a new escape route had presented itself. One of Murat's suite, Francesco Pinto, described the new plan:

'The king persecuted and liable to fall into the hands of assassins had to quit his residence in order to go into hiding in a small house in the country. Every evening, before the city gates shut, each one of us his companions and loyal servants, took our turn to go and spend the night by him, coming back to the city at dawn. This unhappy situation continued several days. The king, tired of the role he was

---

15. As Murat waited in his refuge, he spent time drafting a reply to the French newspapers then slandering him for having been involved in the assassination of the Duke D'Enghien and for the theft of the Spanish royal diamonds. These drafts, which were never sent, showed that Murat was evidently bruised by the royalist jibes that formed the new wave of French journalism.

being forced to play, a refugee and deprived of information as to his ultimate fate, ordered that a boat be chartered so that he and his suite might be transported to Le Havre.'[16]

It was in fact someone in Murat's suite who thought of the idea, not Rossetti, for he and a certain Jean-Baptiste Blancard, a former naval artillery officer, were busy advocating for an escape through the mountains:

'As I walked through the port accompanied by Roccaromana and Giuliani [sic] we saw a merchantman newly fitted out and ready to sail. We went on board and learned that the vessel was called the *Elisa* of Captain Cor and that he hoped to depart in three or four days' time to Le Havre. The Duke de Roccaromana and the Marquis de Giuliani inspected the ship, asking various questions, and then declared that they hoped to be able to travel as passengers to Le Havre saying that they preferred to travel this way rather than by stagecoach. The Duke de Roccaromana went over to Captain Cor and learned from him that General Verdier, Maréchal de Camp Lesueur and various staff officers were to be amongst the passengers but that there was sufficient place for five or six persons more. The duke instantly resolved to have the king take advantage of this opportunity, thinking it a thousand times better than my idea to escape through the mountains. What was worse we learned of the assassination of Marshal Brune at Avignon. The duke mounted his horse and set off through the Gate of France but, after only having gone a little way, he came back into town and rode off to see the king. When he came back he informed us that His Majesty had given up the idea of travelling overland and opted instead for the *Elisa*.'

The idea of a quick escape by sea evidently appealed to Murat. Le Havre offered safety and grace, and also meant that Murat, still hoping that he might persuade the British to grant him exile,[17] or improve on Austria's offer, would be closer to the centre of negotiations around his own fate.

---

16. Pinto, Francesco (Prince d'Ischitella), *Mémoires et souvenirs de ma vie* (Paris, 1864). ·
17. Maceroni had not ceased bothering Wellington and, on behalf of Murat, was offering to exchange an asylum for the surrender of Gaeta. Gaeta, however, would surrender before Wellington had time to assess the proffered bargain.

The *Elisa* was suitably large, at 120 tons, with plenty of space to hide, but there was still one significant drawback that Rossetti, all too willingly, explained to his master:

> 'Sire, I have learned from the duke that Your Majesty has changed his mind and that our overland voyage has been replaced with the determination to undertake a voyage on the *Elisa*. Being very much aware of the risks both these proposed projects incur, I feel it is my duty to inform Your Majesty that the one involving a voyage is practically impossible on account of the port of Toulon and all the vessels in it being so closely watched by the police.'

Once again, Rossetti was right. However, the following day Murat replied, justifying his choice:

> 'My Dear General, I agree with you that a voyage brings a certain number of risks but I am sure you will assist in overcoming them and I have every confidence that you will help bring this affair to a happy conclusion. I shall be open with you by telling you that the only reason I gave up on the overland journey is because I have an absolute disgust for playing the part of a fugitive obliged to live as an outlaw. Trial by combat raised me up to the highest rank but now, amongst these misfortunes, I rely on myself alone to preserve the dignity of my character. Yours, J. Napoleon.'[18]

In truth, Murat relied on Rossetti a little more, and so, instead of sending him to Paris as originally agreed, Murat would opt to send Giuliano overland by coach while the unfortunate Rossetti was tasked with the arrangements being made to spirit Murat away by sea. Rossetti recorded:

> 'There was a meeting held [on 8 August] at the house of the Bonafoux brothers, nephews of the king, in order to determine how we might be able to get the king on board the *Elisa*. The following were present: the Duke de Roccaromana; the Marquis de Giuliani [*sic*]; Eugene Bonafoux, Joseph Bonafoux; me. The gentlemen present suggested

---

18. This was Murat's formal royal title.

the following plan: the vessel was to sail at first light on the 10th so Joseph Bonafoux would quit the port at nightfall on the 9th, setting out in a fishing boat and he would go to collect His Majesty using the same boat on the morning of the 10th. We would meanwhile go on board the *Elisa* on the 10th, taking the king's valet and baggage and, after the police search, the vessel would set off and display a white cloth on the poop to signal to the king by the shoreline and he could be brought over and would board.'

Rossetti thought this too risky[19], believing it was much better to offer the captain 25,000 Francs to hide Murat away like some illicit cargo. In the event, Rossetti was proved right and the operation went badly awry, even though he wrote that it had begun well enough:

'At around ten [on 10 August], with the vessel being ready to cast off, the police came on board for a roll-call of passengers and crew but they did not even go down into the hold. We weighed anchor and sailed out from the port. The weather was calm and the vessel made slow progress and we had time to tie a white cloth on the poop whilst all telescopes were turned to the shore to observe whether the king's boat could be seen.'

The first part of the operation leant unmerited confidence that the next step would go just as well. It did not:

'After an hour-and-a-half's painful wait we caught sight of a boat being rowed out towards us. We rejoiced and each of us told himself "he is saved!". Unfortunately, when the boat came alongside, it was just the person sent by the Bonafoux and he told us he had been unable to find His Majesty. You can judge my despair. All our pleading with the captain and the offer of a considerable sum of money to land us

---

19. The harbour was heavily policed, and even if the boat managed to get away, the royalists were sure he would be caught by their allies. For example, Rivière told the Duke d'Angoulême: 'Our joy will soon be unconditional because the entire province is being pacified and the guilty parties will soon be left without a refuge. It is thought that Murat and Lecointe [Lecointe-Puiraveau] have embarked but the English squadron is vigilant and I hope they won't escape.'

were in vain for, as he said, and with some reason, he could only land us in a port for, if he reached his destination and it was found that two passengers were missing, he would be subject to punishment. We therefore had to accept our misfortune and continue our voyage with the regret of having abandoned the king without money or resources. Only his valet had not joined us and whilst this had initially surprised us it now seemed a blessing, but all the king's property had been loaded on board. The Marquis Giuliani [*sic*], thinking His Majesty had got away with us, had left for Paris to carry out his assigned mission. As we were unaware of this, we thought that Giuliani, Joseph Bonafoux and Armand[20] were still with the king and it was only when we reached Paris that we learned this was not the case. Only Joseph Bonafoux was at Toulon.'[21]

Francesco Pinto was with Giuliano and soon heard about the unfortunate abandonment of Murat:

'On the day the boat was leaving I was due to take a stagecoach to Paris so that I could inform the minister of police, Fouché, that the king had set off for Le Havre by sea and to request passports either for Austria, so that he could be reunited with the queen and his family, or for England, from Prince Metternich or the Duke of Wellington. On the day the boat left the port of Toulon I set off for Paris. On my arrival I saw Fouché and carried out my task. A few days later I was summoned by the minister; he informed me that the boat the king should have been on had been driven away from the beach by the wind leaving the king stranded there as it continued its course.'[22]

20. The valets Armand and Charles travelled overland with Giuliano and would only rejoin Murat in September.
21. Rossetti eventually reached Paris six weeks later, on 26 September. 'The Duke de Roccaromana,' he wrote, 'and myself lodged in the Hotel des Princes, Rue de Richelieu. We learned from Monsieur De Coussy, the king's secretary whom we had last seen at Toulon on 23 June, that the Duke d'Otranto was no longer in office and, a few days previously, had been sent off as ambassador to Lower Saxony.' Rossetti himself remained in Paris until January 1816, when he returned home to Turin. Rocaromana also retired to Tuscany and lived there with 'four dogs, a beautiful German woman and four horses'.
22. Pinto, Francesco (Prince d'Ischitella), *Mémoires et souvenirs de ma vie* (Paris, 1864).

Rossetti's friend, Blancard, would later hear from the king himself why the operation had failed:

'The king was on the beach at the appointed time but, due to an unfortunate misunderstanding, the boat had gone somewhere else and there was just a rowing boat with two sailors. The vessel was some way off the coast and the wind was strong and against him, so they returned to land soaked by the waves and the rain. The king spent the night in the rowing boat and at dawn watched as the vessel sailed off and lost all hope of joining her. He was obliged to hide in the mountains to avoid the search parties for he realised that the vessel had been obliged to leave to avoid the suspicion of those who watched for him and wished him harm.'

Armand, one of Murat's *valets de chambre*, also later supplied Rossetti with some additional details:

'The king, having waited fruitlessly for his nephew, Monsieur Bonafoux, who was supposed to come and fetch him during the night of 9 and 10 August, went down to the shore and found a boat manned by three men and they went out to sea but the wind was against them and it blew fiercely such that they were soon back to where they started from. The sailors tried to row out again and reach the vessel and they came out twice and were blown back twice, such that the sailors were exhausted. The rain was now falling in torrents and night was falling. The king spent it without food and in the open, dressed only in a coat and a silk cap, all soaked and there was no fire to be had or else he would be discovered by it. At about three that morning the weather brightened, the wind dropped and dawn appeared, however the ship could no longer be seen. In this cruel situation, the king, not wishing to risk the lives of the brave sailors, gave them nine of the ten Gold Napoleons he had upon him and told them to go at once to the port and pretend that they had just come back from fishing. No sooner had they left than the king turned to the mountains, worn out by his sad fate and fatigue, tormented by need and in his soaking clothes.'

Having failed to get away, Murat, according to Rossetti, promptly went back into hiding:

'Being as careful as he could he approached an isolated house where, through good fortune, there was an elderly woman who gave him a piece of rough bread and a glass of bad wine. He gave her his last Napoleon. He recovered sufficiently so as to be able to continue for another two hours, continuing into the hills but keeping as close to Toulon as he could as he hoped, at nightfall, there to find the means to find information, and help to alleviate his most pressing needs. He then hid himself and dried his clothes in the sunshine. When darkness fell the king went off to the house [Maroin's] he had quit just a few days ago. He knocked on the gardener's door but she refused to open to him and he had to say who it was, so she opened up, shaking, not for her own account but for the king as she had heard that morning at Toulon that a price had been put on his head. That morning the king asked that she go to Toulon to find his nephew Monsieur Joseph Bonnafoux. Two hours later this gentleman arrived with some money for the king but also urging him to go quickly into the mountains for there were very grave dangers as searches were being made for him. The king briefly described how the boat had left without him, although he did not know how this could be.[23] The king did not ask that Monsieur Bonnafoux remain with him, instead he only asked him to go and find out if there might be another opportunity to leave, and to seek out the unfortunate Leblanc and oblige him to return the money he had been entrusted with.[24] The king then showed Monsieur Bonnafoux a place where they could meet. His Majesty then took some bread and some wine and went off again into the hills. The king spent the night at the gardener's house and she continued to look after him as best she could and she was still as afraid for him as

---

23. Murat's telling of the story confirms this sense of disbelief: 'I had chartered a merchant ship and sent on board my baggage and my aides-de-camp, to whom I had entrusted the sum of 200,000 Francs. I then embarked on a canoe in order to sail over and join them at sea. I was not far off doing so when I saw the ship change direction and sail off. A manoeuvre like that, sudden and dramatic, requires an explanation from my aides-de-camp, Rossetti, Roccaromana and Bonafoux. Thus abandoned I was obliged to return to the shore.'

24. 500 Louis d'Or, according to the valet Charles. There may have been some professional rivalry between Charles and Leblanc. Charles notes that the money was only reluctantly returned: 'Leblanc had it that this money was his and was due to him on account from the time in Naples but, nevertheless, seeing that the king was without funds, he would give the nephew 4,000 Francs and two shirts, which were the king's anyway. The nephew observed that the life of the king was at stake, and so took the money and left this wretch.'

before. The courage and loyalty of this woman were beyond praise. A few more days passed like this, the king spending his days in the mountains and the nights at the brave gardener's.'

This furtive existence almost proved fatal, as the valet Charles noted:

'Forced to hide in the mountains, his boots had given way and his coat had been torn to shreds. One evening, as he came down to spend the night at the gardener's house he spied a group of people on the path ahead and he had just enough time to hide by throwing himself into a pile of leaves. The men were talking loudly, and passed by very close to the king, so he was able to hear them say quite distinctly that "we know full well he is in these parts and, if we find him, we shall cut off his head and take it to our commandant". His Majesty swore that he was within an inch of being assassinated as what he could do with just his two pistols against a dozen or so men even though he was determined that, should he die, he was resolved to sell his life dearly.'[25]

It was the gardener who saved him. Murat later told General Franceschetti she had resuced him on 13 August when the mob came for him:

'She kept me hidden in a hole dug in the ground and covered in wood and leaves, at other times I was hidden under the floorboards and also kept in a chicken coop which was arranged so that I was between the coop and the wall of her house whenever her house was searched.'[26]

Blancard heard about another close shave:

'The old female servant caught sight of a lantern being carried up into the hills and she thought at once that it must be a party searching for the king. She immediately warned him and he barely had time to take his knife and two pistols and to throw himself into a ditch, covering himself with brushwood. A band of 60 men then entered the house and

25. Charles was then in Paris with Armand, but he may have heard these details from Murat after being reunited with his master in September.
26. Franceschetti, Domenico Cesare, *Mémoires sur les événements qui ont précédé la mort de Joachim 1er, roi des Deux-Siciles* (Paris, 1826).

they sacked it before spreading out through the garden, on a number of times passing close to the ditch where the king was in hiding, but the lantern they had brought with them, and which had warned of their approach, threw the area beyond its light into greater darkness. Then they thought they had caught him for they heard a noise and chased after it, running in different directions, but it was only a dog and it began to bark at them thinking, no doubt, they were a band of robbers. The king was seized with the desire just then to climb out of the ditch and to throw himself at them, and he might well have chased them off had he done so for they would not have believed that one isolated individual would attack 60 men. However, our 60 brave men had given up the chase and were leaving, cursing the king, but, as they would no doubt go on and search the immediate neighbourhood, the king decided to postpone his departure to the following day. One can imagine the prince's anxiety that night as he saw, once again, an opportunity to quit Provence disappear. However, the following morning, one of our party appeared and things looked better and, that evening, without waiting for Bonafoux's return, he quit this last place of refuge and set off followed by Maroin who would not leave him until he was sure he was safe. However, assuming a serious demeanour, and one perhaps a little melancholic, he concluded by asking "why are they pursuing me with such hatred. I'm a fugitive asking only for hospitality and not to entangle myself in the country's politics, indeed in the recent crisis I refused to take any position. What have I done to the French to be hated so, me, one who would give his life again for France?"'

Blancard himself then became involved in the king's fate, as Rossetti explains:

'This young man was brave and enterprising and had served as an officer in a regiment of hussars. The king told Monsieur Bonafoux of this man Blancard and asked him to go speak to him. Two days later and Monsieur Blancard came to see the king and to assure him of his support. From that moment on everything was done to spirit the king out of France, the arrangements requiring five or six days, although with each passing day the king's situation grew worse, obliged as he was to constantly move through the rocky and barren mountains.'

The plan was to take Murat to Corsica and three men – Jean-Baptiste Blancard and his friends Joseph André Anglade, a naval officer, and Antoine Donnadieu – thought they had found a way to do it. Armand later told Rossetti what this plan actually consisted of:

'A few days later and Monsieur Blancard came and informed the king that he had found two men as determined as he was to save the king or perish in the attempt and that one of them was a frigate captain, but they had not yet hired sailors as they could not be relied upon at this time when the whole people were so stirred up, but they themselves would do what they could to get him over to Corsica just 80 miles away and where they were convinced His Majesty would be well received. The king, seeing there was no hope of any other way of escape, agreed and, on the evening of the following day, he gave the good gardener 100 Napoleons and told her that, in better times, she would have had everything she might have desired. The king then quit his refuge and went to the point on the coast agreed with Blancard. His Majesty found those gentlemen ready to leave and brave all difficulties.'

Before he left, Murat wrote once again to Fouché, addressing his mournful letter 'from the depths of his dark hiding-place', and indeed it was so badly written that it does look to have been written in the dark. Rossetti, by then in Paris, later heard about this appeal:

'Monsieur De Coussy added that, on 22 August, the king had written to the Duke d'Otranto of the sad events that had led to him becoming separated from his friends and that, in order to avoid the daggers of his assassins, he was obliged to make for Corsica, indeed he was on the cusp of heading to that island and therefore begged the duke to send the passports just as soon as possible so that he could go and rejoin the queen at Trieste. He urged that I be informed, as soon as I arrived at Le Havre so that I could bring them to him, wherever he might then be. His letter was given as being written "at the deepest, darkest hiding place". In fact, the duke had, on 10 September, sent Monsieur Macirone [sic; Maceroni], one of the king's ordnance officers, so he could bring the treaty Prince Metternich had signed as well as the passports for Trieste.'

Maceroni, having failed to get much support from the British for asylum in England, had then briefly been arrested for having corresponded with Murat. It wasn't so much his time as a guest of His Most Christian Majesty that had delayed him, for he had only managed to leave on the 10th because, by his own account, he was enjoying the 'company of a very pretty lady'. He eventually set off with the long-desired documents, Murat's valets Charles and Armand, a few bags of linen and clothes and, if the police were correct in their suspicions, some 200,000 Francs from the ship that had docked at Le Havre.

It had actually been Fouché who had organized the practicalities of the passport, while Maceroni had gone about feeling important. The duke sent word to Murat that:

'I received the letter by which you told me you had disembarked on the shores of Provence and of your state of want. I hasten to send you the funds you need and the passport from Prince Metternich so that you may go to Austria where your family has established itself. I invite you to quit France soon and to set off for Trieste. I can give you no other advice today than to totally resign yourself to your situation. Unhappiness sometimes leads to happiness. You may find private life more restful than being on a throne. What tranquillity could you find on a throne under threat and which might give way beneath the one sitting on it? Believe one who knows humanity's illusions and who has not ceased to take an interest in you however far away you are.'[27]

Help was on the way, but Murat had already quit mainland France. He had been escorted down to the beach at Castigneau on 22 August by two peasants, as well as Monsieur Marroin and his friend Degreaux, and a rowing boat then took him out to a rickety barque where Blancard, Anglade and Donnadieu were waiting for him. As the rowing boat approached, one of the rowers threw two stones into the water and the officers on the barque responded with an air from Gretry's opera *Richard the Lionheart*. This was

27. Lumbroso, Alberto, *Muratiana*, p. 13.

the agreed signal, and so Murat, once Grand Admiral of France, clambered aboard the barely seaworthy vessel that would take him over the water.

Fortunately, the barque was a temporary measure. Blancard later recounted the actual plan to Rossetti:

'The king boarded and we pushed off right away and, making our way carefully, for we did not wish to be hailed by the coastguard or encounter any other boats, we found ourselves beyond the cape when dawn broke. We continued on as the sun climbed high and then the king told us "well, we are out of reach now but this is surely not the boat that shall take us to Corsica?" "No, Sire," replied Donnadieu, "in a few hours' time we shall encounter the xebec that serves as packet-boat between Toulon and Corsica and our aim is to place Your Majesty on board that. The captain will take you to whichever port there you wish. We thought this the wisest course of action but, regardless, we stand ready to follow your orders and, if necessary, sacrifice our lives for you. The captain will follow your instructions." "I shall ask nothing of him," replied the king, "but to chart his course and I shall find what I need in Corsica in order to go on to Trieste or anywhere else." We kept the harbour mouth in sight, riding the waves, but the packet-boat had not yet come out even thought it was supposed to have sailed by now. We decided to wait but in order to disguise our intentions, and confuse those authorities then on watch, we made as if to fish and only that evening, despite our increasing anxiety, did we turn away from the coast to avoid being intercepted. For most of the day, and so as not to reveal how many we had on board, the king and one of the officers would remain lying on one of the benches. That morning we ate a rather humble meal but for some reason, which was not clear to me, the king seemed reluctant to partake of it. Our officers had wished to serve themselves after him, in deference to his rank, yet he would not take anything and it was only in the evening that he would take nourishment when, like good travelling companions, we shared what we had. In truth we had much need of refreshment. We were far from land and the wind had shifted and strengthened, such that we were threatened with a rough night.'

The rough weather almost foiled this scheme and, with their vessel taking on water, the four companions faced a tense and increasingly desperate situation. Blancard continues:

'Shortly after the king spied a merchant ship sailing from the west and which seemed to be lining up to join our route. We did everything we could to draw nearer and when we were within speaking distance we hailed her and learnt that she was the *Santa Maria di Pieta* of Captain Stephano Benvenuto of San Remo. The king bade us offer the man a vast sum if he would take us over to Corsica for it was clear to me that it would be impossible for us to now make it back to Toulon. The sum offered probably made him suspicious, and the sight of armed men at sea in a boat such as ours, probably did not reassure him. He must have thought us pirates for not only did he refuse our request but he even changed course in order to ram and sink our frail vessel. Had it not been for our quick reaction in heaving to one side we would not have escaped this danger. The king was initially indignant, wishing to go and board the merchant ship and seize it, but the prince, reflecting that it was probably not a good idea to commit an act of aggression, of whatever kind, calmed himself and we let the merchant ship continue on its way.'[28]

Then, at sunset, or 12.00 hours Italian time,[29] and just as they were going under some 50 miles from the French coast, Murat saw sails. Blancard carries on with his narrative:

'Then, on the morning of 25 August, three days after our departure, we caught sight of the packet-boat keeping the cape to the south east as it began to turn in our direction so that it must soon pass close to us. We pulled down our sail so we could wait for it there but, in order to attract its attention, we hoisted a cashmere scarf the king had used as a sash, now using it as a flag. Half an hour later and the packet-boat was drawing near but we could not wait and came towards it. It hailed us but we did not reply but came alongside and climbed on board.'

Michel Bonelli, captain of the packet-boat that ran from Toulon to Bastia every Tuesday, had been briefed by a certain Captain Oletta[30] that he

---

28. La Rocca, Jean, *Le roi Murat et ses derniers jours* (Paris, 1868).
29. Italian time, which was falling into disuse, started the day at dusk, or at the *Ave Maria*, and ran for 24 hours from that point.
30. Oletta was a friend of Blancard's and, says Blancard, had told him all about the plan when the two met on the Champ-de-Bataille in Toulon. Oletta had then persuaded Bonelli to adjust his route so that the packet-boat would meet Murat and his companions.

should pick up some mysterious passengers. Oletta was on board, as was Matthieu Galvani, another Neapolitan refugee and a former commissary from Barletta, and this new eyewitness described the king's rescue:

'There were no sails to be seen and we were both overcome with grief. Just then, however, we saw, far off, a little boat which seemed to be heading in our direction. This was a ray of hope and we felt it. Oletta cried out "Langlade [sic; Anglade]!" and his response reached our ears for we heard him shout "Oletta!". The boat pulled alongside and I had the honour to offer my hand to the much-awaited king who, after he set foot on the deck, then warmly embraced me.'[31]

Blancard was happy that the mission had been a success, but, as his barque was sinking, he too was obliged to continue on to Corsica:

'Our initial idea had been to return to Toulon once the king was on board this boat but we saw that this plan was impossible. The damage done to our boat by the bad weather or when we avoided the merchant ship, meant that it was in no condition to undertake the voyage. Besides, after the conduct of Captain Benvenuto, I doubted they would allow us to enter Toulon. They handed me down a rope and just as the king climbed up the packet-boat's ladder I steadied myself by grasping a handle which came away with one of the ship's planks and the water flooded in and the boat went to the bottom 15 minutes after we left.

'We told the captain of the packet-boat that we had set off the evening before for an excursion but we had been blown out to sea. Seeing it impossible to return to Toulon, we told him we would accompany him to Corsica. He believed us, or seemed to. No sooner had the king climbed on board than he was recognised by some of the passengers and it was in vain that we pretended he was just an ordinary member of our party. The captain then came over and begged him to come down to his cabin where he was served some refreshment. We remained on deck all morning whilst the king rested but, that afternoon, he called us down to share a meal with him. He

---

31. Galvani, Matthieu, *Mémoire sur les événements qui ont précédé la mort de J. Murat* (Paris, 1850).

looked sad, kept quiet and seemed awkward in the company of the captain but once he had left us alone, telling the king he was to treat the cabin as his own, Joachim's good humour returned and he began to laugh about our voyage and then chat about the dangers he had faced onshore.'

As well as Oletta and Galvani, the passengers included Count Raphael Casabianca, who was rather peeved to see the king as it would further compromise him in the eyes of the new authorities – and perhaps delay the relaunch of his political career – as well as Pascal-François Boerio, an intendant and author of a volume on the revolutions in Portugal, and a Monsieur Rossi (nephew of Prince Baciocchi). Murat was glad to be among them, but months of being hunted from hill to shore had taken their toll. Galvani, still sporting his ribbon of the Order of the Two Sicilies in his buttonhole, was surprised to see his formerly resplendent king now reduced to a bespectacled and very dishevelled fugitive:

> 'Joachim was different from how he usually looked and was badly dressed. He had a long beard, wore rough shoes and blue trousers, a caped russet coat and a cap of black silk as he had lost his hat whilst at sea.'

The castaways had brought some hardtack and a barrel of wine, but dined on board in better style. An exhausted Murat was then invited to spend the night in Oletta's berth next to his 5-year-old daughter, and after the tribulations and excitement of the day he promptly fell asleep.

Corsica would be his refuge after France had rejected and tried to kill him. There Murat would be safe and might find support; after all, his numerous in-laws hailed from there and he had employed hundreds of Corsican officers in his armies. There, too, he would be granted the time to reflect and gather strength, or, as he was Joachim Murat, to act. Allied passports and guarantees were supposedly on their way, but being among friends would give rise again to wider ambitions. After all, Napoleon had escaped from a Mediterranean island and reconquered his empire. Perhaps Murat could too.

Chapter 5

Corsica

The packet-boat made leisurely haste to the isle, but the first attempt to land its regal cargo at Macinaggio, at the very tip of Corsica, failed when they were turned away by overly zealous port authorities. They thus sailed down to Bastia and there, on the morning of 25 August, Bonelli's ship was visited by the mayor, Charles Vannucci, two officials in charge of quarantine – Rivarola and Graziani – and Commissioner Antoine Rinesi of the Bastia police. The captain found their questioning mercifully vague, and even better, they declined to inspect the vessel despite the mayor having caught sight of Casabianca and a bespectacled man in a riding coat with a black cap strolling around the deck. The captain confessed that he had picked up four men whose vessel was sinking but the authorities did not seem especially interested, the police commissioner merely asking to see the passengers' passports and adding that those without documents should report to the town hall before ten o'clock the following morning. The officials then left with the captain, who was taking his despatches to the post office, and when Bonelli returned to his vessel he found that all his passengers had gone.

Murat had been among the first ashore, assuming the name of Campomele, but free at last he seemed at a loss as to what to do next. Fortunately, Galvani was to hand to spirit him away, as Murat later recalled:

'I remained on the shore with my three naval officers but as chance would have it, a former commissary in Neapolitan service, a Monsieur Galvani, saw my predicament. He had recognised me on the packet-boat, being one of the passengers, and he thought he should help me.'[1]

The three naval officers lingered by the port, where they were briefly detained[2] before Oletta sprung them free, but by that time Murat had

---

1. The valet Charles, who was not there, asserts that a boat came out from Bastia at ten that morning, picked up the king and brought him safely into town.
2. Blancard, Anglade and Donnadieu were later compensated 20,000 Francs each by Caroline.

disappeared. He had been taken into town by Galvani and the pair had tried to find some refreshments at Fourcy's hotel near the Jesuit church overlooking the port. Unfortunately, it was closed, so Galvani suggested instead that they go to Coutourier's in the Strada Nova. On the way there, they were spotted by Major Andre Biguglia, a Corsican who had once served in Murat's 3rd Neapolitan Regiment. Biguglia pulled Galvani to one side and warned him they must leave town at once and that there were friends at Vescovato. Both Galvani and Murat knew General Dominique César Franceschetti lived there, and given what Franceschetti had told Murat in June, they knew he would shelter them. The tired king just had time to down a *café au lait* at the hotel before donning Galvani's round hat and setting off. They went south and when the pair reached Torretta they again found Biguglia waiting for them, this time with horses. The good major then waved off this modern Don Quixote and his Sancho Panza, watching them trot down their dusty road to salvation.

Murat would be safer away from Bastia, but Corsica itself was not an island at peace. Napoleon's homeland was still one of warring clans and factions, and it had been an island even Napoleon had found hard to govern. For the newly restored Bourbons, governing was proving impossible. They were trying hard that summer, appointing royalist governors and commanders in the key coastal towns, but their rule barely extended beyond their citadels. Real power lay in the hands of close-knit clans and families, and their loyalty was rarely to Paris. Some, such as the Petriconi and Vidau families, were agitating for British rule,[3] as had been the case in 1794 when King George III had briefly been declared King of Corsica. Others were adamant that Corsica should be given to the Grand Duchy of Tuscany, the successor state to Corsica's old master, Genoa, or even declare its independence. Murat's friends, however, were drawn from an equally militant faction still loyal to the beaten Bonapartes, even if that family was, for once, trying to keep a low profile in Ajaccio.

As Murat was stepping ashore there was a real danger that these violent cliques, exploiting frustrations caused by economic depression and political instability, might again tip Corsica into civil war. A vendetta of words and pointed looks dominated the cities, while in the countryside armed men

---

3. The Duke of Padua had, in late June 1815, attempted to suppress the English faction in Corsica and the authorities had laid siege to the house of a certain Grimaldi, leader of the faction's armed wing. He wounded four gendarmes and killed one before surrendering.

had been trying out the old ways of war with the stiletto and burning down farmsteads.[4]

Into this combustible mix rode Murat. Borgo, the last village before Vescovato, was peaceful enough, and Murat and his companion stopped for bread, cheese, pears and wine. They continued on to Vescovato, where Andrea Colonna-Ceccaldi was mayor and where his daughter, Catherine, lived with her husband, General Franceschetti, the former commander of Murat's Royal Guard. Murat and Galvani tethered their horses before the Ceccaldi mansion and Galvani climbed the stairs, entering the living room to find Franceschetti in his shirt busy folding the pages of a short study on the 1814 campaign. Franceschetti recorded his version of this unexpected reunion:

'I was quietly at home on the day of Saint Louis, 25 August, when they came to tell me that there was a stranger at my door asking for hospitality. I bade him enter. A man came in wrapped in a greatcoat, with a silk cap on his head, a thick beard, and the trousers, gaiters and shoes of a common soldier. He looked exhausted. Consider my surprise when, despite that horrible disguise, I recognised King Joachim, a prince who once dazzled with his costumes. I cried out and fell to my knees. The prince raised me up and embraced me, saying "you have to take me in, you have to rescue me. Are you still a loyal subject? I am in your hands!"'[5]

While Murat rested, shaved and recovered, the royalist French authorities, shaking themselves from their own slumber, awoke to the dangers inherent in Murat's arrival. They feared Murat might make use of the newly returned soldiers who had once served him in Naples, for he, like Joseph Bonaparte before him, had found the Corsicans reliable soldiers and had raised battalions of them. These men, newly unemployed and increasingly bitter, when combined with the disaffected and those who had most to fear from a restoration of royal order, might – under a charismatic leader – turn the island against them. Murat, with his pedigree, along with an aptitude for demagoguery and fondness for risk, might just be that man. So Colonel

4. At Lumio that August, some 700 armed peasants had seized the town hall and threatened to pillage the houses of local officials they deemed Bonapartist.
5. Franceschetti, p. 6.

Verrière, the cautious and – luckily for him – provisional governor of the island, thought it best to try to arrest Murat and then deport him back to France. He sent out a troop of gendarmes under the Genoan Lieutenant Serra, ordering the officer 'to check the passports of the traveller and to make him aware of the authorities' intentions, and also to serve as escort to his point of embarkment'.[6] The gendarmes rode out on their mission, but at the entrance to Vescovato they found their passage blocked by armed retainers who forced Serra to dismount and brought him before the mayor. The local official persuaded the gendarme that he was just hosting his visitor while alternative arrangements were being made, although General Franceschetti interjected to threaten that it would be impossible for the authorities to take their guest away without there being disastrous consequences. Serra was sensible enough to take this seriously, but also asked if he could see the king. He was thus ushered in before a cordial Murat, who told him he intended to keep out of politics and that he would of course respect the government of Louis XVIII while he waited there for passports to Germany or America from Serra's superior, the Minister of Police. Serra tried to persuade Murat to turn himself in at Bastia, but Murat repeated he was doing no harm and that he intended to pass the time quietly enjoying the hospitality of the Corsicans.

Serra enjoyed a little of that hospitality too while he sent a subordinate back to Bastia for further orders. These soon came, but they were limited to asking the mayor of Vescovato to encourage his guest to leave as soon as possible. Murat told the gendarme he was planning to move on in any case and that he would probably charter vessels in Bastia so he could sail in early September. With that the gendarmes departed, and they quit the village under the gaze of Franceschetti's armed men.

Before long the village began to receive other visitors. These were more friendly and came in larger numbers. As word spread that Murat had arrived, the village was swamped with well-wishers and those seeking employment from the notoriously generous king. Just a week after his arrival, the authorities in Bastia were warning the mayor that 'your guest has raised a small troop of some 200 men and more are added each day. It is also said that he is paying these men, and rewards them, promoting and decorating

6. Franceschetti, Domenico Cesare, *Mémoires sur les événements qui ont précédé la mort de Joachim 1er, roi des Deux-Siciles* (Paris, 1826).

the officers; all this is in direct contradiction to your protestations and will cause trouble in Corsica, sowing discord in several provinces.'[7]

One of the volunteers, Bernard Poli, explained his reasons for seeking service with Murat:

'I decided to go and serve Murat. I did not know him, never having served under his orders, but he was part of the imperial family and this alone was sufficient for me to go and offer him my services. I therefore set off with my best friend, Commandant Cauro, who had served under the flags of the ex-king, and in the company of General [Jacques-Philippe] Ottavi [or Ottavy]. Arriving in Vescovato we found that a quasi-imperial court had been established and one had to wait in an antechamber before having the honour of being admitted into the illustrious presence of the host, a member of the Colonna family. Soon, however, we were received by him [Murat] and we were charmed by his gracious welcome. He asked us if we were disposed to follow him.'[8]

Most of those gathering around Murat were soldiers or officers on half-pay who had served under him in the Real Corso Regiment, a unit of Corsicans in Neapolitan service. Those mobilizing out of loyalty were supplemented by some glad of the opportunity to support any cause for regular pay, especially as most official salaries or pensions were not being paid because of the non-arrival of funds from the central government. The task of organizing the volunteers and recruits into an army in miniature was given to Colonel Sébastien Natali, an artillery officer who had only just reached Bastia from Livorno. While Natali formed them into companies, Murat fed them and paid them well, decreeing that the soldiers would receive 25 sous a day, which, according to Tuscan spies in the island, was a generous amount on the impoverished island. Murat was even more bountiful to his old officers, paying them but also hosting them to dinner at a cost of 30

7. Letter by Colonel Verrière dated 6 September 1815. Franceschetti, Domenico Cesare, *Mémoires sur les événements qui ont précédé la mort de Joachim 1er, roi des Deux-Siciles* (Paris, 1826), p. 132.
8. Poli, Bernard, in *Etudes Corses: revue trimestrielle*, 1 (1955).

Francs a day and paying out 60 Francs a day for their accommodation at the village inn.

What he intended to do with his 'army' was a mystery even the efficient Tuscan spies could not solve. Murat had already informed his hosts that he would charter some boats in Bastia, but for now, as he gathered his soldiers about him, he kept quiet as to his final destination. One option was Trieste; after all, the long-expected passports were on their way. Another possibility was nearby Elba, recently vacated by Napoleon and once claimed by the Neapolitan monarchy. General Jean-Baptiste Dalesme, Napoleon's appointed governor, was in charge of the island and still flew Napoleon's flag, even while Napoleon was being spirited away to exile on an even more barren island. Murat considered leading an expedition there to use Elba purely as a stepping stone to further conquests in Italy, for it was Italy that really transfixed him. And in all of Italy it was Naples that mattered the most. Not long after his arrival in Corsica, a conversation with Galvani revealed the depth of his obsessions and his desire to return to his precious kingdom:

'Vast projects agitate my spirit and my mind for the kingdom of Naples shall once again come to be mine. I shall retake the throne as I am loved by my subjects, my children. Yes, the Neapolitans call out for Joachim, they see me as a father. Ferdinand is hated. I have only to appear. Thirty or 40 Corsican officers shall be with me, quite sufficient for me to overcome the first obstacle placed before me, and the rest will be down to attachment and loyalty [of my subjects]. Now is the time. Come.'[9]

The idea that Naples was calling out for him showed that Murat's old bravura was returning, but it was an idea born from some interesting, but hardly impartial – let alone accurate – intelligence the king had been receiving from some of his old supporters in Italy. One of those letters in particular made a great impression on Murat's agitated mind. It was from General Camillo Borgia, then at Elba and on his way to exile in Tunisia, where he would help discover the ruins of that other fallen empire, Carthage. Borgia's

9. Chuquet, Arthur, Documents historiques concernant La Corse en 1815 in Revue de la Corse (35) (1925).

impassioned missive persuaded Murat that King Ferdinand was universally despised by his subjects, and most particularly by the army, which had 'sworn eternal hatred against Ferdinand', adding melodramatically, but in a style that was sure to please Murat, that 'everyone in Naples, without exception, prayed fervently to heaven to look after beloved Joachim and bring him back'.[10] Borgia added that certain generals in particular were praying for his return, notably Carrascosa, Fortunato, Ambrosio, Colletta (then supposedly at Salerno), De Gennaro and Pepe.[11]

This information, along with Franceschetti's and Desvernois' earlier protestation that the Calabrians were only waiting for him to appear before rising, convinced Murat he would be warmly welcomed. The dearth of any detailed facts, however, should have worried even an optimist, let alone a military commander. Murat would make just one attempt to gather intelligence on the real situation in his kingdom, but he put into effect his plans well before that attempt returned anything useful. It was almost as though he believed that facts were irrelevant and one could win battles with a confident pose. The man entrusted with that difficult intelligence-gathering mission was Simon Lambruschini, a Corsican man of confidence and an agent who had also been in Murat's employ in Naples. Carrying an amateurish note signed by Murat that read 'place your entire confidence in what the bearer of this letter has to say', Lambruschini set off from Bastia on 29 August carrying the king's instructions with him. It was apparent that, even at this early date, Murat's gaze had turned to Naples, for he had tasked his envoy with the following:

---

10. Lemmi, Francesco, 'La fine di Gioacchino Murat', in *Archivio Storico Italiano*, 26, 220 (1900). His chief informant seems to have been his brother, Fabrizio Borgia, formerly in Murat's Guard. The royal guard was incensed at how it was being treated by the returning Bourbons, and also resented Austrian influence over the government and its armed forces, but the disbanded guardsmen had limited influence. There was also resentment at the 'financial support' the Neapolitan government was being obliged to pay for an Austrian garrison, even King Ferdinand thinking 'these new guests just as greedy and just as menacing' as the French had been. The Austrians therefore trod carefully, aware as Count Saurau noted that June that 'any little thing, such as an event turning out badly for the government, might set off a revolution which, even if not an existential threat to the government may still cause considerable disorder in the kingdom'.

11. The valet Charles noted: 'Whilst he remained there he received no news of developments in France but learned much as to what was passing on Elba, and in Italy and Naples, from certain persons loyal to the king. These people intimated to the king that he only need to show himself for the entire population to take up arms in his cause. News such as this would arrive each day.'

'Disembark at Livorno, find out about the Neapolitans in Tuscany, especially Tito Manzi, Macedonio and Princess de Caramanico. Find out if Princess Pauline [Bonaparte] is still at Lucca. Send back a boat with what news you have on the situation in Naples, Calabria and Gaeta. From Livorno go to Naples passing through Siena and from there take the road to Rome or the Foligno road, passing through Aquila should there be any obstacles in getting to Rome. Either at Siena or Rome, if that route is open, Madame and the cardinal [Napoleon's mother and her brother, Cardinal Fesch]. At Naples see General Carlo Filangieri and tell him that you have been sent to inquire as to his health, something which is of considerable interest. Make him aware of our arrival in Corsica and watch how he reacts and only then enter into confidence with him. Ask him on what, and on whom, we can count should the determination be made to return to Naples. Tell him you have the same question for Carrascosa and Colletta if he finds this difficult.

'It is vital that the general tells you how the army has lately been reorganised, what strength it has, who commands which garrisons, regiment by regiment; whether the former generals have resumed service or have been replaced, whether Colonel Russo has been employed. Find out who has replaced Intendant Flac at Cosenza and Gentile at Salerno and any other changes that have taken place amongst the intendants and at the ministry of police.

'It is vital that he is kept informed as much as possible and a system of correspondence needs to be arranged and one in cipher. Gallo and Campomele must be seen and they must be told my news; tell them I have reached Corsica and find out from them what has happened at court. Ask Gallo for a cipher saying that I have lost the one he had given me. Tell the Duke de Campomele to give me information on the Duchess d'Avalos, Casoli, Caramanico, Torella, Belmont and other courtiers, and on the Filangieri household and that of the Altri, Carignano, Belvedere, Saint Arpino, Calabretto, etc.'[12]

Lambruschini's first port of call was actually Elba, where he was to hand the French governor a strangely worded letter that stated that 'following

12. Fortunato, *L'ultimo autografo politico*, p. 4.

the Great Napoleon, to whom none should compare himself, I dare flatter myself that I am the only one capable of refloating the ship of liberty'. However, that particular ship had sailed as the French governor, General Dalesme, in charge of the island on and off since 1810, was just then surrendering Elba to the Grand Duke of Tuscany. Asked if he might delay the surrender on behalf of Murat, Dalesme scoffed, 'six days earlier, and the affair would be settled; today, it is impossible to carry out'.

Lambruschini sent this bad news back to Murat, via Bastia, then continued on to the Grand Duchy of Tuscany, landing at Livorno on 8 September and reaching Florence a day later. There, equipped with a Genoan passport, he began to carry out his instructions, gathering intelligence on the Neapolitan exile community and dodging the Tuscan police. The government was alert to the danger Murat posed and its police agents were on the lookout for any sign of trouble. They knew Murat was probing for opportunity, and feared that the man who had proclaimed Italy united might easily use Corsica or Elba as a base to organize yet another intolerable attempt at revolution. When the French Consul in Livorno, Monsieur Mariotti, informed the authorities that the 'former king of Naples' had reached Corsica,[13] alarm bells rang out all along the Tuscan coast and that of the neighbouring Papal States. The chief of Tuscan police heard from his spies that Murat had reached Corsica, having been 'found by the packet-boat in a small boat dressed as a sailor; he has found supporters and has started issuing instructions'. His concern was that Murat could then 'seize a Mediterranean island and make of it a refuge for the discontent and desperate', thinking that either Elba, Pianosa or Monte Cristo were likely destinations. Consequently, the governor of Livorno, Spannocchi Piccolomini, put the port on high alert and told his men to be vigilant for 'vagabonds, those with dangerous opinions, *murattiani* and *napoleonisti*'.[14]

Many people had 'dangerous opinions' that summer, and febrile claims as to Murat's true intentions were being trafficked at an alarming rate. There was speculation that Murat might raid Italy, but also that he was bound for Tunis to place himself at the head of a fleet of Barbary corsairs, or that he was raising mercenaries to fight for the Ottomans in the Middle East. Nevertheless, the Papal consul in Bastia, Lota, was sure that Murat's real

---

13. The information reached Paris later. In a letter of 15 September, Talleyrand informed Fouché that Murat had reached Corsica.
14. Valente, Angela, *Gioacchino Murat e l'Italia meridionale* (Turin, 1963).

objective was Naples. Lota had heard that Murat had more than an army, he had also put together a fleet:

'There are eight of the largest boats in this port, some bought, some chartered by secret agents of Murat, although the cost is not known. Still, at least one well-equipped flute [a trading vessel] has been hired. They say that this is so the former king can flee should he need to. There is great secrecy concerning this but his former soldiers are in movement and seem to form part of the plan. Murat landed in Corsica with nothing and they say the boats are to carry all those Corsicans who want to risk an adventure by following him in his destiny, for which a number of boats will be needed. Still, the destination of Murat is still a mystery although most agree that he will embark for Naples and try to get to Gaeta.'[15]

Tuscany and the Papal States were on edge, but for the authorities in Naples, who never really trusted their own people, news like this was seriously alarming. That September, they sent out gunboats under Commodore Caffiero to patrol between Tropea and Naples, while at Messina the commander, Admiral Preville, a republican sailor who since 1799 had been a loyal Bourbon servant, ensured that the waters between Corsica and Naples were regularly swept for trouble. Orders went out that if Murat was caught at sea, then Neapolitan naval officers were fully authorized to execute him. Should he linger in Corsica, then the Neapolitan ambassador in Paris, Prince Castelcicala, hoped that the French would assist by sending some troops to the island so that Murat's enterprise could be nipped in the bud:

'His Majesty the King of the Two Sicilies, having been informed that Joachim Murat had enlisted, paid and formed troops in the island of Corsica, with the twin aim of raising the said island against its rightful sovereign and sending an expedition against the kingdom of Naples, has ordered that a squadron of two frigates, a corvette, a schooner and several gunboats, all under the command of Admiral Preville, be sent to watch Corsica and thus prevent any such expedition. This

---

15. Lemmi, p. 268. Gaeta had actually surrendered to the Austrians on 8 August.

officer has been instructed to act alongside the British commander there. His Majesty requests me to inform the minister of His Most Christian Majesty that such measures are essential to secure the realm and to ask the French minister to send sufficient troops to Corsica to put an end to Murat's revolt before the bad weather commences and these ships are unable to remain at sea off Corsica.'[16]

The idea that troops might solve the Murat problem was being heard in other corridors of power, too. On 15 September, Captain Phipps Hornby's HMS *Spartan* reached Livorno bringing an envoy from Corsica, a certain Antonio Galloni, who breathlessly informed the British and Tuscan authorities that Murat was about to declare himself King of Corsica and requested Tuscan, British or Sicilian troops to stop him.

However, soldiers – whether French, British or Italian – were apparently unavailable for now,[17] so another attempt to bring Murat to reason was launched. This time it was the British in Genoa – in the form of Admiral Josias Rowley, the cantankerous sweeper of the seas, and the ubiquitous Lord Bentinck – who conceived the notion that Murat, hemmed in from all sides, might still be wishing to give himself up for the promise of life and an asylum in an undisclosed exile. The British sent over an envoy on a brig, which reached Bastia on 7 September, and its captain accompanied the envoy to Murat's quarters at Vescovato where they were introduced to a king rightly suspicious of their intentions. Murat denied all the many rumours that were being whispered about him, telling the Britons that

'the fortunes of war forced me to leave my kingdom with circumstances, which could never have been predicted, obliging me to seek asylum on this island. I have not come here to bring or sow discord, but to seek out hospitality. I expected to be received well here by the people, for support of the unfortunate is a sacred thing amongst them. I made

---

16. Sassenay, p. 232. Ironically written on 11 October.
17. Some Corsicans in British service, then idling in Genoa, would accept Antonio Galloni's call for volunteers to capture Murat, and there was even talk that an Anglo-Tuscan-Sardinian expedition, perhaps of 500 men, could be formed within a month. However, Britain did not want to interfere too much and ruled out landing on French territory without French permission. Wellington, in Paris, hearing that Murat was intending to seize all of Corsica, determined there would be no action against Corsica unless a specific request came from the authorities there.

more than 2,000 Corsican soldiers into officers. I live here as a private individual. The flag of the king of France is respected and I will not allow my name to be used as a pretext to stir up trouble. In any case, I await passports from the Allied powers and if I am to receive them from you I am ready to leave Vescovato and go on board your brig.'[18]

The British rather curtly replied that he did not have the passports, although the brig was at Murat's disposal should he wish to embark. In the absence of any firm guarantee, and rocky Saint Helena having made quite a dent in British guarantees, the king elected not to take up their offer. The brusque interview thus ended and the British left. They would soon be back, however, and in more force as the growth in Murat's power and influence could not be left unchecked. Soon after, Admiral Rowley sent Captain John Bastard, a 'sensible, gentlemanly man' in charge of the frigate *Meander*, accompanied by four Neapolitan gunboats to Bastia.

Captain Bastard's show of strength leant some additional spine to the legitimate but anxious French authorities in Corsica. Those in Bastia had exerted themselves a little, confiscating the boats Murat had purchased from Joseph Gregori and preventing others from leaving port. Murat had planned to load some men and supplies on board his little fleet at Golo on 10 September, so the intervention of the authorities was frustrating. However, of more immediate concern was Colonel Verrière's attempt to raise some local troops to hunt down Murat, the colonel having finally managed to raise a ragged band of royalist men under Major Carlo Luigi Galloni. Fortunately for Murat, these did not make it as far as Vescovato, instead preferring to settle scores by plundering some homesteads closer to home. Still, the noose was being tightened and the royalist authorities gave it a further tug on 15 September by declaring that Murat and his supporters were to be considered outlaws.

When Captain Bastard arrived, he assumed that Murat would realize that, with the appearance of a Royal Navy frigate and some Bourbon gunboats, escape by sea was nearly impossible, while on land the royalists would, sooner or later, have sufficient strength to overawe or scatter his allies. He therefore presumed that Murat would see the writing on the wall,

---

18. Franceschetti, Domenico Cesare, *Mémoires sur les événements qui ont précédé la mort de Joachim 1er, roi des Deux-Siciles* (Paris, 1826).

sending a badly worded and undiplomatic summons to the king declaring that it would be better for him to surrender himself to the Allies, come directly aboard the *Meander* and there await the Allied decision as to his fate. Murat had no such plans. Instead, he opted to evade the law and put some distance between himself and Bastia.

Corsica was welcoming and wild, so there were a number of places in which a fugitive king or a persecuted soldier might hide. One of his officers, Bernard Poli, advised him to lay low at Fiumorbo, where Poli's clan would ensure the king's safety. However, Murat had other ideas, and on 17 September he quit his asylum and marched out with an escort that, according to Papal spies, numbered '150 armed men'. Rumour had it he and his band of outlaws were heading south to Porto Vecchio.

Murat was actually marching west to Ajaccio, where he understandably assumed the Bonaparte clan might offer shelter or even share with him some of their wealth, judiciously accumulated over two decades. Money lubricated the wheels of war and mounting an expedition, even a modest one, was never cheap. Access to his accounts with Falconnet in Naples was obviously impossible, nor could he reach his deposits with Sir William Forbes' bank in London. His ready money had gone to Le Havre, and then on to Paris, and while he hoped that Rocaromana or Maceroni might find a way to send it to him, for now there was no sight of it. However, the Gregori brothers in Bastia do seem to have accepted bills of exchange drawn on funds in the Barillon Bank in Paris, a gesture which, from 8 September, granted the king access to up to 178,236.95 Francs. The difficulty was in getting his regal hands on it. Although the king's accountancy was never state-of-the-art, and subsequent squabbling over who owed what to whom complicates any audit, it seems that when he quit Vescovato he only had 6,500 Francs available to him as disposable income. To increase his immediate funds, he sent Poli off in advance to Ajaccio in the hope of raising 25,000 Francs from his wife's family, offering diamonds as surety, while the trustworthy Franceschetti was also sent to see what he could get for a diamond-encrusted epaulette worth 50,000 Francs.

While this money-raising vanguard went off to Ajaccio, the rest of Murat's column, with the king always to the fore, marched down the coast before swinging inland at Cotone. There he met and awarded Galvani's two brothers, both priests, the Order of the Two Sicilies. The next day he entered Ghissoni, where Ottavi's estate was located, and he was escorted through by a mounted troop under Captain Riolacci. Vivario was just as welcoming, although there an old priest named Father Pantalacci ruined the atmosphere when he frankly informed Murat that 'he could not see how he was to regain his throne in the present circumstances when he had not been able to hold on to it when he had been at the head of a strong and numerous army'.[19] Murat, taking the rebuke in good spirit, hurried on to Bocognano, known locally as the Thermopylae of Corsica as it dominated a key mountain pass, and there he stayed with François Bonelli, a hero of the revolutionary struggle in Corsica who also had a brother who had served in the Neapolitan gendarmes. The Bonelli home was far from Spartan, so Murat remained a few days to recuperate, spending his time in lively discussions, scanning the newspapers for news from Naples or working with his new secretary, Galvani, on a proclamation that he wanted published to mark his triumphal return to his capital. But he was also waiting; he needed to hear back from the emissaries he had sent to haggle in Ajaccio and to learn from them what his reception might be in Corsica's capital.

Any plans for a triumphal entry into Ajaccio were thrown into doubt when news came back that Caroline's family were declaring openly that they would have nothing to do with Murat, the Bonapartes and Ramolinos collectively turning their back on him. General Franceschetti had been to see Napoleon's second cousin, the Duke of Padua, Jean-Toussaint Arrighi de Casanova, who had been governor of the island just a few months beforehand. After hearing Murat needed money, the duke made it abundantly clear that it would be far better for Murat not to come. Only Maria-Antonia Paravicini, aged just 14 and a very distant relative, offered some support, but the more senior members of the family then leaned on her and she had been forced to agree to close her doors to him, too. Still, there was some good news: the population was apparently waiting to see him with bated breath.

On 23 September, Murat mounted Father Moraccinole's bay mare, invested Bonelli with the Order of the Two Sicilies and rode out of Bocognano. As he approached Ajaccio at four o'clock that afternoon, he found Poli and Pietrasanta waiting to assure him of his welcome. The

---

19. Franceschetti, Domenico Cesare, *Mémoires sur les événements qui ont précédé la mort de Joachim 1er, roi des Deux-Siciles* (Paris, 1826).

royalist officials had fled to Bonifaccio, and although Colonel Laforet was made of sterner stuff, he could not be so sure about his men. Laforet therefore slammed shut the gates of the citadel, locking himself and his garrison inside and passing the baton for keeping order to Major Cauro and the National Guard.

The first job of the National Guard was to erect a cordon so that the jubilant throng might be prevented from crushing their new idol. Murat then rode in with some of his old panache, taking the town without a shot being fired. He pointedly rode straight past the Ramolino residence, where Caroline's mother had once lived, and smirked his way past the house of the Bonapartes before taking up quarters at the shabby Hotel La Croix de Malte on rue Napoleon.[20] From there he wrote a letter to those remaining authorities, reassuring them he intended no harm and that there would be no unrest or disorder. As for violence, none would be necessary.

After months of persecution and woe, Murat's coup and the scenes of rejoicing inevitably went to his head and affected him deeply. That evening, he was reminiscing about similar scenes that had once greeted him in fickle Naples. General Franceschetti jotted down some of Murat's maudlin memories:

> "And that's how I was welcomed into my capital whenever I returned from the army", he said, then, shedding some tears, added "in truth, I shall live or die but amongst my people. We shall see Naples again, let us go at once."'

Franceschetti says he urged his prince to at least wait for the return of Simon Lambruschini and some reliable intelligence from the old country, and then added, perhaps for the sake of posterity, that 'God is my witness, arguments, tears, prayers, I spared nothing in the hope of persuading him not to go.'

Bernard Poli also had his doubts, and on one occasion had the audacity to tell Murat: 'I do not think your true intention is to go to Naples. I believe, rather, that you wish to trick the Allied powers and disguise your true purpose.' To this Murat replied: 'No, you are wrong. I shall go to

---

20. The inn was run by Joseph Qui, father of Joseph Antoine Qui, Napoleon's steward when he had been on Elba.

Naples, my decision has been made.' Poli then says he told the king: 'It troubles me to confess that I see no good coming of your expedition. You wish to copy the Emperor but you are not the great Napoleon and the Neapolitans are not the French. Neither do you have the means required for such an expedition.'

These rather frank words, if Murat had stayed to hear them, would have irritated the king, but they were unlikely to discourage him. His warm reception after months in the wilderness was encouraging Murat to develop, just like Napoleon, a firm belief in his own star, and in a destiny that promised a second chance if not a second coming. This meant that Murat had little time for doubters such as Poli. The king had equipped himself with the conviction that he would prevail and that he had the ability to imitate Napoleon, crossing the sea and bursting forth to reclaim his old lands. Ajaccio was little more than a pause on the path of this glorious return, for it was a sizable enough place and an important enough port to equip him with the means to follow his star and crown himself anew in Naples.

There was, for example, a printing press. Murat, having finished off the proclamation he had composed with Galvani, made use of Ajaccio's official printing press to print off 500 copies, paying Monsieur Battini 1,990 Francs for doing so. His decree, or constitution, some thirty-six Articles on what he would do when his power was restored, was not yet ready to be printed, but he kept a draft of it by his side, annotating and adjusting it. He also spent time revising a text denouncing Ferdinand's treatment of his former army, which he hoped to distribute when he landed in Italy.[21]

The forces available to him were also being checked and readied. His miniature army was in robust health. The prefect at Ajaccio thought that Murat had with him sixty mounted men – mostly officers from the Royal Corsican Regiment of Naples – fifty soldiers and some sixty armed peasants when he entered the town. This had expanded to some 600 volunteers within a few days of his arrival, and Natali was again given the difficult task of organizing them into companies. Some were veterans from Naples, while others were soldiers keen to escape the monotony of garrison duty in the National Guard or in the ill-paid Corsican battalions the authorities were struggling to raise. There was also a handful of youths and students,

---

21. This was dubbed 'The Cry of the Neapolitan' and attacked Ferdinand's letter to General Bianchi insensitively describing Murat's Neapolitans as 'enemy bands'.

untested by war but keen to play the part of modern Argonauts. Murat, an able persuader, used his charm to flatter those who stepped forward to take part in his own little odyssey, but he soon realized he had more men than he could make use of. Nevertheless, he told those who were surplus to requirements that should his expedition prove to be successful, then he would give Corsica its independence or, if not that, he would join it with his restored kingdom of Naples. Whatever the case, he said there would be positions for everyone and his Royal Guard would be formed exclusively from 4,000 loyal Corsicans.

Such bravado made up for the fact that Murat only really had supplies to arm and equip fifty soldiers and officers, although a hundred or so more could sport his cockade. He placed orders for more uniforms and muskets at a cost of 4,419 Francs, and these were delivered on the eve of his departure. The king, always popular with tailors, also looked after himself, purchasing a coat and six pairs of gloves from Touranjon for 230 Francs. For a man who had dressed to kill on the battlefields of Europe, this seemed paltry, but Murat, feeling his star in the ascendant, was beginning to shine in ways that had been impossible these last few months.

First, of course, to travel to his beloved Naples he would need ships. The port had been closed soon after his arrival, but this hasty ban, combined with the fact that some other boats had been driven in during recent bad weather, meant there were at least a few merchantmen idling in the harbour. After some keen bargaining, all Murat's representatives could secure were five 15-ton barques known as *trabacoli*, or *gondole*, single-decked vessels with two sails and crewed by just four or five sailors. There was also a single felucca, or *scorridoja*, that was more adept at putting on a show of speed and might prove useful for sending messages, or for a quick escape should Murat's star reveal itself a meteorite.

None of these vessels were ideal for a voyage across the autumnal Mediterranean, but Murat had little choice. Nor could he afford to haggle too long, which meant that the cost of following his star and chartering this flotilla proved astronomical. It cost 36,000 Francs to hire the barques and the felucca, although Murat's agents managed to agree on payment for each of 2,000 upfront and 4,000 when they returned, while the twenty sailors demanded 500 Francs a man. Then there was the cost of obtaining enough food and drink to keep a few hundred men satisfied for two weeks, which added up to a further 10,000 Francs. The masters and captains, afraid they may be charged with assisting enemies of the realm, also insisted that the expedition's paperwork be in order. A large deputation, some of whom were armed, accordingly paid a visit to the offices of the maritime authorities, demanding that they be given permits to sail to Tunis, a convenient story for any subsequent insurance claim. Fortunately for them, the commissioner was away and his assistant, Peri, felt too intimidated to refuse.

With charters and patents in order, the crews and captains readied their ships to transport troops and were told by their new admiral that the first leg of the voyage would be down to Sardinia. That commander was Baron Vincenzo Barbara, a Maltese born in Cottonera and a former Knight of Malta, who had been promoted to frigate captain and baron by Murat. Barbara had served forgettably in the Neapolitan navy until it was generously donated to Commodore Campbell, and he had then slipped away to Porto Longone in Elba. While there, he heard that his king was preparing to mount an expedition, so that September he sailed over to Corsica and offered his services. Murat was pleased to see him as he was familiar with the kingdom's coastline, and Barbara duly assumed charge of Murat's modest armada.[22]

Everything was ready by 26 September, although the bad weather plaguing the island kept the boats at bay and discouraged a few of the volunteers. Murat, however, was having none of it and continued to act as though willpower alone could transform a rash and risky endeavour into a glorious exploit. When Galvani, anxious like most administrators, shared some of his doubts, Murat shot back with some of the fighting talk more routinely found in seedy bars or cabinet meetings:

'What is the risk we are running? I see none. They might capture us, so what? In the situation I am in now, I don't fear that as, sooner or later, I will fall into the hands of my enemies. Let it be honourably and after having braved adversity. No, a happier fate awaits us. The moment is ripe, let us seize it and before long, I doubt not, fortune shall smile on us as we receive universal acclaim.'[23]

---

22. Barbara had quit the Knights of Malta in 1798 to side with the French, and his appearance in Corsica seems to have been a genuine gesture of support. However, after the botched landing in Calabria, there were hints, as we shall see, that he had been sent by the Bourbons to betray Murat and deliver him into their hands.

23. Galvani, p. 46.

Fortune, lucky stars, fate, destiny... these were all very well, but it is a truth universally acknowledged that a man in possession of good fortune should be in want of a plan. The elements of chance inherent in a sea voyage were too great, and the reception in Naples too doubtful, for this to be an easy endeavour, and nothing had been done to mitigate such risks. Murat and his men were sailing into the unknown, and if ever there might be a lesson on how not to stage a coup, then this was it. In truth, Murat had no real clue as to how he would seize his capital and place himself back on his throne. He had fled in May when his army and his people had abandoned him, and only wishful thinking – and the inimitable example of Napoleon – persuaded him that the time was ripe to turn that disgrace around.

When it came to detailed planning as to what might happen should the flotilla reach the Kingdom of Naples, Murat's ideas were subject to the whims and caprice of his overactive imagination. When he first began to form his fancies into something suitable to balance the dangers he was requiring everyone to brave, all he could say to Galvani was:

> 'My plan has matured and I shall carry it out alone if everyone refuses to follow. I shall land on the coast by Pozzuoli. From there I shall head to Vomero to the Duke of Gallo or the Prince of Belvedere and there rally those who are loyal to me. Then I shall see myself again master of Naples.'[24]

A few days later, Galvani found Murat wandering around in his shirt. The king probably realized his outburst had worried Galvani rather than reassured him, so at the sight of his diffident secretary, he changed tack and made it known that he had been working on a much more specific scheme. This time, Pozzuoli, five hours' march above Naples, was abandoned and 'our plan' involved targeting the royal palace to the south of the capital:

> 'I have changed our plan when it comes to landing. We shall enter the gulf of Naples. Ferdinand is at Portici so we will land at Granatello and march on the palace where we shall surprise the Guard and, using a secret staircase I know about, and which lead directly to Ferdinand's rooms, seize the king.'[25]

24. Galvani, Matthieu, *Mémoire sur les événements qui ont précédé la mort de J. Murat* (Paris, 1850).
25. Galvani, Matthieu, *op.cit.*

Murat thought they could overpower the guards and surprise Ferdinand, but Galvani naturally wanted to know what would happen next and so naively asked: 'In that case, wouldn't Your Majesty be required to kill Ferdinand?' 'No,' replied Murat rather too quickly, 'I would force him to abdicate and ship him at once to Sicily.'

On other occasions Murat mentioned Bagnuoli, Cetraro or Salerno as potential landing places where his men might disembark. Salerno seemed the most sensible, as the remnants of his army had been dissolved there and so at least some of the 3,000 soldiers remaining in the region might have welcomed him. From there, Murat's men could have cut the telegraph system before perhaps sweeping inland and, via Avellino, storming the capital. Such a plan hinged on his enemies not reacting and on the Austrian garrison of Naples looking the other way. Murat also considered striking at Calabria, the troubled province that stretched south of Salerno to Italy's toe. Quite why Murat believed the stories he would be welcome here is a mystery; although a few of the towns boasted a middle class that had benefitted from Murat's rule and Napoleonic modernization, they were easily outnumbered by those who had lost a relative to Murat's campaign of hanging the province's youth and calling it peace. This, and the British presence at Messina, made Calabria a dubious starting point for a war of national liberation.

The absence of a strategy did not deter Murat, and his little army had sworn allegiance that they would follow him come what may. An impromptu ceremony was held, a modest *adlocutio* during which Murat presented an even more modest regimental standard to his assembled legion – or more properly cohort – unfurling a large handkerchief of light blue bordered with a checkerboard pattern of red and blue. Beneath this symbol of better days and grander parades, Murat promoted Colonel Natali of the artillery to major general, Lieutenant Viggiani to captain and Second Lieutenant Pietro Pasqualini to lieutenant, among others. Those officers not yet belonging to Murat's royal order were made Knights of the Order of the Two Sicilies.

The king was now ready to lead those adventurers who had bound their destinies to his. However, as the king returned to his inn, and the soldiers to their quarters, there came a rude reminder that Murat was not quite in charge of his own destiny. Indeed, it seemed as though the Great Powers of Europe wished to remind him that they held a controlling share. The long-anticipated passports for Trieste had arrived.

Murat in happier times. An equestrian portrait by Antoine-Jean Gros. Murat wears one of his characteristically flamboyant uniforms.

Murat's family: his wife, Caroline Bonaparte, and their children Achille, Marie Laetizia, Lucien and Louise. A courtly portrayal by François Gérard.

Prince Achille Murat, Murat's son and heir, sketched by Ingres in 1814.

A sketch of Princess Louise by the same artist.

Queen Caroline, Murat's capable wife, and, until 1814, Napoleon's most respected sister.

King Joachim Napoleon, as Murat styled himself, as commander-in-chief of the Neapolitan army. When he heard that Napoleon had escaped from Elba, Murat lead his army northwards into Italy in a rash and disastrous attempt to seize the entire peninsula.

Glorreicher Einzug der K.K. Oesterreichschen Armee zu Neapel den 23 May 1815.
Nachdem das tapfere Heer, unter Feldmarschall Bianchi, in den unglaublich kurzen Zeitraume von 6 Wochen, ganz Italien erobert und den Feind gänzlich vernichtet hatte.
Nürnberg, bei Friedrich Campe.

As a result the Austrians, and the Bourbons of Naples, were able to chase Murat from Naples and place the elderly, senile and vindictive King Ferdinand back on his throne.

Komisches Ende des Neapolitanischen Feldzugs.
König Joachim Murats Flucht zu Wasser,
nachdem seine feinen Plane zu Wasser geworden waren.
London bei Ackermann 101 N101 Strand.

A contemporary print of Murat's flight from the coast near Naples. In fact, Murat set off with just a handful of loyal supporters and barely any baggage. His initial idea was to continue his war on the Austrians from Gaeta or Calabria but, in the event, he fled to Ischia and then France.

One of Murat's loyal followers: General Dominique César Franceschetti. Franceschetti was a Corsican who had served in Murat's Guards in Naples. In September 1815 he took part in Murat's final expedition to Calabria.

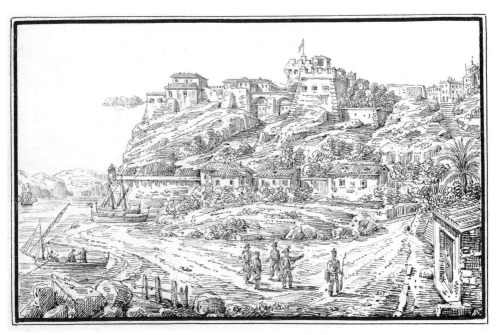

Murat's followers landed at the little town of Pizzo in Calabria. Fishing boats would beach themselves below the castle walls whilst, to the right, can be seen the path and steps up to Pizzo's little piazza.

PIZZO

Another view of Pizzo. The tower of the San Giorgio church can be seen and, just to its left, the castle of Pizzo.

Murat's prison warden and executioner, General Vito Nunziante. Nunziante was a Bourbon officer who conducted himself with a great deal of dignity.

Colonel Maceroni had left Paris on 10 September in the company of Murat's faithful valets, Charles and Armand, making their way slowly to Toulon and then leaving the port ten days later. Maceroni had reached Calvi first, sending a letter to Murat alerting him of his arrival, and then proceeded to Bastia. There he met Captain Bastard and, over punch, urged the Royal Navy frigate captain to delay blockading or intervening in Ajaccio. This would allow Maceroni time to deal with Murat, and he coyly suggested that Murat was sure to surrender and go – or be taken – to Trieste and that Bastard could then play his part in bringing this unfortunate episode to a close. This was all nicely described in Maceroni's subsequent and rather heavy-going explanation to Prince Metternich:

'I have the honour of informing Your Excellency that, upon arriving here this morning, and having made myself known to the authorities here, I was informed by them that King Joachim, seeing himself threatened by Colonel Verrier, commander, by interim, of the 23rd Military District, and by the presence of a British frigate, had, on the 13th of this month, left Vescovato and gone towards Bogognano and was, as recently as yesterday, there with 100 friends who were providing him with personal security. The English captain Bastard has been sent here by the admiral stationed at Livorno and he has his frigate, the *Meander*, and some sloops, and aims to cooperate with the local authorities and the English troops that are to be brought from Genoa in order to secure King Joachim and they summoned him to surrender himself yesterday to the English frigate or to Commandant Verrier. This summons was in the name of the King of France and the principal Allies but it is unlikely that the former King of Naples will comply voluntarily as it does not stipulate any future destination for him. Having put in at Calvi yesterday I took the opportunity of sending a letter off to King Joachim informing him that I had arrived in the island and of the nature of my mission and there is no doubt he will comply with that. I leave tomorrow to go to him and I agreed with Captain Bastard that I would inform him at once of the outcome of my mission and that, in the meantime, he should desist from further action. I shall come back to Bastia with King Joachim and the British frigate shall be at my disposition to take us to Toulon, where an Austrian officer has been ordered to attend to us by Count

Anton Starhemberg; no other vessel offers such security as there is a squadron of seven Algerian three-masted warships cruising in these waters which intercept and pillage everything that falls into their hands. Captain Bastard has offered to have this letter taken to Livorno from where it will be forwarded to Your Excellency by the English ambassador, Lord Burghersh. The summons by the aforementioned gentlemen was for King Joachim to surrender himself voluntarily until the will of the Allied powers on his future fate is known.'[26]

Maceroni, delighted to once again be at the dark heart of intrigue, then set off for Ajaccio with the Allied offer. Instead of appearing in Bastard's frigate he decided to head overland, taking with him his fishing rod, the valets, a small escort of seven soldiers and the mysterious Carabelli brothers, Ignazio and Simone, who had coincidentally arrived from Naples.[27] Simone spoke English, having served in the Corsican Rangers, and after overhearing Maceroni talking to his servant in that language in his Bastia inn, the brothers had introduced themselves. The Carabellis said they were on their way home, fearing that, given the tumult in Corsica, their family and estates were under threat. But they had come to Bastia on Captain Bastard's *Meander*, which suggested more official business and influential friends. Maceroni did not put two and two together, but some French spies were more alert and reported back to General Partouneaux in Marseille that 'some important people have arrived in the island from the kingdom of Naples and they bring some political schemes with them. This information comes from a reliable source.'[28]

It was probably the rough seas that induced Maceroni and his odd companions to travel by land, but it meant slow progress and they only reached Ajaccio after three days on bad roads. By then Murat knew

26. Letter dated 25 September. Lemmi, p. 293.
27. Another brother, Giovan Battista, had served in a French unit that became the Legione Corsa in Neapolitan service. Ironically, he had fought against Simone, who was in British service, at Capri in 1808.
28. Chuquet, Arthur, *Documents historiques concernant La Corse en 1815* in *Revue de la Corse* (35), 1925. The Governor of Livorno, probably referring to Carabelli, reported that 'Commandant Mussio tells me that, on 21 September, an English vessel came into Port' Ercole and that a certain Sir Flin, an English officer, was on board and was to land in Corsica. This officer said that he was the bearer of a message from the royal court of Naples and was most insistent he should be allowed to land so he could carry out his mission.'

they were coming, for he had received Maceroni's letter from Calvi just as the party approached. The timing of the arrival of this Anglo-Italian plenipotentiary bearing Allied-approved salvation must have come as a complication. Murat had, after all, resolved on a military expedition, but now here came an offer of peaceful exile. A complication is not, however, an insurmountable obstacle, so upon his arrival, and as Maceroni was pleased to relate, the envoy was summoned into the king's presence:

'I arrived in Ajaccio on the afternoon [3 pm] of 28 September 1815. The house occupied by the king was distinguishable by his standard and by the sentinels which were planted at his door. I immediately sent to the king to inquire when he would be pleased to receive me, and he returned for answer that I might come to him immediately. I thought it requisite, however, to communicate to him by letter, in diplomatic form, the object of my mission. I wrote the letter and was myself the bearer of it.'[29]

Maceroni had found Ajaccio in rather an agitated state, and his next report to Prince Metternich gives a sense of the febrile atmosphere:

'King Joachim was staying in an inn. The prefect and the other authorities, with the exception of the mayor, had quit the town and left it entirely in the hands of the friends and partisans of Murat. The garrison in the citadel is animated by the same zeal and has threatened to kill their commander, Colonel de le Forest, as he sought to curb their enthusiasm and bring them back to their duty. There is much disorder. Still, it is remarkable that throughout this time when everyone is armed and acts according to his desires, the disorder has not been worse.'

---

29. Maceroni, cited in *A few Specimens of the Ars Logica Copleiana*, p. 173. The letter Maceroni mentions is in Add MS 41534. It stated that if Murat decided to accept the Austrian offer then he could travel overland under escort of an Austrian officer or by sea using the passports he was bringing as a safe-conduct. Maceroni also stated that, should he wish to travel by sea, Captain Bastard had offered to bring the *Meander* to Ajaccio and to receive him on board. Maceroni closed by mentioning that he had 'found two servants of Your Majesty's at Paris who had been in difficult straits and in discomfort' and that they wished to rejoin him. These were Armand and Charles.

Ignazio Carabelli was with Maceroni when he arrived, and he soon learned that Murat and his men were on the cusp of departing:

'Reaching Ajaccio, and before I had even dismounted, I was surrounded by a group of officers whom I knew and who were friends, and amongst whom I especially noted General Ottavi, asking for news of Naples and telling me that the expedition would leave tonight. I could not believe such folly and at first I thought it was a joke and then that the passports Maccirone [sic] had brought with him would soon change their minds.'[30]

Whether the passports would convince Murat to go quietly was now put to the test, for very soon afterwards, Galvani found Maceroni at the door of the inn and with him a portmanteau containing those important documents:

'Maceroni came in and, without saying a thing, bowed deeply before the king. The king also kept quiet but with his right hand indicating the door through to his study. They went in together and remained shut in there together for two hours.'[31]

There, in Murat's improvised office, Maceroni informed Murat that as well as his passports, he also brought details concerning the Allied offer of exile. Maceroni recorded that he tried to convince Murat to comply with Allied wishes, and thus to surrender himself to a life in exile:

'He received me with the utmost kindness and cordiality, and upon my giving him a brief account of the manner in which I had obtained for him, from the Emperor of Austria, the offer of an asylum, he expressed his warmest acknowledgements for my exertions in his behalf, and his entire approbation of my conduct. I now had recourse to every argument and supplication in my power to induce him to

---

30. Carabelli, p. 28. Carabelli had been in Murat's civil service, probably as a military intendant or administrator.
31. Franceschetti, Domenico Cesare, *Mémoires sur les événements qui ont précédé la mort de Joachim 1er, roi des Deux-Siciles* (Paris, 1826).

accede to the proposal, and I informed him that an English frigate waited at Bastia to convey him to Trieste.'[32]

If supplication was involved, then we can be sure that Murat was not quite as keen on an Austrian exile as everyone supposed he should be. It would be a life-sentence of obscurity and oblivion, not conditions a man such as Murat could accept or prosper under. As Maceroni ran through their terms and conditions, it soon became clear their best offer was Murat's worst fear. Maceroni had originally hoped that Wellington would intervene on behalf of his royal patron, but in the event it was the busy Prince Metternich who took it upon himself to also decide Murat's fate, and his decisions were rubber-stamped by another hastily arranged Allied congress. Unsurprisingly, that meeting of Allied minds had agreed that Metternich's offer was best,[33] and Maceroni had therefore been given a general agreement, or treaty, drawn up and signed by Metternich on 1 September and a passport to travel to Trieste. A version of that passport was endorsed by Stuart on 9 September, with the phrase 'good for the voyage to Trieste', which suggests the intention was for Murat to make use of a British ship for his final voyage. The passport itself wasn't controversial, but the general agreement, which stipulated Allied terms and conditions, certainly would be. Despite describing Murat as 'King Joachim', it stipulated that Murat must henceforth assume the name of a private individual, and Count Lipona was suggested. It also prescribed that he would be free to choose his place of asylum, so long as it was in Austrian lands, more specifically a town in Bohemia, Moravia or Upper Austria, or a country house; in short, anywhere apart from Vienna. Third, the document insisted that 'the king shall give his word to His Imperial and Royal Majesty that he shall not quit Austrian territory without the express permission of his aforementioned

---

32. Maceroni, cited in *A few Specimens of the Ars Logica Copleiana*, p. 173.

33. Not everyone agreed that Murat should be granted an asylum. The court at Naples was livid and the Austrian ambassador, Count Jablonowski, was admonished by Ferdinand's Minister of Foreign Affairs, Circello. Jablonowski says he replied: 'Shouldn't your king prefer that Murat should stay 200 miles from Naples, under the eyes and supervision of a powerful ally of His Majesty, rather than having to constantly fear that the adventurer might land at a point on the coast which, because of its great extent, can never be properly guarded, and disturb the peace of the kingdom? Of course he won't succeed, that's what our troops are for. But he can cause enough unrest and disorder, especially if, as is not at all improbable, he joins forces with the Barbaresques [Barbary corsairs] and sets out to do mischief.'

Majesty and that he shall live the life in the style of a private person of means and submit to the law in vigour in Austrian territory'.[34]

This made it, of course, a gently phrased ultimatum to abdicate and renounce his throne, and the rights of his children to that throne. He was also being informed that he was to be kept prisoner, a private person and not a royal one, but one never permitted to leave the country. All in all, it would be a genteel incarceration, perhaps even more insulting for being voluntary. Unsurprisingly, as Maceroni set out the Allied offer and Murat began to understand the ramifications, the king grew increasingly furious. He even went so far as to tell Maceroni: 'I do not wish to offer myself as a prize to the house of Austria, I refuse their asylum if it comes with these conditions; I shall only see the queen again on the throne of Naples.'[35]

Murat had already made up his mind not to offer himself as a prize; his eyes were on a greater reward, after all. He gladly told Maceroni that, in any case, he had 'come too late, that the die was cast, that he had waited nearly three months with the utmost patience, and at the constant risk of his life for the decision of the Allies. That it appeared evident to him that he had been abandoned by the sovereigns who had so lately courted his alliance, to perish by the revengeful daggers of his enemies, and that he had at length resolved to attempt to regain his kingdom.'[36]

Maceroni again tried hard, or so he tells us, to persuade the king to give up, 'but found him immovable', so this strange envoy decided to leave it at that. It is difficult to tell if Maceroni was merely trying to persuade the readers of his memoirs that he had made a valiant attempt to stop Murat, something that looked good for the historical record given what was to follow, because his accounts are often contradictory and his

34. The text is in Add MS 41534 in Maceroni's papers.
35. Maceroni, Francis, *Interesting facts relating to the fall and death of Joachim Murat, King of Naples: the capitulation of Paris in 1815 and the second restoration of the Bourbons: original letters from King Joachim to the author, with some account of the author, and of his persecution by the French government* (London, 1817). Murat was also not sure Austria would be safe. He was soon telling Galvani that he would likely be poisoned there. 'I'd rather go to Constantinople,' he added, 'but they'd have me strangled there; no, gentleman, only in Naples can I be safe, only Naples. Therefore I shall go to Naples and, moreover, all my friends are in Italy and I should not be too distant from them.'
36. Another version toned down the anger, replacing it with a more noble discourse: 'He had at length been driven to the resolution of seeking death in a more honourable shape, adding that having now associated to his fate several hundred brave officers and men, his honour would not permit him to abandon them to persecution.'

conduct is rather singular. After all, he had never shown much urgency to bring the documents that he said could seal Murat's fate, and had also left Bastard and his troublesome frigate behind rather than sailing in to collect his patron. This might suggest to suspicious minds that Maceroni was out to win time for Murat to get away before the passports reached him, or to indicate to Bastard that all was in hand and settled. Nor can we properly know what Maceroni meant when, after handing over the passports, he told Murat he should accept them 'in the hope that he might during the course of his voyage determine to avail himself of it, and abandon his hostile enterprise'. He may genuinely have been hoping for a change of heart from Murat on the road to Damascus – or in this case passage to Naples – but equally, and here suspicious minds again sense something disingenuous, Maceroni was perhaps suggesting that Murat should use these documents as an insurance policy should his voyage prove unsuccessful; for example, should he be castaway during a storm on the coast of southern Italy. Then he might produce them to explain his surprise appearance, or should he be caught in *flagrante delicto* by the Neapolitan gunboats sweeping the seas between Corsica and Italy, then they might also save his life.

At least Maceroni had carried out his mission, so the pair quit Murat's office and Maceroni was then introduced to some of the others involved and implicated in the enterprise that was still going to be launched that evening. First came food, however, and everyone was ushered through to dinner. There, conversation focused on Murat's friendly British aristocrats, and inevitably, given the company were all military men, on Waterloo. Maceroni, forgetting his diplomatic mission and manners, hailed the steadfastness of the British infantry, which, given the company were soldiers who had spent their lives fighting Britain, was awkward. His assertion particularly irritated the great cavalryman in the room, Murat counter-attacking with 'had I been there I would have driven them in!'. Perhaps unaware that he too was in danger of being trampled underfoot, Maceroni, possibly emboldened by Dutch courage, responded with: 'Your Majesty would without doubt have crushed any Austrian or Prussian squares, but not those of the English.' This salvo forced Murat to draw on his last reserve of royal patience before swinging back with a *coup de grâce*, in which he declared: 'Monsieur Maceroni, I see you are loyal to your nation; even so, I would have broken the English squares, as I would those of the Austrians and Prussians, and Europe knows I would. But the way the French cavalry was used and sacrificed was faulty.'

After the forks – and sharp knives – were put down and the guests drifted away, Maceroni asked Murat for a formal reply to the Allied offer. Murat complied and sat down to write two very different letters. In the first one he kept things formal, keeping negotiations open by neither quite rejecting or fully accepting the offer:

> 'I accept the passport you have charged to deliver to me and I shall use it to repair to the destination fixed in it. As to the condition which his imperial and royal majesty annexes to the offer of an asylum in Austria, I reserve to myself the privilege of treating upon this important article at the period when I shall be united to my family. The disrespectful summons which the captain of his Britannic Majesty's frigate has addressed to me, prevents me from accepting the offer which you make me, in his name, to receive me on board his vessel.'[37]

His intention seems to have been to mask his warlike intentions by agreeing to go to Trieste, not with Bastard or under guard, but freely, in his own time and in boats of his choosing. This would be understandable to most who cared to query it; after all, the British were then seen as too inclined to cart eminent prisoners off to barren islands in the Atlantic. The letter closed by saying Murat would 'be leaving Corsica that evening' and implied it would just be with his valets, Charles and Armand, as unwarlike an enterprise as any pleasure cruise.

It was true that Murat would be leaving Corsica that evening, yet he would not just be taking his valets with him but hundreds of armed men, which meant that the letter was a ruse, as both men knew. Maceroni, again covering his master from any ensuing criticism, deliberately noted that Murat 'now observed to me that the letter he had just addressed to me contained a deception which he regarded as unbecoming his dignity and that it was his intention to address me another in which he would inform me of his real intentions and enter into some explanations concerning the motives of his conduct'. Murat summoned Galvani and, after jotting down some notes, began dictating a second letter to his secretary. This

---

37. Maceroni, *Interesting Facts*, p. 91.

letter was more honest and seems designed to serve as a justification for his actions, whether they turned out to be successful or not, and also to absolve Maceroni of any blame for abetting or aiding Murat.[38] Still fuming at the Allied offer, Murat could not help himself from opening the letter with a fresh tirade against those Allies who had so wronged him:

'I do not accept the conditions, Monsieur Macirone, that you are charged to offer me. I see them as being nothing short of an abdication pure and simple and all this in return for them permitting me to live, although even that in eternal captivity and subject to the arbitrary whim of the laws of a despotic government. Where is there any fairness, any justice? Is there anything here which shows consideration for an unfortunate prince formally recognised throughout Europe and who, at a critical moment, decided the campaign of 1814 in their favour. These powers now, against their own interests, weigh him down with their own persecutions.'

He continued with reflections on other matters that irritated him and set out a rather unrealistic appraisal of the army he had spent so much time and treasure forming:

'There is not one individual in that army who does not recognise his error. I am leaving to join them. They burn with the desire to see me at their head. Their affection for me is undiminished, as is that among each class of my subjects. I never abdicated. I have the right to retake my crown and God will give me the strength and the means.'

Then came the artifice intended to exonerate Maceroni and excuse him from not having prevented his departure, but also, perhaps, one that might serve – and with a flourish – as Murat's final testament:

---

38. The full text of this letter can be seen in Annex II. As for when he received it, Maceroni's testimony varies. Maceroni told Metternich 'a few days after the departure of King Joachim and upon coming back to my quarters, I found a second letter on my table which was addressed to me and which was dated 28 September. I take the liberty of sending a copy to Your Excellency.' In his memoirs, he says he was presented with the letter when he was at the citadel the morning after Murat's flotilla had sailed.

'You will not be able to prevent me from leaving, even if you wished to do so. By the time you have received this letter I shall already be on my way to my destination. Either I shall succeed or I shall end my troubles. I have braved death a thousand times fighting for my country; can I not do so once again but this time for myself? I shudder only for the fate of my family.'

Maceroni was fully appraised of Murat's secret and, knowing what those intentions were, happily provided cover to his master by shielding him from the British and the Austrians, and therefore felt entitled to send this not entirely truthful report to Metternich:

'I informed King Joachim of the mission I had been charged with by Your Excellency. We spent some time discussing this but, in the end, he seemed quite disposed to accept the conditions I presented him with without, however, coming to a firm decision. I left him at nine that evening after he asked me to come for lunch the following morning.'[39]

Before quitting the inn, Maceroni says he received a bill of exchange for his expenses and handed over Murat's trunk of clothes, which Murat's valets brought in. He told Metternich he left at nine o'clock, but this is certainly not true for Maceroni was still there when Murat was interrupted by his next visitor just after eleven. This was the equally enigmatic but far less talkative Ignazio Carabelli. Murat had sent an aide, a certain Monsieur Fournier,[40] to find him and invite him for an interview, even though Murat had already received information from Naples that Carabelli could not be trusted. Indeed, a certain Cristiani, who had also arrived from Naples, was openly denouncing him as a police agent.[41] Certainly, most of what passed

---

39. Lemmi, p. 294. The mention of lunch was probably to persuade Metternich that Murat was taking his time to deliberate, rather than launching himself immediately into an operation the Allied offer had been designed to prevent.
40. Fournier was also against the king going, having even presented Murat with a gloomy volume on a failed medieval attempt to seize Naples. It dealt with Conrad, or Conradin, of Hohenstaufen, who had declared himself king of Jerusalem and Sicily but was captured by Charles of Anjou and beheaded in Naples in 1268. Franceschetti also warned Murat he should wait: 'Too much haste will open up an abyss into which you and the brave officers and men attached to you will be swallowed up.'
41. Franceschetti was the source of this, and he had received a letter from a friend he calls 'GM' in Naples that told him to trust in Cristiani and stated: 'Ignace Carabelli has made secret

that evening would reach the ears of the Bourbon Minister of Police, Luigi de Medici, and although Ignazio Carabelli vehemently denied it – saying he was only in Corsica by chance – it does seem as though the Bourbons had sent him on a particular mission and using a British ship. What that mission was is still far from clear, but the Carabellis may have been sent to rally local support to enable the French authorities to either seize Murat or at least prevent him, or any of his men, from leaving Corsican soil. It was clearly impossible to hand Murat over to the French authorities, given those authorities had fled and Murat was surrounded by armed men, so the Carabellis had arrived too late to do much more than try to dissuade Murat from sailing. This Ignazio Carabelli was prepared to do, and he therefore obeyed the summons:

'I had barely entered the room before he asked me whether I came from Naples and if it is true that King Ferdinand had revoked the endowments he had bestowed on his generals and favourites and I replied that it was true that he had. After a few other general and vague questions he stated that he could not hide the fact, as everyone knew it, that he was about to embark to set out and reconquer his kingdom.'[42]

Carabelli says Maceroni was still present, as were Galvani and Franceschetti, and that it was after eleven when they started talking. Neither side found much solace from the conversation. Galvani was taking notes and says that he heard the king tell Carabelli that he intended to return to Naples, to which Ignazio replied that if he did so 'he would be lost' as there was no popular support. Carabelli's account confirms this: 'I told him that without soldiers, without weapons, without much help of assistance, he would achieve nothing but failure, and that this, the most rash and mad adventure one could imagine, would end miserably.' Murat argued back against this

arrangements with the prefect of police in Naples and has received passports to travel; secrecy surrounds his mission, even at police headquarters, but I hope that Carabelli has not been tricked into doing something that would offend his friends and compatriots. Be on your guard with Carabelli, place your trust in Cristiani and in me and the others as we wish to safeguard the health of a prince that merits our trust and our service.' Franceschetti, p. 40. This seems correct. Carabelli had been deprived of his position by Murat and may have had a grudge against the king.
42. Carabelli, p. 32.

brutal assessment, but Carabelli's barbed comment lead him to wonder out loud, why it was that his people had shifted their loyalty to Ferdinand so quickly. He went on to reveal a naïve belief in the faith of the clergy, thinking they at least should have remained true as 'they had sworn an oath of loyalty on their knees'. Carabelli broke that particular spell by informing Murat that 'they had just done the same to Ferdinand'. After an awkward pause, there followed some more pragmatic questions, Murat asking about the Austrians, to which Carabelli, true to his mission to ward off Murat, told the king there were 7,000 or 8,000 at Naples and that the 'newspapers in Tuscany said another column of them was on the way'.

Fortunately, this difficult encounter was now drawing to a close. Earlier, Carabelli had heard from General Ottavi that Murat would offer him a position at Salerno if he would join them. Carabelli used the opportunity of being in the king's presence to publicly refuse, telling the king: 'I do not wish to go and be killed in Naples.' 'Well,' Murat shot back, 'I will go and die like a king.' This ended the rather fruitless exchange and Carabelli was politely ushered out of Murat's quarters:

> 'I went out to the lobby with Galvani and found gathered there around 30 officers getting ready to leave, among them Colonel Natali and Capitan Ettore; I told them that I thought they were heading to their certain doom as someone in Murat's state of mind was sure to ruin them. It was midnight [sic] and Captain Ettore, who would be in charge of one of the boats of the expedition, offered to accompany me back to my quarters and on the way I repeated my reasons as to why they should not go. He was a young, sensible man and he made the following reply: "I am persuaded by what you say and know that we are going to die, but I have promised to leave and do not wish to break my word."'

Murat's times, like our own, saw as much loyalty as duplicity, but it was generally assumed that officers were held to a higher standard of conduct, even if, as we shall see, that was never completely guaranteed in practice. Those men Murat had selected to follow him were professional, experienced soldiers, and most would prove dependable; none more so, of course, than the loyal Franceschetti. He had been left alone with a Murat perhaps a little shaken by Carabelli's bitter reproaches. So now, at that late hour, Franceschetti – good soldier and loyal friend that he was – sought to shake Murat out from his reverie and asked: 'When do we leave?' 'Tonight at midnight,' came the clear reply.

The boats were ready, although Poli noted a certain unease among the crews and some of Murat's officers:

'That evening, the sailors who had, earlier that day, seemed prepared to sail without being paid now declared that they would only leave if they were paid an advance. So this was done, [but] even so a number of them failed to show up for the roll call. A few important personages, amongst others, General Ottavi, who were supposed to be leaving with Murat, betrayed their promises. General Ottavi had, until half past ten, assured him he was ready to leave. Then, as we were to set sail, it was impossible to find him.'[43]

It was sometime around half past eleven when Murat exited his hotel arm in arm with Franceschetti, and, leading his officers, went down through cheering crowds to the Greek chapel, where, chatting to his staff, he waited as his men clambered aboard the boats in the harbour. Then, when all was ready, he marched over to what is still known as the Quai Napoleon and also embarked.

Galvani says that in total, 298 people accompanied Murat.[44] Not all were soldiers, for there were twenty-two sailors and at least four servants, but the troops ranged from a drummer aged 14, and many other teenagers, to one veteran aged 57. Murat was taking only Corsicans, save for three or four Frenchmen, one Tuscan, one Maltese and one Roman; it did not seem to trouble him that no Neapolitans were with him.

Before long, all was ready. The five *trabacoli* and the little felucca were loaded with food and water for just eight days, and the soldiers made themselves as comfortable as possible so anchors could be weighed. The first of the vessels, Dominique Forcioli's *Saint Erasme*, would transport Murat, Baron Barbara, Franceschetti, Natali, Major Silvio Ottaviani, captains

---

43. Poli cannot be entirely trusted here. Later, in February 1816, Ottavi joined the government troops sent against Poli during the Fiumorbu insurgency, so the two were certainly not friends.
44. Other accounts state there were only 188 soldiers. There was one woman, the wife of Charles Marion, Maddalena Osmond, aged 26.

Antoine Félix Lanfranchi and Giovanni Battista Viggiani, Mathieu Galvani of the commissary, the servants and twenty-eight non-commissioned officers and soldiers. On the slightly more capacious *Misericorde*, owned by Dominique Tavera, was Major Philippe César Courand, Captain Pietro Pernice, lieutenants Jean Multedo, Domenico Medori and Luca Pelligrini, and second lieutenants Pisani, Susini, Bailli and Lorica. This boat also housed seventy-three non-commissioned officers and soldiers. On Thomas Drago's *Conception* were Lieutenant Cuttosi and second lieutenants Ettore, Lega, Nosoi, Naltrini, Leonetti and Pietro Pasqualini,[45] plus thirty-seven non-commissioned officers and soldiers.

Master Andrea Cauro also had a boat named the *Conception*, which contained Captain Pietro Paolo Giacometti, lieutenants Domenico Mattei, Alessandro Graziani, Nicola Costa and Francesco Marchetti, and thirty non-commissioned officers and soldiers. The final merchantman was the *Vierge du Carmel* of Xavier Antonio Pozzo di Borgo, who hosted Captain Luigi Semidei with thirty-four non-commissioned officers and soldiers. The only other vessel in the fleet was the swift little felucca, the *Voltigeante* of Master Vincent Cecconi, which Murat hoped would serve as a messenger or scout and also store some of the inevitable baggage. It carried just seventeen soldiers.[46]

It was strange that the passengers were unevenly distributed across vessels that were supposedly of the same type, and it was also odd that no more of the 600 Corsicans who had declared themselves willing to follow were permitted to board.[47] This suggests that the embarkation had been rather hurried, perhaps precipitated by Maceroni's arrival or by fears that Bastard may soon arrive to block the port. Certainly, everyone was now acting as though there was no time to be lost, and as the crowd continued to shout 'Vive Joachim!' and 'Vive le roi Murat!', a pistol shot rang out, giving the signal for departure. The boats cast off and began to quit Ajaccio just as 29 September began. The citadel watched quietly, but to keep up appearances the gunners were ordered to fire, which they did – reluctantly – sending

---

45. He later transferred to Murat's vessel.
46. Cecconi's account ran: 'On 28 September I was at Ajaccio with my felucca the *Voltigeante* and I was chartered by General Franceschetti for the sum of 6,000 Francs, the same price as paid for the other ships that were to make up the flotilla for the expedition under King Joachim.' He says he received an advance of just 1,000 Francs.
47. Tuscan spies reported that 'for want of transport some 1,000 more volunteers were left behind'.

some half-hearted roundshot wide of the last boat. This shot that was just enough to look good in their commander's subsequent report:

'The ex-king of Naples has slipped out of Ajaccio where he had been with five gunboats and in which he had embarked two generals, some officers and 250 Corsican soldiers who had served in Corsica [*sic*]. It is believed that he has said he is going to Calabria. However, on the night of 28 September, when he was leaving Ajaccio, the commandant of the fort fired two roundshot at the gunboats to make them obey but they had no effect and they were seen sailing for Calvi and Saint Florent. This suggests that they are heading for France probably as they had learned that King Ferdinand had taken measures to arrest them at sea should they try to attempt any landing in his territory.'

Others said, or planted the story, that Murat was destined for Tunis. But the reality was, of course, that he was bound for Naples. Maceroni, who had heard the gunshot,[48] knew Murat's real intentions but was again able to play a small part in helping Murat get clean away. This time his actions were more overt, doing what he could to delay the pursuit. Of course, this did not stop him lying to Prince Metternich that he had done his best to raise the alarm:

'On the 29th, at seven in the morning, I was woken and given a letter from King Joachim and learned, at the same time, that he had rashly set sail an hour after midnight taking with him one or two generals, some Corsican officers and around 200 armed men as well as a small calibre piece of artillery. The vessels they embarked on consisted of five small boats of lateen sails called feluccas and it is supposed that he is sailing for the kingdom of Naples. I did not lose a minute and sent a message to Captain Bastard, captain of HMS *Meander*, who was waiting for news in Bastia. My despatch happily reached him after 26 hours and he set off at once in pursuit of the flotilla and also sent off gunboats to various points along the Italian coast to raise the alarm.'

---

48. He went to the citadel and heard from the gunners that their shot had been deliberately aimed wide. Later that morning he heard from their commander, Colonel Delaforest, that this was true as the garrison was all for Murat.

However, this was not true; Maceroni's message to Captain Bastard was only sent twelve hours after Murat's departure, and it actually took thirty hours to reach the frigate captain, neatly giving Murat time to get beyond Sardinia as the earliest Bastard could set out in pursuit was on the night of 30 September. This supposedly urgent message Maceroni sent to Captain Bastard is interesting in the way it mixes truth with fiction:

'I have the honour to inform you that immediately on my arrival here yesterday afternoon I communicated by letter to King Joachim the purport of my mission. He refused to sign the proposals of the Austrian government, declaring that they contain nothing more or less than a simple abdication with the only condition of delivering up his person into the custody of the Austrian government. I enclose you, sir, my letter and his answer, *which he did not send me before this morning* [my emphasis], when at the same time I was informed that he had sailed suddenly in the night with about 150 men, several generals and officers, most probably for the coast of Calabria. I think you may be in time to intercept him as I am in hopes that you will receive this letter tomorrow night. I think it my duty to make all possible haste to Paris.'[49]

When Captain Bastard received this message, he set sail, writing to Lord Burghersh as soon as he reached Livorno and trying hard to excuse his delay:

'I take the opportunity of informing you that I left Bastia yesterday evening in consequence of a letter I received from Colonel Macirone [*sic*] who, I believe your lordship knows, was charged with a mission from the Emperor of Austria to offer Murat an asylum in his dominions, at Ajaccio, acquainting me that Murat, having refused to sign the proposal, embarked suddenly in the night of 28 September and sailed with about 150 officers and men, as you will observe by

49. *Correspondence of Lord Burghersh*, p. 197. Maceroni did leave for Paris. Murat had presented him with a bill of exchange for 40,000 Francs to compensate him for his expenses and for the debts he had incurred in London when purchasing lace and cashmere for the queen and the wife of Gallo, Murat's foreign minister, during the spring of 1815. He was promptly arrested when he reached Marseille, the authorities suspecting him of aiding Murat's escape.

the extracts of Colonel Macirone's letters which I have the honour to enclose.

'I regret that Colonel Macirone, in the hurry of writing, did not mention the size and description of the vessels in which he embarked, to enable me to judge of his probable destination. I believe, however, from the information of the person who conveyed the express to me, that he sailed with three vessels called gondolas capable of containing about 50 men and a week's provisions, but I can inform no opinion where he is gone.

'I despatched yesterday two of the gunboats under my orders at Bastia with the information to Naples and the coast of Italy,[50] and I left one there to convey any particulars of Murat's departure and embarkation the governor of Bastia might learn after my quitting it. It appears that Murat was favourably received by the inhabitants of Ajaccio, in spite of the governor's endeavours to prevent his entering the place. I have obtained the names of some of the officers supposed to have accompanied Murat, which I have the honour to enclose.'[51]

Maceroni, assisting everyone – but some more than others – had bought valuable time for Murat and his followers. By the time Bastard's superior had read his hasty despatch, the erstwhile king of Naples was on the open seas and heading for the rocky coast of his old kingdom.

---

50. Bastard reached Livorno on 3 October, while Gunboat Nr 4 went to the Papal States, allowing the governor of Civitavecchia to inform the Austrians that Murat had quit Corsica. General Lezeltern promptly sent a courier to General Lauer in Rome advising of this and adding: 'Murat has so little credit and support in Italy so the results of his mad behaviour need not trouble us; however, as his actions may have an impact on a few extremists or the discontent then it would be wise to consider the possible effects of the actions of this desperate adventurer.' Lauer sent the warning on to Naples and informed Count Jablonowski on 4 October: 'I have just received notice of Murat's flight from Ajaccio during the night of 28 September with 150 armed men on board three ships. One thinks him directed towards the coasts of Naples. This news dated Bastia of October 1 adds that the English gentleman [Maceroni] who came to speak to Murat on the 28th could not obtain his adhesion to the decisions of the Allied Sovereigns in his respect.'

51. *Correspondence of Lord Burghersh*, p. 196. It is odd that Bastard does not mention that Murat left 'most probably for the coast of Calabria'. The list of officers Bastard cites is in Add MS 41534. It calls Franceschetti a colonel, and 'Gavalni' [*sic*] a major, and alongside Natali it says in error that a certain Cauro also embarked. The list is signed 'Blanchard', the surname of Armand, Murat's valet.

Chapter 6

At Sea

While the Allies scurried to their action stations, Murat's expedition was making good progress. When the last of the vessels to leave port, the *Voltigeante*, caught up with the convoy, morale was raised a little further as favourable winds carried the little armada south towards Sardinia. Even though Murat was buoyed by a firm belief in his own abilities and the righteousness of his cause, nobody really knew what their reception might be should they make it to the kingdom of Naples. Murat had no real plan for the landing; indeed, he had spent more time drawing up a constitution and specifying who should wear his cockade for the weeks after his assumed victory than he had in finessing the details of what he would do if he managed to step ashore. This was unfortunate, as his belief that his kingdom was ripe for his amateurish putsch was just that, an assumption, and a rather unrealistic one at that.

Murat had received no impartial intelligence on the state of the country before he set sail. His agent, Lambruschini, had, after all, still not returned. The spy had been diligent enough in his task, seeking out General Filangieri, who was 'overcome with joy' when the envoy told him he had come from the king. According to Lambruschini, as related through Galvani, the general had given a guarded summary of the situation in the country and the mood in the army, stressing how 'the situation as it stood renders the king's objectives difficult'. Filangieri then described 'how the troops were positioned, the situation in the kingdom, the opinions of the Neapolitans, the preparations being made to defend the kingdom from attack, the changes in the administration and the ministries, and, of course, the police'.[1] The wise soldier also told him who Murat might trust, and what Lambruschini might do to evade the police, a band of men then uncharacteristically active for Neapolitan government officials.[2]

---

1. Valente, Angela, *Gioacchino Murat e l'Italia meridionale* (Turin, 1963).
2. Lambruschini spent a further four days in Naples, seeing the general again and being told by him to leave as soon as he could for his own safety, but also meeting a banker called Falconnet

None of this cautious and still rather vague information would reach
Murat in time, however, as Lambruschini only quit Naples on 3 October,
eventually reaching Bastia on 12 October and there learning that Murat
and his band of followers had sailed.

Filangieri had been right to be wary. Naples was certainly tired of war, of
conscription, of seeing its young men sent off to Spain, Russia or Germany
whenever Napoleon needed reinforcements. Murat's fall, and the general
triumph of the Allies, had ended that seemingly perpetual conflict. The
return of the Bourbons at least meant peace, which made the corruption
and stagnation that came in their wake more tolerable. The influx of royalist
courtiers and generals looking for their old positions and sinecures was of
course resented, as was the presence of an Austrian garrison, but there had
been no time for these irritations to fester. Those ministers and generals
who had actively served Murat had gone into exile or, understandably,
undergone a complete and public conversion into loyal upholders of the
new order. The consequences were there for all to see. Few – very few –
among the elite were nostalgic yet for Murat, and the British ambassador,
William A'Court, Baron Heytersbury, who seemed to pray daily for the
utter destruction of the Bonapartists, relished the change in regime and was
soon enthusiastically promising his superiors that Murat's day was over:

'All is going on smoothly and the number of Muratists daily
diminishes. I do not quite approve of their being taken completely
into favour, or that Ambrosia and Filangini [sic] should so soon have
been appointed members of the board, which conducts all military
affairs. I am however positively assured that the business could not
have been carried out without them. The downfall of Napoleon may
possibly make them very good subjects.'[3]

The upper classes may have been diffident, but attitudes among the urban
middle classes and the civil service – the two sectors in society that had

---

in Naples, a man whom Murat hoped could forward him 100,000 Francs. However, the
banker, who would be arrested by the Neapolitan secret police on 5 October, noted that the
Count de Mosbourg had largely emptied the king's accounts in May, hopefully with a view
to saving them from the Bourbons, so Murat's account contained only 14,952 Ducats. This
had been sequestered by Medici, the Bourbon Minister of Police.

3. *Correspondence of Lord Burghersh*, p. 215. Written on 18 July 1815 but given the incorrect
date of 1816.

prospered most under the more meretricious French policies – were harder to judge. Raymond-Jacques-Marie de Narbonne-Pelet, A'Court's French colleague, hinted at some difficulties over loyalties when he told Paris that 'the majority of the more junior positions are filled by those who occupied them when under Murat, amongst whom there are those who are not quite so attached to the government they currently serve. The royalists are therefore unhappy and complain that they are being overlooked but the different branches of the administration value experience so it is therefore inevitable that the civil service includes many who proved themselves loyal to the other faction.'[4]

This did not, however, mean that such functionaries would welcome Murat's return, or risk their lives or salaries for a man who had, after all, so recently run away. Further down the social scale, the common folk were fiercely Bourbon, all king and church and 'death to the French!', which meant that, given the very small and hesitant numbers nostalgic for the old order, weighed against the very vociferous urban and rural underclass with a penchant for butchering revolutionaries, the greatest fear of the ambassadors was not that Murat would sweep away the regime with popular support, but that his return would trigger a popular massacre of the kind that had rendered Naples notorious in 1799. As summer turned to autumn, William A'Court told his superior, the foreign secretary Viscount Castlereagh, that what he feared the most was a repeat of just such a bloodbath:

> 'Should he effect a landing in this kingdom, the principal thing to be dreaded would be the rising of the people and the general massacre of his adherents in this city. The number of his friends is small and of the number not one probably would have the courage to join him.'[5]

Murat's best bet lay with his army, and here, as with Napoleon's return from Elba, it was not so much the generals who could be relied upon, but the junior officers and, here and there, the civic guard and provincial legions raised among a middle class terrified of the lower orders and the ubiquitous banditry of the south. As for the soldiers in the regular army, they had run

4. Ersilio, Michel, '*Vicende dei Corsi che seguirono G.* Murat al Pizzo, 1815–1817', in *Archivio Storico di Corsica*, V, 14 (1929).
5. Burghersh, Lord (Fane, John), Weigall, Rachel (ed.), *Correspondence of Lord Burghersh, 1808–1840* (London, 1912).

away from Murat, and they could also accuse him quite fairly of having abandoned them; but even if their regiments could be rebuilt, and given their performance in May, it was not clear if they would be a match for the Sicilians and Austrians who then occupied the kingdom's strategic centres.

Still, the Bourbons were the untrusting kind, and Ferdinand was especially given to bouts of paranoia, so news that Murat was in Corsica, and that he had loyal supporters there, sent shivers down the royal spine. Ferdinand's ministers were therefore commanded to make preparations, and his chief of police, Minister Luigi de Medici – a man who loved intrigue, which is not the same as being good at it – emerged from the shadows to coordinate arrangements designed primarily to prevent Murat from reaching Italy. Gunboats had been sent out to patrol the seas, and Medici had also despatched his agents to serve as advance warning or, as in the case of Carabelli, to ward off Murat or weaken the resolve of his followers. In the kingdom itself, his spies and men of confidence listened out for signs of sedition; anything anti-royal or Muratist was of interest, and one agent was soon reporting back that, in Calabria, he had heard it said that a new republic would be proclaimed on 4 November, and that Joachim Murat would be made its First Consul.[6] Another agent at Sorrento reported, even more bizarrely, that Murat would establish a republic and rule it alongside Lord Bentinck.[7]

These were rumours, symptoms of uncertain times, but Carabelli had failed, and even while Medici's agents were chasing wild geese, Murat was on his way to reclaim his lost throne. After quitting Ajaccio with his flotilla, he had been held in check by contrary winds near the island of Asinara off the north-west of Sardinia. There they had encountered a Spanish ship also seeking shelter, but when it caught sight of the little fleet it took them for Barbary corsairs and veered off towards the island of Maddalena. This was probably just as well, for Murat had considered seizing it in an act of piracy that would win him a more seaworthy vessel but make him an outlaw on the sea as well as on land. The winds relented, giving the fleet time to slip round the pointed tip of Sardinia, and then came back in full force,

---

6. The Countess of Albany, wife of Bonnie Prince Charlie, then in exile in Florence, heard that 'the man of the mountain' is in Corsica and that 'word has it he wishes to land in Calabria and he has lots of money but they think they can catch him in Corsica'. Archivio Borbone, F 656.
7. There was a rumour at court that Bentinck was involved in inviting Murat back to seize the throne. Ferdinand loathed Bentinck, which might explain the rumour.

driving the frail vessels into the bay of Pozzo on the north-eastern coast of the island. On 30 September, as they again made headway, they were spotted by a Sardinian watchtower on Maddalena and the coastguard fired a warning shot, followed by an actual roundshot, at the ships, which, to the king's delight, bounced harmlessly off the rocks of Sardinia. The flotilla then continued on to the limestone cliffs of the island of Tavolara,[8] where, at two o'clock in the afternoon, they secured the boats and the soldiers were disembarked for the night. The king then organized his men into companies and handed out another forty blue uniforms with white buttons and red turnbacks, and ten cartridges were also issued to those who had muskets. Everyone rose early again on the morning of 1 October and the expedition continued eastwards.

Had they travelled the shortest distance from Tavolara to Naples, they would have found themselves before Gaeta, or had Barbara been a little more skilful, then they would have selected a destination south of the capital. In the event, caprice or misjudgement meant that when they sighted land on 5 October, they were surprised to be so close to the menacing slopes of Vesuvius and realized they had blundered too close to the capital for their own good. Murat's star had led them a little astray, but for now, not fatally. However, just as the boats, and Murat, were drifting a little, hesitating before events, the weather seized the initiative.

The flotilla was turning to head south when, in the late afternoon of 6 October, a storm hit the ships before they could seek shelter in the bay of Policastro, around the headland from Salerno. As men make history, the weather holds them in its hands and now the winds scattered Murat's carefully appointed fleet, driving the helpless boats dozens of miles apart. By the following morning, only Murat's vessel, flying a French ensign in the hope other boats would see it and rally,[9] and the felucca remained of his navy. Murat lingered off San Lucido, briefly sending the felucca in search of the others while, according to Galvani, he himself gave way to despair. There, lonely on his flagship, he 'sat in the ship's barge, totally absorbed by

---

8. The valet Charles is mistaken when he writes that 'On 2 October, with the winds contrary, the king put in at the island of Caprara', as it was certainly the isolated Tavolara, with its steep cliffs, that briefly hosted the expedition.

9. There had been signals agreed before the storm, namely beating out a tattoo on a metal bar on the bridge rail, rather than lighting lanterns that might have alerted the authorities, but this measure proved useless in the circumstances.

his thoughts, and, resting his head on his right hand, looked up to heaven as though begging to know the cause of the misfortune which so dogged his destiny'.

Nobody answered, but there were others whose eyes were turned to Earth, and they spotted two men on the shore, one on a mule and the other walking alongside. What caught the attention of those on board was the fact that the pedestrian was wearing the uniform of Murat's Guards. Murat wanted to land at once, but preparations were interrupted by a shot from Schooner N.4, one of King Ferdinand's patrol boats, which had just entered San Lucido's harbour. Its captain, Francesco Barba, then on his way south to Pizzo, was wary of the strange craft, thinking they must be pirates or smugglers. To show goodwill, the visitors again hoisted the white Bourbon ensign, and Major Silvio Ottaviani and a sailor were sent off in a launch, rowed over by two other Corsican sailors, to explain to the captain of the schooner that they were friends. The captain wanted to know their business. Ottaviani said they were from France and were heading to Trieste. Two of the sailors were sent back for documents to prove this, while Ottaviani and his illiterate companion, Gianbatista Cerisolo, were detained and, escorted by a lieutenant, handed over to the port authorities. They then found themselves subjected to a lengthy interrogation, as follows:

Question 'Your names, first names, origin, profession, what boat you were on, the strength of the crew and destination?'

Answer 'I am Silvio Ottaviani, a major of Corsican Chasseurs under the Napoleonic government, and the other is Gianbatista Cerisolo, sailor in a Corsican vessel of 11 sailors and 10 passengers, all Corsican. The former is from Erbajolo and the second Ajaccio, from where we sailed.'

Question 'How do you find yourselves in this port?'

Answer 'Having left Corsica, and being in the waters off this coast with another two boats from our own country, we were dispersed during the darkness of the night and found ourselves off the coast by this port, although we did not know where we were. We were waiting here to see if the others would return, and a third boat join, when we saw a xebec of His Majesty King Ferdinand which fired a warning shot at us and we hastened to obey and we sent a launch over to tell him that we were from France, and under the French flag, and that we were bound for Trieste on business. However, we did not have with us our boat's charter or the crew's manifest, or the other required documents, and so we were brought into the harbour by the royal xebec's captain and a lieutenant of the National Guard.'

Question 'What documents do you have?'

Answer 'I, Silvio Ottaviani, have no documents save my pay book from the time I was in service and which was issued by the Minister of War under Napoleon, last dated 24 June and signed by General Baron di Hasorelli, orders indicating I shall return to Corsica [to report to the Duke of Padua], also signed by three communes there, and with the seal of Napoleon and Louis XVIII, plus a certificate signed by the major of the commune.'

Question 'Who are the other passengers?'

Answer 'They are gentlemen who, because of the war in France, are obliged to seek exile far away.'[10]

The poor illiterate Corsican sailor was less forthcoming, and when asked what he was doing there he limited himself to explaining:

'I was part of the crew of a barque belonging to Domenico Fricciuoli of Ajaccio. We left the port of that place around eight days ago with another five barques of around the same size and belonging to masters from different places in Corsica and we went off in the direction of Sardinia and then into these waters to go to Trieste. Arriving off Paola, and around 10 miles off, we were struck by a storm which scattered the boats.'[11]

The authorities were understandably more interested in the soldier, Ottaviani, and the other mysterious French gentlemen waiting out to sea,

---

10. Archivio Borbone, Fascio 656.
11. Archivio Borbone, carton 656 (*Carte relative l'arresto e il processo di Gioacchino Murat*, includes interrogations of Murat's followers).

so he was forced to explain away their presence, and what he was doing here. Ottaviani therefore confessed that they had been 'on half pay in Corsica, and unsure of our fate, when I, with many of my compatriots and friends, decided we would leave Corsica and travel to the Levant to find a decent living. Meeting the former King of Naples, Gioacchino, quite by chance in Ajaccio, he told us he had an Austrian and English passport allowing him to go as he pleased, and he said his intention was to travel to Trieste or Constantinople, or some other place in the east, and that he wished to take with him as companions a number of officers.'

This was enough to have these two suspicious visitors placed under quarantine under the watchful eye of a lieutenant of the National Guard while the authorities worried whether King Joachim really was a few hundred metres away. He was, and while the two returning sailors amused his officers by informing them that the authorities thought the visitors were Barbary corsairs, the king was more serious. He saw that he was not going to be welcome here and that the schooner made any landing impossible, so he decided to continue on down the coast to Amantea. The Corsicans therefore abandoned their two unhappy companions and set off into the gloom.

They had not gone far when, all of a sudden, another boat appeared. Thankfully, as the valet Armand recalled, it was a friendly vessel, one of the stray sheep scattered in the storm:

'After two hours, we saw a boat and it was the one with Monsieur Courant [sic], three other officers and around 30 soldiers most of whom had served in the king's Guard.'[12]

It was the *Misericorde* of Dominique Tavera. But all was not well, and shortly afterwards, two officers – Pietro Pernice, a loyal soldier who had persuaded many Corsicans to follow Murat,[13] and Jean Multedo – transferred to the royal ship to complain of the conduct of their commander, Philippe Cesar Courand,[14] a man they dramatically accused of cowardice. Courand was summoned to the royal ship and seemed offended that his subordinates

---

12. Account by the valet Armand in AN, 31AP/21, Dossier 361.
13. For example, the soldier Antonio Matteo Catanej, a student in Ajaccio, was persuaded to follow Murat to Trieste by Pernice.
14. Born in 1784, Courand was a distinguished captain in the king's velites.

had questioned his loyalty. Even so, Franceschetti went to the trouble of asking 'Barbara to take Courand's vessel in tow as it contained 50 veteran soldiers on whom the king was counting'.[15] The advice was sound. Barbary corsairs were operating in the area, and someone thought they spotted the British flag on a distant brig, so all were resolved to leave no one behind. However, when an enemy struck it proved to be one closer to home, as Captain Cecconi on the felucca related:

> 'Courand went back to his boat without the two officers. Commandant Barbara towed the boat of Courand along the shore and, around midnight, we were at Mantea [Amantea], where we thought to put in, when Major Courand's boat cut the cables without us noticing and made off. We were astonished by such a vile act.'[16]

Courand did indeed sail off, telling his men and a second boat he encountered, Master Drago's *Conception* containing Ettore and forty more officers and soldiers, that the expedition had been called off and that as the king was going on to Trieste, he had no need of them. Giving up rather too easily, the brave soldiers promptly returned to Corsica.

Courand's departure, following quickly after the stormy reminder of the caprice of the sea, and of fate more generally, clearly disheartened Murat and placed him in a dilemma. His solution seems to have been to give up on the idea of an invasion and reconcile himself to failure and exile. Franceschetti, who had the enviable ability to remember long rambling speeches in their entirety, was surprised to hear the king declaim:

> 'My idea had been to see my capital and my subjects again and to spare them from the revenge of a government that wished to punish them for having assisted my government of the kingdom of Naples.

---

15. Franceschetti, Domenico Cesare, *Mémoires sur les événements qui ont précédé la mort de Joachim 1er, roi des Deux-Siciles* (Paris, 1826). Armand said thirty soldiers, but the valet Charles says that 'he had with him 40 of the best soldiers who had served in the king's Guard in Naples'. It should, however, have had seventy soldiers. It is presumed the men were redistributed among the other vessels during the pause at Tavolara.
16. Franceschetti, p. 172. Before we shout treason, there is a possibility, although Franceschetti does not mention it, that Courand was told by Murat that the expedition was being called off and he could return to Corsica. As we shall see, shortly afterwards, Murat himself declared he was giving up.

The idea that so many talented and brave men would be persecuted for their opinions, for their service, troubled me. The fate of my friends made me unhappy but I now see that my plan was a risky one. The wind has scattered my ships and just a handful of men are still available. Let us go on to Trieste and I shall accept the offer of asylum that the Austrian government has offered me.'[17]

The more matter-of-fact Charles merely remembered that 'given there were hardly enough people remaining, the king decided to abandon his project'.[18] Some among his subordinates were probably quite relieved as just about everyone was, by this stage, tired, hungry and – perhaps worse – thirsty.[19] Just as worryingly, Murat's remaining vessel and the *Voltigeante* felucca had been badly damaged in the storm and repair was not possible at sea. Fearful of the Messina straits, Baron Barbara insisted that continuing on to Trieste in these vessels would be impossible. Murat tried to persuade him otherwise, but Barbara pushed back and exclaimed that, in this season, it would be too dangerous to attempt a crossing of the fickle Adriatic in such rickety boats. The Maltese admiral in charge of what remained of Murat's flotilla had briefly suggested putting in at Messina before changing his mind and opting for Pizzo, a small fishing port, thinking it might supply food and water and allow them to exchange their battered vessel for something that could survive the voyage to Trieste and exile. Armand, who was close to Murat, remembered their exchange of views and Barbara's insistence on heading for a port:

'The king now intended to head to Trieste with the passport the Emperor of Austria had provided to him, and which His Majesty had received on the very day he had departed from Ajaccio. As the boat had been damaged by the bad weather, and as supplies and water were starting to run short, the king suggested to Monsieur Barbara, [the] frigate captain, that it would be necessary to procure another

---

17. Franceschetti, p. 48.
18. AN 31AP/21, Dossier 362.
19. Thirst was evidently an issue. A British report to Admiral Exmouth later stated that 'the total number who left Corsica with him was 141. … In the boat in which Murat was, only one bottle of water remained which was kept for his own use.' Add Ms 35651, written on HMS *Queen*, at sea, 25 October, probably by Admiral Charles Vinicombe Penrose.

boat if they were to cross the Adriatic, and that it was also important to collect supplies, and the captain replied that this might be done at Pizzo (Calabria Ulterior) as it had everything that might be needed and was, moreover the nearest port and that he had contacts there.'[20]

This seemed sensible and Barbara did indeed have connections there, as he had once worked on the coastal battery that now protected the harbour. So a decision was agreed and preparations were made. The 500 copies of Murat's stirring proclamation were thrown overboard as being surplus to requirements, as an anonymous eyewitness, who signed his narrative NN, confirmed:

> 'The main mast was damaged and provisions were running low. Joachim wondered whether he should sail for Trieste but he first thought to send someone in to Pizzo to hire a better boat and one furnished with supplies. I then took the proclamations we had had printed in Corsica, as well as a pamphlet *we* [my emphasis] had produced attacking the Bourbons, placed them in a sack, weighed them down with two stones and threw them in the sea. One of Murat's valets made a list of what might be needed in terms of supplies in order to continue and all [that] was needed was for someone to go ashore and buy the supplies and hire the boat.'[21]

This seemed like a straightforward matter. A little haggling, a little bargaining and some trade. And yet all eyes turned to shore nervously, just as the boats, caught between sea and land, paused, becalmed. Murat, still caught between dreaming and waking, squinted up at the little harbour and its castle on the cliff, marooned by the significance of the task. The currents and winds had brought him here only so he could resign himself to defeat. But Pizzo was his kingdom. And here, quite unexpectedly, was its king.

20. Armand, *op. cit.*
21. Lumbroso, Alberto, *Muratiana*, p. 35. The 'we' is a giveaway it was Galvani. Galvani sent this report to Fouché following his release from captivity. Fouché says it came from a commissary officer wounded in the leg at Pizzo.

Chapter 7

Pizzo

Pizzo had seen them coming. These unlooked-for visitors had been spied approaching early on the morning of Sunday, 8 October. A lookout among Captain Girolamo Del Gardo's gunners, manning the four guns on the battlements of Pizzo's medieval fort, caught sight 'at about 15 miles distant of two vessels one, known as a bova, or ox, and the other, not quite so big, sailing towards the harbour'.[1] Nobody, however, knew what these strange vessels were, let alone that their old king was sailing over to join them. Some merchants, back from the fair at Salerno, thought they must be Barbary corsairs and calmed the curious by saying that they would soon head north for richer pickings in the bay of Naples.

But these two strange vessels, the *Saint Erasme* and its swift but smaller companion, did not – or would not – leave. Indeed they came on, calmly, sedately, towards the shore. Those on board were, however, far from calm or sedate.

Barbara and the valet Armand, clutching the shopping list of supplies, were designated as the ones to go ashore, but as they prepared to go off in the *Saint Erasme*'s barge, Barbara, sitting on the deck to pull on his boots, asked Murat if he could take with them the Austrian passport to serve as a safe-conduct. Perhaps he hoped it would persuade the authorities to give him a better boat, or maybe more sinister forces were at work.[2] Whatever the truth, Murat, who knew how critical this document would be should he be captured, refused. Barbara abruptly declared that he would not then go ashore, and instead the pair held a sharp exchange of views on board. This quickly escalated and Murat, giving way to the strain of the last week, really lost his temper. This is how the valet Armand remembered this unanticipated explosion:

---

1. Archivio Nunziante, V Parte.
2. Barbara was accused after the event that he intended to run off with the document and thus deprive Murat of this important insurance policy. Rumours that Barbara was in Bourbon employ circulated after 1815, but there is no evidence he wished to undermine the king; he may just have needed the passport to raise credit for the new boat.

'The captain asked the king to supply him with his passport but His Majesty replied that he did not wish to give him it as it would lead to him being recognised and arrested. The king added that he had chartered the boat and the crew and that if the captain did not now wish to obey him he would seek out another. The captain absolutely refused to obey the king's orders so the king, growing angry, said this was intolerable and that, as he was so despicable as to refuse to go onshore then the king himself would land even if he should be killed doing so or would do so rather than suffer this any longer.'[3]

This largely tallies with the account left to us by General Franceschetti, and it resulted in an unfortunate outcome:

'It seemed that Barbara would embark on barque number 6 [sic] so as to leave for Pizzo but as he did so he asked the king to hand him the passports he had received from the Allies so that, he said, he would not be troubled by the authorities. His Majesty, surprised by this request, refused to hand over these important documents. Barbara then refused to leave without having them to hand. The captain's refusal shook the king and he shot an indignant look at the man and shouted to me in a loud voice saying "I am not to be obeyed. So, as necessity obliges me to land, so I shall disembark myself *with you at my side* [my emphasis]. My memory still lives in the kingdom of Naples. I have done the inhabitants good; they will not deprive me of assistance."'[4]

The faithful subordinate adds: 'These words were pronounced in a way which rendered argument useless. Moreover, it was one which could only alarm the soldiers and the crew and so I affected a calm voice and my own anxiety did not show on my face and I said that we shall obey, thus using the danger to lend the soldiers courage.'

Whatever was said and why, the end result was the same: the king had determined to land. Seeing this, and at least according to Galvani, his companions bravely volunteered to remain by his side:

---

3. Armand, *op. cit.* Charles says that Murat's words were 'it would be better to die sooner than suffer any longer'.
4. Franceschetti, Domenico Cesare, *Mémoires sur les événements qui ont précédé la mort de Joachim 1er, roi des Deux-Siciles* (Paris, 1826).

'Sire, there are too few of us, there are no more boats. Your Majesty's life is too precious to risk like this. However, if we have to we shall spill our blood to the last drop for you.'[5]

To which honourable proposal Murat gave assent and, conscious that his armada had shrunk so greatly, admitted to Galvani:

'It is not the number of followers that will win me my throne, it is the love and loyalty of my subjects that shall do so. Unshakeable in the midst of so many battles, I shall not be cowed now. Come, friends, this place gives me confidence.'[6]

Charles the valet did not share that confidence, and Galvani heard the servant put up a brief rearguard action, telling his master 'do not disembark, Sire, if you do so you are lost', before adding, quite truthfully, 'but then you never listened to your faithful servants'. Charles does not mention this barbed retort in his own account, but claims his objections had an effect on the king and that they at least made Murat think twice and confess that:

'I do not think it sensible to land with so few followers in a place nothing is known about. It might mean the needless sacrifice of the brave men who have followed me. Go back home, gentlemen, take the felucca. As for myself, I shall abandon myself to the current and be taken who knows where. Wherever I end up, I shall remember you and the noble hospitality of the Corsicans. They shall forever find in me a father, a friend.'[7]

This was too much for the loyal band that surrounded him. These were men of honour, selected by ordeal, tested by adversity, and having come thus far, they could not now abandon their king. Only Franceschetti spoke out, rising to the occasion as writers in their own memoirs are wont to do, swearing on behalf of those assembled that they would not abandon him.

---

5. Franceschetti, Domenico Cesare, *Mémoires sur les événements qui ont précédé la mort de Joachim 1er, roi des Deux-Siciles* (Paris, 1826).
6. Charles noted a slight variant, saying that Murat declared that 'it is not by force of arms that I shall conquer my kingdom, but by the feelings that animate all of the people'.
7. AN 31AP/21, Dossier 362.

Then, with a nod to the legacy of those men, he followed this steadfast oath with the rousing thought that it is 'fine to carry out great deeds with such poor means, that is the stuff of heroes. Let's land, long live Joachim!'[8]

This was music to Murat's ears. After all, glory corrupts just as absolutely as power, and these cheers roused the old king like an old warhorse hearing the sound of a distant trumpet. Intellect or prudence might have steadied his hand or cautioned his nerve, but Murat lived by different principles. His strength had always been his impulsiveness, his unpredictability before any odds, charging forwards come what may with his cavalier disdain for risk.

It is often said that fortune favours the bold, and Murat had always been audacious. He had enabled Napoleon's daring coup in 1799, charmed his way over the Tabor bridges outside Vienna in 1805 and persuaded Prussian castles to surrender to mere cavalry. There was also the recent example of Napoleon's escape from Elba, when, starting out with just a few hundred companions, he recaptured Paris and sent Europe's crowned heads into meltdown.[9] But while fortune may indeed favour the bold, this is only ever said when some surprise success is being recounted; here, on the coast of Calabria, the surprise was to be of a very different kind, and the bold would see that fortune can be all too fickle with her favours.

Yet Murat cared not, rousing himself and readying for battle. Jumping down from his bed of a mattress in the barque's barge, he turned to Galvani and asked, with a meaningful glance, 'whether there were still any examples of the proclamation that had been thrown into the sea'. Galvani saw that 'one of the officers present handed a copy to him that he had found in his pocket having, I don't know how, procured it from the printing house in Ajaccio'.[10] The proclamation contained more fine talk and began with this rousing appeal:

---

8. Franceschetti, Domenico Cesare, *Mémoires sur les événements qui ont précédé la mort de Joachim 1er, roi des Deux-Siciles* (Paris, 1826).

9. That morning, two of Murat's officers were heard recounting Napoleon's winning over of a regiment at Laffrey, where, shortly after his escape from Elba and on the way to Paris, he had marched up to them and told them 'Soldiers, open fire on your Emperor, if you dare', at which point they rushed to join his ranks. Murat, hearing this, exclaimed: 'I too shall do thus!'

10. Masson, Frédéric, *Napoleon et sa famille*,; volume XII. Another account by anonymous eyewitness 'NN', still probably Galvani himself, states: 'Joachim turned to me and asked me if I had kept the original manuscript of the proclamation and, on my affirmative response, he asked for it and I gave it to him.'

Murat enters Ajaccio, Corsica, at the head of his volunteers. The men look well turned-out, and at least two of them are in the uniform f Murat's old Neapolitan Guards, and the population is appropriately enthusiastic. One of a series of watercolours by an eyewitness. *(Reproduced by permission of Yves Martin)*

Murat lands on the beach below Pizzo. He is accompanied by General Franceschetti and, in civilian dress, General Natali. Behind them can be seen Pizzo's fort whilst, close to the beach, we can see Murat's two vessels readying to leave and hover offshore.

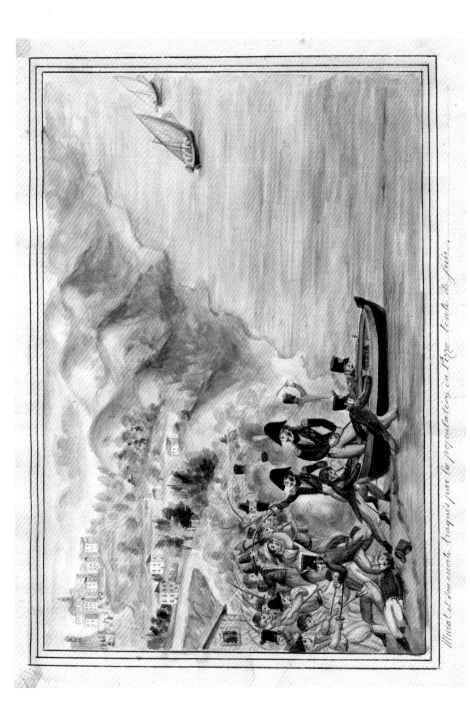

Murat et son escorte, traqués par la population du Pizzo, tente de fuir.

In this violent scene, Murat is captured by the shore whilst Captain Pietro Pernice lies dead in the foreground. Murat's soldiers are being overpowered in the olive groves in the distance, whilst, away at sea, Murat's boats are too far off to come in and rescue the king and his companions.

Another, more fanciful view, of the taking of Murat. In fact there were very few Bourbon troops amongst those who seized the king, most of those who overwhelmed Murat's party were armed servants or townsfolk.

Murat et ses compagnons d'infortune dans la prison du Pizzo (Calabre)

Murat and his companions in the prison in the castle of Pizzo. The man in the civilian coat was Natali, whilst the officer in white and red is probably Antoine Félix Lanfranchi dressed in the uniform of Murat's Guard velites.

The most accurate representation we have of Murat's execution. The firing squad, composed of grenadiers from the 3rd Foreign Regiment, are too many in number but their uniforms are correct and the watercolour correctly places the execution in the castle courtyard.

Murat _vormt König von Neapel._ _wurde zu Pizzo in Calabrien erschossen den 13. October 1815._

Er zeigte große Festigkeit in seinen Augenblick, ließ sich die Augen nicht verbinden und nahm den Schwefel nicht an, sondern commandirte selbst den Schützen das tödliche Wort: Feuer!

Nürnberg bei Friedrich Campe.

Another image of the execution, this time by Friedrich Campe. He suggests the execution took place in the town square, which is wrong, and that a large crowd was present, which is equally erroneous.

This sketch is of a proposed memorial to Murat, commissioned by General Franceschetti, that was never built. In fact, Murat's body was dumped in a common grave and his remains have never been identified.

'Brave Neapolitans, your king has returned, he is amongst you. Your woes have come to an end. Your king shall not talk of pardon, for you have done nothing wrong, but he does renew his vow to render you happy. ... I lived a lonely and modest life of exile, as the poor but virtuous always have, and there I avoided the knives of the assassin and those cannibals who, during the time of the French revolution, bathed in the blood of their own people.'

After this strange, faltering start, calculated to win pity for an itinerant king rather than impose respect, the proclamation needlessly summarized Murat's adventures, then gave a rambling account of the political situation in Europe before concluding by promising the army and civil service pay, restoration of rank and general prosperity. Murat certainly knew what grieved old soldiers, but this wasn't a document designed to inspire the fishermen and peasants of the Calabrian coast, who had only known Murat as their remote hangman, the author of their poverty and father of their oppression.

Pocketing this odd text, which perhaps he thought to have printed later in some regional capital, Murat then asked Galvani for the draft of the 20 Articles setting out his reforms to the kingdom's government, should he recapture his capital. Then, even more oddly given the circumstances, he pencilled in some last-minute amendments.

Having attended to these superfluous final touches, Murat turned to his followers and readied them for reconquest. Franceschetti saw how 'the king ordered his officers to put on full-dress uniform' but Natali fell foul of this command and Murat, 'seeing [Lieutenant General] Natali in civilian dress asked him the reasons for it. The general replied that he had no other clothes, a reply which angered the king, who was then in such a foul mood nobody could restrain it, and he replied "civilian clothes are not fit for following me into danger".'[11]

As his officers and men got ready as best they could, Murat took out his frustration and spent a bizarre few minutes taking pot-shots at some porpoises that swam around the vessels before watching them move out of range. Feeling better, and feeding off the imminent danger, he then

---

11. Franceschetti, Domenico Cesare, *Mémoires sur les événements qui ont précédé la mort de Joachim 1er, roi des Deux-Siciles* (Paris, 1826).

prepared himself for his long-anticipated return. He asked to be shaved, then, according to Galvani, he 'put on a blue tunic with the epaulettes of a colonel, nankeen breeches and riding boots and a tricorne decorated with black lace'.[12] Then, with warlike intent, he strapped on his sword and stuffed two pistols into his belt.

Murat ordered Charles to arrange matters so that the baggage would remain on the boats but for it to eventually be landed and transported on to Monteleone,[13] a more sizable town a little inland and to the south. Barbara and Cecconi were instructed to have the felucca tow the barque slightly to the south of the port, but out of range of the fort or the shore batteries he had himself constructed, and wait there for a signal before coming back. Charles also adds that Barbara was told to 'remain standing off to the right with the two boats, and, if you hear of any disturbance or any musket shots, then come and fetch me with the felucca'.

At around 10 o'clock on the morning of 8 October,[14] the barque came in as close as the shore would allow and paused so that Murat and his officers and men could be ferried out on the boat's barge. Jean Multedo and Pietro Pasqualini wanted to be the first to jump onto the sand, but Murat brushed them aside and declared: 'I am the one who should land first.'

He did so and was quickly followed by his small landing party, which consisted of the following:

Joachim Murat
Domenico Cesare Franceschetti
Sebastiano Natali
Matthieu Galvani
Captains Giovanni Battista Viggiani, Pietro Pernice and Antoine
    Félix Lanfranchi
Lieutenants Jean Multedo, Pietro Pasqualini and Giovanni Luca
    Pellegrini

12. This hat also seems to have been adorned with a showy cockade of twenty-two diamonds.
13. Now known by the more Roman, and less Norman, name of Vibo Valentia. Dominique Forcioli's deposition states that the baggage consisted of one of Murat's trunks and one belonging to Franceschetti, which was later returned to his family. There were also three portmanteaux, one of which was later taken away by Charles when they returned to Corsica, while Barbara took two others to Malta. Murat's coat was also left on board.
14. Natali stated that it was 10 o'clock French time, sometimes given as 15 o'clock Italian time, although some official reports state the landing was nearer 11.30.

Sergeants Pietro Paolo Casabianca, Matteo Santoni, Giovanni
    Sartolini, Francesco Tartaroli (or Tortorelli), Giovanni Felice
    Perretti, Giovanini, Giulio Perretti and Francesco Perrelli
Soldiers Maurizio Artusi, Antonio Lavezzano (the 14-year-old
    drummer), Giovanni Domenico Angeli, Giuseppe Maria Varese,
    Antonio Matteo Catanej, Simone Paolo Battestini, Sebastiano
    Angeli, Giuseppe Santoni, Carlino Battini and Giovanni Vincenzo
    Garelli

Then there were the servants Armand Blanchard, Salvadore Poggi,
Domenico Franceschi (Franceschetti's servant) and the cook acting as
bookkeeper, Luigi Ferrari.[15]

One account, written more than twenty years after the events by a local
eyewitness, the sailor Giuseppe Panella, has it that only '14 officers and
26 soldiers all armed with sabres, muskets, bayonets and pistols and one
man who carried a more elaborate sword, a pistol and with a hat with a
cockade and 18 diamonds'[16] came ashore. Murat actually had only twenty-
nine companions, including four servants, and this odd landing party was
not particularly well-armed. Sergeant Giovanni Luca Pelligrini was glad
to have a musket, but he adds that 'not all the soldiers had muskets, but
instead of those they had pistols or daggers'.[17]

Murat's men therefore swept across the beach more like an insignificant
eddy than an inexorable wave, but some 300 paces from the little town
itself they paused among some beached fishing boats and close to various
shacks and stores. They were to violate the peaceful bustle of an ordinary
Sunday, for all along the shore there was a fair amount of activity among
the boats as the fishermen spent their day of rest mending their nets. These
sailors, and some curious bystanders, watched as Murat's company formed

15. There should have been more. The barque had left Ajaccio with nine officers and servants
    and twenty-eight non-commissioned officers and soldiers, and the felucca was supposed to
    have seventeen more. It is presumed these were placed on other boats when the companies
    were reorganized off Sardinia. No account mentions leaving any soldiers with Barbara and
    the valet Charles, who stayed on the barque as he was ill. Dominique Forcioli's deposition
    states that this was the case, it being just these two plus the crew.
16. Orefice, Antonella (ed.), 'Gli ultimi giorni di Gioacchino Murat. La cronaca da un
    manoscritto del 1838', in *Nuovo Monitore Napoletano* (September 2013).
17. Archivio Borbone, carton 656 (*Carte relative l'arresto e il processo di Gioacchino Murat*,
    includes interrogations of Murat's followers).

up on Calabrian soil and set off in a modest column for the town's modest piazza. Murat was leading, a little overwrought with emotion and tension, and a little out of breath from the exertion. Meanwhile, those behind him were shouting, as Antonio Perri, a merchant acting as the British consul in the port of Pizzo, later recalled:

'During 8 October of the year 1815 there came before this port a barque and a felucca with, so they say, a white flag. A pistol was fired from one as it came to the place where such boats usually beach and as soon as it touched the shore, 28 or 29 men were instantly ashore and set about shouting "Long live King Gioacchino, long live King Murat!" with such force that these shouts from the marina were heard in the town but, even so, the inhabitants were astonished when, before long, Murat and his companions, appeared at the so-called harbour gate and entered into the main square of the city.'[18]

Before they got there, Pellegrini said the landing party encountered a 'man who was curious to know who we were; he was a customs official dressed in civilian clothes but with a tricorne in silver lace'. The party had, after all, landed 'without waiting for permission from the sanitary commission'[19] and Vincenzo San Andrea, thinking they were probably smugglers or had contraband on board, had sent an official to inquire. His subsequent report stated that:

'Today, around 16.00, a French xebec came into the harbour. We sent one of our officials down there and he found Gioacchino Murat with arms in his hands and some 16 others from the boat including generals, officers and others who had landed.'[20]

The official with the clipboard was Antonio Barba, and Murat asked the astonished man if he recognized him; Barba replied 'yes, Sire', to which Murat answered 'good, follow me'. Barba was clearly left speechless by this and it was only later that he managed to recall:

---

18. Add MS41537.
19. Archivio Borbone, carton 656 (*Carte relative l'arresto e il processo di Gioacchino Murat*, includes interrogations of Murat's followers).
20. *Rivista di fanteria*, XII, p. 849.

'Those who had disembarked marched up to me constantly shouting "Long live Gioacchino Murat" and it was then that the former general Murat approached me and said: "Don't you recognize your King Gioacchino", but I was so surprised I had not the means to answer him and those officers who were with him, seeing how shocked I was, spoke up, calling me Signor Commandant (because I was wearing a military-style hat), and telling me "do not be afraid, come with us". One of them, whom I did not know, took me by the arm.'[21]

This odd procession then carried on, and the men continued to shout. Captain Antoine Lanfranchi recalled that 'no sooner had we stepped on the beach than the sailors in our boat cheered "long live Joachim" and the soldiers, who were there to escort us, did the same although I ordered them not to', while Lieutenant Pietro Pasqualini seemed quite at ease that his men were 'shouting Long live Gioacchino Murat, just as we used to do'.[22] As the column approached the town, Franceschetti adds, almost as an aside, that Murat, too, was bellowing out that half-forgotten refrain.

Pizzo was too provincial for a messiah, even if it was a Sunday. It had just 5,000 inhabitants, and many of those spent their days at sea, but today things were a little busier as those from the surrounding villages had come to attend mass for the good of their souls or pick through the produce in the market for that of their bodies. The square was the busiest part of town and the sudden appearance of these new, rather more militant, visitors among the bustle came as something of a rude shock. Murat quickly dismissed any doubts as to who these men at arms might be, shouting: 'Long live Gioacchino Murat, do you not recognise me? I am your true king, your father Gioacchino.' His followers again followed this with a hearty 'Viva Giacchino, Re di Napoli'. Very few of the inhabitants cheered back; most recoiled, seeking shelter in the church or slinking away through the town's dark alleys, while the brave or more foolhardy stood and gaped. Barba had already managed to slip away from Murat's entourage, using as an excuse an errand he had been given to collect horses so Murat could ride on to

---

21. Archivio Nunziante, V Parte.
22. Archivio Borbone, carton 656 (*Carte relative l'arresto e il processo di Gioacchino Murat*, includes interrogations of Murat's followers).

Monteleone to slip away for good.[23] However, a group of fifteen soldiers, waiting to go into mass, were equipped with rather less initiative and, either through a sense of duty or confusion, stood hesitating in a corner of the square. These were men of the provincial legion and coastal gunners from the Monacella battery, and as they stood there in their rather threadbare blue uniforms – issued to them by Murat's government – they became the object of Murat's attention. Their king marched over to inspect them and again demanded to know whether they recognized him. Their sergeant, Francesco Sanandres, had them present arms to the man in the splendid hat. Murat apparently asked the sergeant if the men had a drum so his drummer could beat a call to arms and summon the garrison. They did not, so a soldier was sent for a drum.[24]

Murat then tried to persuade the soldiers to join his ranks, and it seems that two sheepishly stepped forwards. Seeing the rest rooted to the spot, he took the folded flag from one of the Corsican officers and handed it over to one of the soldiers, telling him to go and raise it,[25] while another soldier was ordered to fetch a horse. Murat stood waiting for ten long minutes; his kingdom for a horse, or for a drum. Time was slipping away and the windows of opportunity were starting to close and be shuttered tight like those of Pizzo's shops. Franceschetti, with a soldier's sense for trouble, felt a subtle change in the atmosphere. The landing of Murat and his men had come as a surprise, but now the tide was about to turn, and not in their favour. The people weren't rallying. They, too, were slipping away:

23. Barba recalled: 'Nearing the piazza, I asked of them "what do you want from me?" They answered "we need horses to go up to Monteleone"; I replied "I can go and fetch you horses but I cannot follow you". Then the soldier who was holding me by the arm said "you are right" and left me standing on the main road by the house of the mayor.' Archivio Borbone, Fascio 656 f 502.

24. In January 1816, Baron Koller had written to a friend that Murat had at this point called out 'where is my Guard, call for the commandant of my Guard', suggesting that Murat thought his royal Guard was stationed there and that is why he landed at Pizzo. This is rather far-fetched. The *garde* is a drumbeat, so it seems that he was only calling for the drums to be beaten to assemble the garrison.

25. An anonymous British report to Admiral Exmouth says Murat had brought with him the flag last shown at Ajaccio: 'He landed when almost all the people were in church and soon collected a gazing crowd of stragglers. He called out that he was their King Joachim and "follow me". Of the people that landed with him he made one a colonel, another a captain and so on and seeing the Sicilian colours he called out "hand down that white rag" and one of his officers took from under his clothes one of Murat's flags.' Add Ms 35651. Written on board HMS *Queen*, at sea, on 25 October, probably by Admiral Charles Vinicombe Penrose.

'Some of the inhabitants of Pizzo watched us talking and their faces betrayed either their bewilderment or feelings akin to anger; then we saw them disappear off. The king spoke to a few of the townspeople but they just stood staring back at him.'[26]

Barba had not returned, nor had the drum been fetched, and any hope that Pizzo might rally and rise up against the Bourbons was evaporating in the late morning sunshine. Had Pizzo thrown in its lot, then Monteleone, the provincial capital, would surely have followed. But Pizzo was turning hostile and Murat, no doubt also growing aware of that ominous shift in atmosphere, opted to move down the coast and hope for better luck and a more loyal reception in Monteleone.[27]

Pizzo was loyal, but to the Bourbons. The population had shown little more than contempt towards Murat and his intruders, but as he dawdled in the piazza, some rather energetic royal officials and local dignitaries were seeking to transform that latent hostility into action. The most capable of those dignitaries was Francesco Alcalà y Cebrian, a steward of Pedro Alcantara, the Duke of l'Infantado, who had lands in the province.[28] He knew Pizzo well, having been a former governor of the town, and he was not a man to lose either his head or his opportunity:

'On the 8th of this month of October at around nine in the morning, considerable tumult could be heard from the port. Then a frightened servant came into my apartment and told me "Your Excellency, can you hear them shouting 'long live King Joachim?'" I went out onto the balcony which looked over the harbour and using a telescope I saw that there was a launch and a boat of around 20 tons with their bows pointing to the shore and that various soldiers and officers in

26. Franceschetti, Domenico Cesare, *Mémoires sur les événements qui ont précédé la mort de Joachim 1er, roi des Deux-Siciles* (Paris, 1826).
27. Lanfranchi, Natali and Pasqualini also later claimed that they intended to march to Monteleone, and from there to Cotrone to take ship and continue the journey. Lanfranchi's subsequent interrogation includes his bold statement that 'we left the town [Pizzo] and went off towards Monteleone where Joachim thought to present himself to Your Excellency [Nunziante] so as to ask for an escort to go with him to Cotrone'. Murat mentions this in his own written testimony to Nunziante, so Natali may have taken the idea from there.
28. Since 1505, the family had owned the principality of Mileto, the dukedom of Francavilla and the barony of Pizzo, among others.

French uniforms were leaping onto the land. It took them just a few minutes to reach the main square and Murat was shouting "don't you recognise your King Joachim? Patriots, follow me!" at the top of his voice. In fact the square emptied and the shops and houses locked their doors. I went down towards the square through the crowd which filled the street and found the captain of gendarmes, Don Gregorio Trentacapilli, readying with some of the people preparing to go and meet Murat."[29]

Gregorio Trentacapilli was a captain of gendarmes; with, however, no gendarmes. He had come over from Cosenza for an enjoyable weekend and that morning was, along with his brother Raffaele, enjoying the hospitality of Baron Giovambattista Melecrinis. He saw 'a crowd of fleeing peasants race past' and learned that Murat had landed. For all the sloth in his gait, this shuffling servant of the crown showed a degree of energy and was soon, along with the more learned Alcalà y Cebrian, overseeing the distribution of weapons to counter this unexpected incursion. This is how another royal official, Justice of the Peace Francesco Mazza, remembered this decisive rallying of royal power against this usurping king:

'At around 17.00 hours [Italian time, i.e. around noon] Gioacchino Murat and some of his followers came ashore at this marina from two boats. They came at once to the piazza and he started shouting "I am Gioacchino, everybody shout 'long live Gioacchino Murat!'" At the sound of this the people were at first confused but there were those who ran to arms so as to open fire against him and his followers. Hearing of this extraordinary commotion we hastened to rally them as did the governor general, Francesco Alcola [sic; Alcalà], the officer Gregorio Trentacapilli and many property owners.'[30]

Meanwhile, Murat, despairing of support, had finally made the decision to leave Pizzo's piazza and to continue overland to Monteleone. He had once been headquartered there for several months, so knew the roads, and also

---

29. Raffaello Mole, p. 119. Francesco Alcalà y Cebrian later told Nunziante: 'Having been told the news, I instantly armed myself, and with people of my own I could trust, I immediately ran to the Piazza.' Archivio Borbone, Fascio 656, f 481.
30. *Rivista di fanteria*, XII, p. 848.

hoped that, given its reputation as a base for Masonic or secret societies – many of which had sympathized with the principles of the French Revolution – it might prove more welcoming. The consul, Antonio Perri, left this account of Murat's change of plan:

'Not one of the people of this town joined in but all were rather astonished and afeared that this might be make-believe and so Murat, seeing that none wished to follow him, turned to General Franceschi [*sic*] and said "these are all brigands, let us go to Monteleone" and turned to the legionaries and bade them follow him but none did so and so he set off towards Monteleone with his followers while nearly all the worried inhabitants shut themselves up in their houses and the shops were shuttered.'[31]

Murat again attempted to make the local soldiers join him, ordering 'you are my soldiers, follow me', or – as an account by an old soldier, Francesco Antonio Salomone, then idling in the piazza, puts it – urging them to 'come follow my brave men to Monteleone'. Franceschetti thought that five men offered to join him while the majority of the platoon returned to the fort, closing the gates and rejoining the rest of Captain Girolamo Mattei's provincial legion on the battlements. Meanwhile, another former soldier, a certain Francesco Alemanni, who had served under Murat in the 1813 campaign, also appeared. He urged the king to speed his departure as crowds were forming just out of sight and their intentions were hostile. Murat needed no further prompting and so, again in the lead, and guided by Alemanni and Salomone and with some dejected soldiers in tow, the king quit the square. Turning right, and keeping the fort to their left, they started off down the road to Monteleone, but they had barely gone 100 paces when Franceschetti saw that the 48-year-old Murat 'was soon finding it difficult to walk and, indisposed, stopped for breath'. This was out of character and the general felt required to explain away his embarrassment by adding that this was happening 'after a dozen days without any exercise of any sort, as we were so tightly squashed in the boat'.[32] The wheezing Murat then abruptly pulled his men off the main road to the right and

31. Add MS41537 (Antonio Perri's account).
32. Franceschetti, Domenico Cesare, *Mémoires sur les événements qui ont précédé la mort de Joachim 1er, roi des Deux-Siciles* (Paris, 1826).

up onto the Parriera olive grove. Nobody knows why he did so; perhaps it was in the hope the high ground would give him a better view, perhaps to find the local telegraph semaphore. Nevertheless, Alemanni, the former soldier, shouted to Murat, telling him he was making a mistake. Murat, however, continued to climb until, from close to the summit, he turned to see the unsettling sight of columns of civilians armed with clubs and a few firearms issuing out from Pizzo.

The mob was more than a thousand strong. Antonio Perri says it had set off just fifteen minutes after Murat's departure, spilling out in three columns down the street of San Antonio, San Pancrazio and the more ominously titled Strada dei Morti. The main column of hastily armed locals intermingled with the footmen of Baron Annunziato Tranquillo, and some of the artillerymen and troops from the fort were being led out of the town by an officer recognizable by his epaulettes. A second column lagged behind it, while a third, of just twenty armed retainers under Giorgio Pellegrino, a young pharmacist who doubtless welcomed the excitement, strove to outflank Murat. It was the main body that caught up with Murat first, however. Murat and his men had come to a halt in the shade close to the Church of Piety, sometimes known by the more appropriate name of the *Congregazione dei Morti*, not far from the banks of the Parrera stream. They all carefully watched the mob as it began to climb the slope towards them, with the column's plump, and similarly out-of-breath, officer attracting Murat's especial interest. The officer was Captain Gregorio Trentacapilli. Unfortunately for Murat, one of Trentacapilli's brothers had died in Murat's prisons and another had been persecuted by General Manhès[33] during Murat's reign. The desire for a settling of scores may have given the gendarme just enough energy to propel him up the slope that October morning.

Murat, never one to be intimidated, decided he would personally confront those in pursuit. He stepped out from among his men and shouted 'come forward' down to the crowd, but it was only Trentacapilli who came forward to speak to the king. There was a brief exchange of words with Murat, who spoke first to the assembled, again demanding to know whether they – and more specifically Trentacapilli – recognized

33. Manhès had pacified Calabria in 1810 and 1811 by executing 900 brigands, or insurgents, just some of the 5,421 'bandits' who would perish in the first five years of Napoleonic rule. Many were mere peasants who supplied food to the bands.

their king. Trentacapilli, who had been mistaken for a colonel by Murat's officers on account of his braided epaulettes, replied: 'I most certainly do, he is none other than Ferdinand IV.'[34] Murat, having lost the opening sally, sought to persuade the gendarme to let him be or come with him. While an anxious Franceschetti, Natali and their soldiers nervously handled their weapons, Murat attempted to mask that he had just tried his hand at armed insurrection by explaining that he was simply going on to Monteleone and from there would likely continue to Trieste. Franceschetti, as usual, developed this straightforward statement into a much more expansive and eloquent appeal to his royal master's subjects:

> 'My children, do not bear arms against your former sovereign. I have not landed in Calabria to do you harm. I just wish to seek assistance from the authorities in Monteleone so I might continue on to Trieste where I shall rejoin my family. If you had given me the chance to explain this in the square of Pizzo then you would have learned that I had passports which Ferdinand himself has to respect.'[35]

Trentacapilli, not persuaded by these fine words, or perhaps simply not wishing to let slip the arrest of the century, refused to let Murat continue. In consequence, according to Galvani, Murat, who was already brandishing a pistol, made to draw his sword, prompting his soldiers to present arms. It was then that General Franceschetti forced the issue, seized the initiative and, quite literally, took matters into his own hands:

> 'I thought it pointless for the king to try to continue the discussion with the peasants so I approached Trentacapilli and demanded to know who he was. Trentacapilli gave his name and rank, and added that he wanted the king to return with him to Pizzo but Murat, waving a pistol, said he had no ill-intent, and that he and his followers could

---

34. Francesco Alcalà y Cebrian relates the exchange as follows: 'At about 400 paces beyond the last of the houses he [Trentacapilli] made to arrest him in the name of King Ferdinand. Murat, taking him by the arm, asked "don't you recognise me, I am Joachim your king!" To which the captain replied "My king is Ferdinand IV and if you do not halt you are dead." Whilst this dispute was going on a general [Franceschetti] in Murat's entourage waved two pistols at the captain and forced him to step back.'
35. Franceschetti, Domenico Cesare, *Mémoires sur les événements qui ont précédé la mort de Joachim 1er, roi des Deux-Siciles* (Paris, 1826).

follow him. I saw the king was in danger and placed myself between them and the king, brandishing a loaded pistol and threatening Trentacapilli with it, declaring that I would kill him if he did not let the king go free.'[36]

Trentacapilli says that Murat's 'adjutant brandished a pistol and seized me, saying "come with us or die"'. There was a brief struggle but both Galvani and Franceschetti confess that Trentacapilli managed to wrestle free from this deadly embrace and the gendarme stumbled back, others saying that it was actually his brother, Raffaele, who rescued Trentacapilli by pulling at his coat tails. Whatever the truth, both Murat and Trentacapilli fell back to their respective lines. Franceschetti, believing it was now or never, urged Murat to order his men to fire a volley and to charge the enemy with the bayonet, but the king refused, still not wanting to kill those he insisted on calling his subjects. Trentacapilli, however, had no such qualms and Francesco Alcalà y Cebrian says that 'the captain of gendarmes ordered those of his men who were armed to open fire'.[37]

This they did, as did Pellegrino's armed retainers, who had curled round the road to cut Murat off from Monteleone. They sent some shots into the flank of the Corsicans, and although the discharge was poorly aimed, only one Corsican being hit in the knee and falling to the ground, the surprise was sufficient to persuade Murat to opt for discretion over valour. He thus bellowed to his followers to run for the beach and the boats. As Francesco Alcalà y Cebrian later put it: 'When the first shots rang out they shouted "to the harbour, to the harbour!" And they ran off followed by a mass of people.'[38]

The Calabrians reloaded and opened fire at them again, a shot wounding Galvani in the flesh above the right knee, and they now surged forward to

---

36. This seems to be confirmed by Armand the valet, who wrote: 'However, General Franceschetti ran at the captain and pushed a pistol against his throat, telling him that if he fired he would blow his brains out and then he told the king that he should make for the shore and embark while the captain was in their power.' Charles, who was not present, only says the general placed a pistol against the captain's chest and threatened to shoot if the Calabrians did not cease fire.

37. Archivio Borbone, Carton 656. Trentacapilli himself remarked that the French general 'was going to attack me when my brother pushed into the said general, so I turned away and shouted to those men who were armed to fire'.

38. Mole, p. 121.

overpower Murat's dumbfounded soldiers. Only a small band of officers managed to break free and helped spirit their king away through Signor Ochea's field and the olive trees, hoping to get down to the shore where, close to the defensive wall by the Vallisdea stream,[39] they hoped to find Barbara. The Maltese captain was supposedly idling offshore and should have come in as soon as he heard the firing. However, as the following anonymous British report reveals, Murat's hopes were soon to be dashed:

'By the time he had advanced a little way, intending, I suppose, to go to Monteleone, the fishermen and peasants began to recollect themselves and taking their guns ran on his flanks until they headed him and party and then began a fire through the vines and bushes which soon brought on a complete run towards the beach but they missed the place where their own vessel lay and attempted to launch the first they got at but, in their fright, nine or 10 of them got in and grounded her faster. By this time some gendarmes as well as peasantry were collected and as soon as Murat's followers had fired their pistols, while still trying to escape, Murat himself with an oar in his hand [was] pushing hard.'[40]

It wasn't so much that Murat had misjudged the landing place but that Barbara was still out at sea with the felucca and barque. To get away, or to get to them, Murat and his officers had desperately tried to float one of the fishermen's stranded boats, as Antonio Perri confirmed:

'Murat was the first to reach the place where they had disembarked but the bovo was not there, nor was the scorridora, for they had gone off when the first shots had been fired so, instead, they found a boat on the beach and Murat clambered aboard it and they tried to cast off but could not manage as they were being shot at and, indeed, a captain was hit and fell to the ground, dead, and then some of the people managed to surround the boat and clamber aboard it and they dragged him to the ground and abused him as though he was the

39. Now covered by a car park off Lungomare Cristoforo Colombo.
40. Add MSS 35651.

lowest of criminals. He was caught along with all his followers many of whom were wounded from the gunfire or by blades.'[41]

Francesco Alcalà y Cebrian, who had himself fired a few shots at the invaders, saw that Murat was cornered:

'Murat and his men crossed over the Vallisdea stream heading for the shore. I headed in that direction too. The two boats had gone off about a mile and a half from the shore and Murat, seeing all was lost, was trying to launch a fishing boat they had found there.'

It was 18.00 Italian time, or about an hour after noon, and as Murat and his handful of officers clambered onto the boat or sought to extricate it from the sand, the mob of locals caught up with them. Some shots were fired and local legend has it that Pernice was hit in the head by a bullet from the priest Pietro Citanna, while Sergeant Giovannini was beaten to death and the servant Franceschi seriously wounded in the close-quarter fighting. General Franceschetti adds: 'The king saw Pernice killed at his side, and sergeant Giovannini; I fell wounded at his feet as did Captain Lanfranchi and Biciani [Giovanni Battista Viggiani], Lieutenant Pasqualini, the valet Armand and Sergeant [sic] Franceschi.'[42]

There was no escape. Resistance was futile. An adventure built on sand came undone on that Calabrian beach. The baying mob had trapped them and Murat and his men would have to concede defeat or be massacred in the process. Franceschetti says Murat, used to more refined martial etiquette, offered his sword to the crowd as a token of surrender, but it seems that Murat begged Fortunato Catalisano, a miller aiming a fowling piece at him, not to fire and so spare his life, which the miller promptly did. The king's party then ceased resisting. A sailor called Giorgio Grillo manhandled Murat over the side of the boat and into the swirling surf, where a new ordeal began for, while the crowd had spared their lives, they would not spare them from injury. As soon as they were within reach of the king, the people of Pizzo launched an assault on him. Fortunato Sardinelli grabbed Murat by the hair and stole the diamonds from his hat, while a

---

41. Archivio Borbone, Carton 656.
42. Franceschetti, Domenico Cesare, *Mémoires sur les événements qui ont précédé la mort de Joachim 1er, roi des Deux-Siciles* (Paris, 1826).

woman named Megara pulled at his whiskers, shouting 'you talk of liberty but you had three of my sons shot'. Murat's epaulettes were stolen, as was a ring that had once belonged to the queen of Spain,[43] and he was terribly beaten as Antonio Perri's subsequent report of the king's capture relates:

'However the fury was such that Murat and his followers were abused in such a way as to excite compassion in any soul and these poor people were soon covered in blood. Murat was badly mistreated, he was punched in his face, slapped, spat at in his face, beaten around the shoulders and crotch, his uniform torn, beaten in the face with his own hat after the cockade with its 15 valuable diamonds had been taken from it. One rascal had the temerity to hit him in the face with one of Murat's own shoes whilst another pulled at his whiskers and kept the hair that came off as a trophy. You would not believe such things if you read about them, but they are true. And all the others were treated in the same manner apart from just one officer who remained unwounded.'[44]

Not all the people crowding about were so cruel. As the blows rained down, one of Murat's officers, Natali, noted that 'some honest citizens intervened, risking their lives to save ours'.[45] This seems to refer to Pasquale Greco, who saved Murat from an imminent lynching, and Domenico Bandari of the Civic Guard, who calmed the mob while Girolamo Ventura shielded the officers. Francesco Alcalà y Cebrian had also just arrived at the right time and managed to impose a measure of royal authority, helping to put an end to this squalid battle on the sands:

43. Pasquale Greco took or received a ring from Murat that had once belonged to Maria Amelia, the mother of King Ferdinand. He also handed Murat's sword and pistols back to him, although these were then confiscated in the prison.
44. Archivio Borbone, Carton 656. The British anonymous report notes the loss of his diamonds, but also the all-important passport: 'The gendarmes rushed in and seized him and, true to the old principle of plunder and self-interest, in an instant his diamond button and loop and epaulettes were pulled off, his clothes torn with, I believe, a few good blows on his person. He had with him the passport which was to have taken him one way or other to Austria and then declared that he only wanted to travel across to the Adriatic in order to embark for Trieste.'
45. Archivio Borbone, Carton 656.

'There was a rush of anger and it was a difficult thing to save the life of Murat for when the people came forward, swarming in from all directions, they were all pointing their muskets, pistols or whatever weapons they had at him. There was then a scrum of bodies and I had to shout that whoever killed him would ruin the honour of capturing him and that our king would be displeased as he alone could dispose of the lives of those who disturbed his lands.'

The Spaniard's shouting seems to have helped, as he described:

'The initial fury subsided, and some order was imposed on the people whilst Murat was secured and taken into custody, being lead off towards the town. As this was being done, Captain Trentacapilli arrived as he had not been able to keep up with the fugitives. Murat was handed over to him so he could be taken to the castle, which was done.'[46]

However, Murat's ordeal was not yet over and Antonio Perri describes how Murat was abused even after his capture:

'Murat was further abused as he was taken from the shore to the castle, it is impossible to describe with a pen how all the people wanted to do him and his followers harm with the women screaming out against him shouting vendetta, kill him, murder him and if everything said or done had to be written down in detail it would fill volumes.'[47]

The Neapolitan envoy in Rome, Tommaso Spinelli, Marquis de Fuscaldo, told his French colleague a similarly ferocious tale just a week after Murat's landing:

---

46. Archivio Borbone, Carton 656. Francesco Alcalà y Cebrian informed Medici on 2 November: 'In this most faithful city the rumour is spreading that Captain of Gendarmes Trentacapilli takes on the credit alone for having arrested Murat and his followers. He did not have the good fortune to be there at the time of Murat's arrest, but met us at the first house by the harbour about a quarter of an hour after the affair.' Archivio Borbone, Fascio 656, f 438. The gendarme had indeed written to his superiors, saying: 'I took them all prisoner and brought them to this castle.'
47. Add MSS 35651.

'An officer in his entourage was killed and around eight were badly wounded. He himself sought to flee but Trentacapilli cut his retreat and arrested him; *the women then abused him and punched and spat at him to such an extent that his face is all swollen and you might hardly recognise him* [my emphasis].'[48]

Murat, with eight of his immediate followers caught on the beach, was taken to Pizzo's little castle, and as he marched through the tumult and the threats, the king tried to hold his head high and stride out in front, even while the mob bayed for his blood. Franceschetti saw that the regal blood was again nearly spilt just as they approached the castle:

'I was dressed in a similar manner to the king and was about 15 paces ahead. Suddenly a man wielding an axe, leading a group of around 30 individuals, also armed, came towards me and the king demanding to know which of the two of us was Joachim. Despite my utterly exhausted condition I managed to find sufficient strength to cry out "It is me, the general behind me is not guilty; spare him!". He raised the axe above his head ready to strike and end my days but those escorting us and who had hitherto allowed us to be mistreated, intervened and prevented the blow, shouting that such a thing would not be allowed. So the individual who had threatened me then went at the king. We saw what was about to happen and we shook at the thought of it. I begged those who had just saved me to go and save the king. They replied he was safe and there was nothing to fear. I then heard some commotion and saw that the man with the axe and his companions could not get near.'[49]

After this Spartacus moment and this last attempt at unauthorized assassination, the castle must have come as some relief to Murat's party; even if, when they arrived, they were placed in a small cell that had recently been used to house pigs.

---

48. Sassenay, p. 234.
49. Franceschetti, Domenico Cesare, *Mémoires sur les événements qui ont précédé la mort de Joachim 1er, roi des Deux-Siciles* (Paris, 1826), p. 58.

Chapter 8

Prison

Calabria had proven to be Murat's downfall, and Pizzo the forgotten backwater that memorably caught a king. There, the ruler of Naples discovered how his people viewed his legitimacy, even as he pleaded that he had returned to rule over them. He had grabbed at his throne, and in less than two hours of violence and confusion had seen a mob kick his precious crown into the dusty gutter.

Murat had to shoulder the blame for the debacle. A degree of wisdom and preparation was essential whenever throwing the dice for kingdoms, but he had rashly cast himself ashore, gambling all on a place he hardly knew and on a people whom he barely understood. His supporters kept quiet when it came to royal guilt for the debacle, and as Murat and his followers nursed their wounds in their insulting quarters, the royal prerogative of never being at fault was, by and large, respected. Instead, Murat's faithful followers laid the blame for their fate on the one to have escaped it. Consequently, Barbara, the Maltese commodore, was appointed the guilty party. He should have been at his post and engineered their rescue, they argued, but he had not come and nobody in the cells of the castle knew why. General Franceschetti thought Murat's little navy should have saved his miniature army:

'We had placed the king in the boat and made vain efforts to cast off, hoping to make it out to the barque we had been on, the one captained by Barbara, but this wretch remained off the coast despite the orders that he had from the king to remain close by, within the range of two musket shots, and to come to Madraga de Bivone with barque number 6 under Cecconi. Had he obeyed these orders we could have used the 4-pounder gun against the crowd and scattered them, or part of them. And the king might well have got away.'[1]

---

1. Franceschetti, Domenico Cesare, *Mémoires sur les événements qui ont précédé la mort de Joachim 1er, roi des Deux-Siciles* (Paris, 1826), p. 56.

However, the truth was that Barbara had attempted to follow Murat's instructions and had waited forty-five minutes, hovering close offshore with the barque and felucca – and Murat's treasure – until the authorities, not wishing to leave him be, had taken measures to chase him away. Yet according to Vincent Cecconi, master of the felucca, Barbara hardly rose to the occasion:

'At around 45 minutes after the landing we heard some shots being fired. Commandant Barbara had me tow his boat and we rowed away from the shore and, to be safe, he came onto my felucca. He sent his servant up the mast with a telescope, telling him to inform us what was happening on shore but neither I nor the crew could understand what he was saying, or what Barbara was saying, as they spoke Maltese. When I asked what was about he told me that a large number of people had come down to the shore to arm some corsairs to come out and attack us and he begged us to row faster so we could get away. A quarter of an hour later the fort fired two shots against us and the shot fell close by. A little later we saw two sloops come out, rowing towards us, and they pursued us until sunset.'[2]

Barbara had mistaken the mob for sailors rushing out to attack Murat's flotilla, but the two sloops were real; or at least one of them was, for Captain Girolamo del Gado had indeed instructed a sloop moored by the Monacella coastal battery to chase the strangers away. Barbara had fled in indecent haste, not betraying Murat for a reward or favour, but merely to save his own skin.[3] It was not clear if Barbara could have saved Murat even had he been bolder. Their battle on the sands had been of short duration, and Murat had been overpowered before the clamour on the shore could be understood for what it was: a desperate attempt by a prince to escape his people.

That prince was now confined within the medieval walls of Pizzo's fort. Trentacapilli had taken charge of the bloodied prisoners, and had made sure to humiliate and abuse them a little more. He had taken great delight

---

2. Franceschetti, Domenico Cesare, *Supplément aux mémoires sur les événements qui ont précédé la mort de Joachim 1er, roi des Deux-Siciles* (Paris, 1829).

3. Armand says that a request was sent off in the form of a pencilled note asking for Murat's baggage, but those on board refused to send it to Pizzo, p. 172.

in stripping Murat of his remaining possessions, using violence to do so,[4] and his haul of seized documents was impressive: the vital passports; the agreement on asylum in Austria written in French signed by Metternich on 1 September; the permit for onward travel to Trieste and the endorsement by Stuart; a document that, according to Antonio Perri the consul, was a printed copy of the 'proclamation, which the mob had taken'; certificates promoting Pernice and Multedo and four other officers, with Murat signing himself 'King of the Two Sicilies'; the draft constitution; and fragments of a letter, probably that from Borgia, which had it 'that the people await him with open arms and that just one regiment would be enough to carry out his will'. There was also a copy of the article Murat had been working on that condemned Ferdinand's letter to General Bianchi, something he had called the 'Cry of the Neapolitan', and three copies of Ferdinand's letter. These documents showed that Murat still considered himself king and had hopes for a kingdom, and read in conjunction with Murat's arrival in Pizzo in the company of armed men, they seemed pretty damning. The gendarme had thus done well to confiscate them. He seized less useful booty too, including six shirts, six handkerchiefs and six pairs of silk stockings. But the real prize, at least for Trentacapilli, was a tempting bank draft and the splendid diamonds Murat had sported in his hat.

Murat and his officers were goaded into the same small cell, and when the mob had finished rounding up his Corsican soldiers, these wounded and badly beaten men were also lodged in the same cramped conditions. Discomfort and despair ran deep, but General Franceschetti also caught a sense of the bitterness in that defeat:

> 'The king sat down, his officers surrounded him without saying a word and those soldiers who had been taken prisoner and brought here lay down here and there on the ground; they were angry and begged that they should have been allowed to open fire on their enemies and to have died [with] weapons in their hand defending their master.'[5]

---

4. Murat later complained to Captain Frojo that Trentacapilli had used violence. Multedo says that Trentacapilli grabbed 'the passport, other documents and buttons from his coat and when Gioacchino tried to take them back from him he struck him and made off with them'. Luigi Ferrari also says that the gendarme hit Murat.

5. Franceschetti, Domenico Cesare, *Mémoires sur les événements qui ont précédé la mort de Joachim 1er, roi des Deux-Siciles* (Paris, 1826), p. 59.

It was too early, but only just, to talk of graves, worms and epitaphs, but defeat was always a heavy load to bear. Despite his own wounds, Galvani's sympathy was for his hero, the dejected figure of the king who, alone in his failure, sat mourning entombed in these dirty stone walls:

'He who had only recently sat upon a throne swathed in glory, and commanding a vast army, now found himself perched on a bench in a cell, abandoned to the ferocity of men capable of anything, and commanding a poor body of fellow unfortunates covered in blood.'[6]

Antonio Perri would see for himself how pitifully the expeditionary force was incarcerated, but notes that one official, and an unexpected one at that, did feel a little pity:

'They wanted to put them in a small, filthy cell, and this is where they were finally held, but, at first, Murat resisted and would not go in but, eventually, he was forced in and he and his followers were locked into a cell of the kind held for the lowliest criminals and bandits. They were all bleeding, exhausted and naked and were a fearful sight to behold, especially Murat. The agent of the Duke dell'Infantado, a Spaniard, ordered that shirts, tunics, breeches and everything else that might be necessary be sent to clothe those whose apparel had been torn and ruined by the ferocity of the mob. He then came in person.'[7]

Murat felt want, tasted grief and needed friends, and Francesco Alcalà y Cebrian, if not exactly a friend, proved more generous than the Calabrians. Indeed, his act of mercy towards the defeated men was the one redeeming detail in a drama that was soon to take an even more sombre turn. His own account of the charity he bestowed on a vanquished foe runs as follows:

'The number of his followers was 29 individuals including generals, officers, servants and soldiers. They were all taken to the castle and placed under guard in a cell. I re-entered the castle in order to bring relief to the prisoners and arranged matters with the captain of the

6. Galvani, Matthieu, *Mémoire sur les événements qui ont précédé la mort de J. Murat* (Paris, 1850).
7. Add MS41537 (Antonio Perri's account).

gendarmes who took it upon himself to remain there on guard. I saw what a pitiful state the unfortunates were in. Murat was not wounded but most of his uniform was missing as it had been torn off during the fighting; some of his companions were in shirts and the others were barely covered by the remains of their uniforms and were all bloodied from head to foot. Thirst and exhaustion meant they could barely talk. I summoned a surgeon to treat them and had two sheets sent to be cut and used as bandages, as well as sending for some wine, beer and fresh water. This assistance came as a complete surprise to them after the ordeal they had been through and they accepted it most gratefully and it restored some of their courage as, until now, they assumed they would be massacred.'[8]

There was indeed a real danger that Trentacapilli's guards would take the opportunity to massacre Murat and his men, or have them murdered by the incensed locals. This risk certainly occurred to the vigilant General Franceschetti.

'The darkness of the prison, the fact we were covered in blood and the moans that were uttered from time to time rendered the scene one of complete horror, one that still causes my hair to stand on end. The silence we maintained was broken by ferocious cries by the inhabitants as they threatened the king and these cries, more than our fate, filled us with sadness and despair. The king, despite these calls and threats, rose above such misfortune. He did not cease consoling his men, urging them to be resigned to their fate: "forgive the people of Pizzo, they are blind tools of the beasts that control them".'[9]

Fortunately, that generous soul Francesco Alcalà y Cebrian again intervened. He had the fanatic mob of locals dispersed and gave Murat the welcome news that regular troops were on the way to guard them:

'Hearing that I was addressed as governor they imagined that they were being kept in a cell in a tower which formed part of a more

8. Archivio Borbone, Carton 656.
9. Franceschetti, Domenico Cesare, *Mémoires sur les événements qui ont précédé la mort de Joachim 1er, roi des Deux-Siciles* (Paris, 1826).

extensive castle and that I was in charge of it. This lead to Murat asking an apprentice cobbler, then serving as a sentry, whether "I might have a word with His Excellency the governor, I have a couple of words I'd like to say to him." I came to the entrance to the prison and, after expressing his infinite gratitude, and adding that he hoped I would take measures to prevent the population from murdering him and his men, he then added in French: "Monsieur, does it seem that the place where the captain of gendarmes has incarcerated us is suitable for King Joachim? I beg you to have me and my men taken to a more decent prison." I replied in the presence of the aforementioned captain saying "General (here he lowered his head as though angry), I have no authority in this region, I am a private citizen from Spain and I reside here as I manage the affairs of His Excellency the Duke de l'Infantado. They call me governor because that was the title I enjoyed before French rule was imposed and I lost my position. However, I can reassure you that this tower is the only available prison. General Nunziante, who commands in Calabria, shall arrive this evening and he shall take suitable measures, as for your life you can rest easy as the worst has passed and now is the time to treat the wounded and look after the living." Meanwhile a hearty meal was served to them and a delivery of clothes, shirts, handkerchiefs, and a smart blue coat trimmed in black for Murat was distributed. I sent my servant in to serve the meal and to hand out the clothes and I told Joachim who stood watching all this in silence that "General, I hope that, given the state you and your men find yourselves in, these trifles will please you. Much of my wardrobe has been donated and, whilst I think I have thought of everything necessary, if anything is still required do let me know." Covering his face with his hands he leant silently against the wall then, an instant later, he approached me with tears in his eyes and told me in French: "I am more overcome by your words than by the misfortune that has stricken me down." He then spoke about his gratitude but I interrupted him saying "I do not ask for thanks, it is sufficient for me to give proof of Spanish generosity towards a defeated enemy; if, one day, you have occasion to speak of the attentions you have received, you might say that they came from a servant of the Duke de l'Infantado." Although just then I was thinking about the massacres this man had brought about in Madrid and the harm he had done to me.'[10]

The promise of the arrival of some proper soldiers came as a relief to the prisoners. They soon turned up, a detachment consisting of a half-company of fifty men having marched over from Monteleone under Captain Stratti, Lieutenant Imbardelli and Ensign Federico. The government intendant at Monteleone, Petroni, had learned of Murat's landing via courier at two o'clock that afternoon and stated that 'I sent those troops that were available to Pizzo, entrusting the mission to a reliable officer, Captain Stratti of the 3rd Foreign Regiment.' While another detachment was on the way from Tropea, Stratti's men quickly took charge of guarding, or perhaps protecting, the prisoners. Franceschetti jotted down that 'an officer of the line called Stratti, of Greek origin, arrived with 40 men and they sent away the mob, securing the castle in which we were held and making sure we were respected'.[11]

Next to arrive was General Vito Nunziante himself. The general had his headquarters at Tropea and news of Murat's arrest, sent by Baron Tranquillo and Captain Mattei of the Provincial Legion, reached him via the courier who had first called on Intendant Petroni. Mattei's message assured the general that 'the usurper' Murat 'was being kept out of sight and under lock and key'.[12] The news had an electrifying effect on Nunziante and, as his subordinate, Lieutenant Pasquale Bottazzi, informs us, spurred the general into action:

'I had left my quarters in Tropea with the idea of going for a walk when I reached the Porta di Vaticano, where the house of General Nunziante, Commander-in-Chief of Calabria, was, and under whose orders I served. As I did so I heard him bellowing "fetch the horses, the horses!". This made it clear that some important business was afoot; I therefore hurried over to him, and upon seeing me approach,

10. Archivio Borbone, Carton 656. Murat had been in charge of Napoleon's garrison of Madrid during the May 1808 revolt, an event that sparked a wider war for independence, and he had put down the insurrection brutally.
11. *Rivista di fanteria*, XII, p. 850.
12. Archivio Nunziante, Storia della famiglia: Arresto e processo del generale Gioacchino Murat, 02.064. Rapporto di Girolamo Mattei, comandante militare della piazza di Pizzo, sull'arresto di Murat.

he called out to me by name and bade me mount and follow him. This I did and he charged off at the gallop along the Parghelia road with me following. After some four miles I asked him where we were going and he told me we are going to Pizzo to find Murat for he has been arrested.'[13]

Nunziante had reacted quickly to the news, and he informs us that:

'As soon as I had been informed by Captain Mattei, who commanded the [civic] legion at Pizzo, of the landing and arrest of General Murat and his companions, I rushed to that place with the mountain artillery, the garrison of Tropea and my staff. I called in other troops as well to make sure that General Murat and his entourage were secured.'[14]

The general reached Pizzo, riding in with just his staff and some troopers, at around eight o'clock. He promptly ordered that a Te Deum be sung across the province, for after all, no ordinary brigand had been caught. Then Nunziante, the military governor of Calabria, resplendent in his gold braid but with a passing resemblance to a brigand himself, went up to the castle to meet his distinguished captive.

First, however, he had to deal with Trentacapilli, more distinguished by his pride and greed. Inevitably, Trentacapilli proved a disappointment to the regular soldier, but his appearance was nothing compared to his actions for the gendarme had disposed of all the documents he had confiscated from Murat and his men, diligently sending them away to Naples to his superior, Inspector General Filippo Cancellieri, along with three swords and two pistols. He had also, or so he told Nunziante, sent the diamonds to Ferdinand.[15] While the exact fate of the jewels was ambiguous, it was the

---

13. Archivio Borbone, Fascio 623, f 171.

14. Report by Petroni in *Rivista di fanteria*, XII, p. 851. Since 4 October, the coast had been on alert. Nunziante had selected Colonel Carlo Tschudy as his deputy, replacing the less experienced Colonel Labonia, and had called in detachments, including some artillery, to Tropea. Meanwhile, gunboats under Cafiero and Natoli were ordered to cruise off the coast. Warnings were sent up and down that coast by the Chappe Telegraph as the roads were bad (it took forty-eight hours of hard riding even to reach the capital).

15. The gendarme still had them on 18 October, however, as he was, or so he said, hoping to deliver them in person to Ferdinand. He had hoped to arrange this through Prince Canosa, nephew of his friend Bishop Minutolo.

absence of the documentary evidence that irritated the general the most, and his mood did not improve when the gendarme informed him he had not made any copies.

Nunziante was professional enough to not allow his frustration to show, but his next interview was more refined for it was with the suave Francesco Alcalà y Cebrian, as the Spaniard himself relates:

'At around eight that evening Marshal Nunziante,[16] governor general of all the two Calabrias, arrived and I reported to him on the particulars and as he wished to remain here close to the prisoners I invited him to supper and gave him a bed as well as sending a bed for Murat. Murat himself not only had to make do sharing a poor cell designed for no more than 12 people with all his followers, but still had to listen to the people shouting "revolutionary, usurper, thief" or others, more moderate, "general" or just "Murat". I made a note of everything that might be needed and set down everything for His Excellency to satisfy his curiosity.'[17]

Then Nunziante came to see the prisoner himself. His aide, Lieutenant Bottazzi, confirms this first meeting but without giving details:

'We reached Pizzo about an hour after dusk, and dismounted at the castle gate. A company of the 3rd Foreign Regiment had reached there from Monteleone and was guarding the place and the prisoners who numbered 29 including Murat. They were in a cell behind a wooden grating. Soon after his arrival General Nunziante went to speak to Murat for a few moments.'[18]

Nunziante, using the third person, later set down some particulars of this first, inauspicious encounter:

---

16. Nunziante's rank was technically *maresciallo di campo*, the equivalent of a major general in the British Army of the time.
17. Archivio Borbone, Carton 656.
18. Archivio Borbone, Fascio 623, f 171. The 3rd Foreign Regiment, along with the 1st and 2nd Foreign Regiments of line infantry, and the 4th and 5th Foreign Regiments, serving as light infantry, had supposedly been absorbed in August 1815 into a single foreign regiment. The Bourbon foreign regiments had largely spent the wars in Sicily and were primarily composed of Swiss, German, Albanian and Greek personnel.

'On seeing the general Murat said "General Nunziante, I know that you are an honourable man, I would have done anything to have had you in my service. It was not my fault if I did not succeed." He added that "as a man of honour you will treat me as I would have treated King Ferdinand had he fallen into my hands." Nunziante replied but called him "general" and at this word, Murat was much surprised saying that "he was a king and recognised as such by the whole of Europe". Nunziante replied "you will never be my king, one whose throne you have usurped for some time; convince yourself, therefore, that addressing you with the title of general is the best I can do for you." The French generals, Franceschetti and Natale [*sic*], called out that the nation should be ashamed to lay its sacrilegious hands on a man who four months ago was their king and who had made them happy. General Nunziante left them all, and went off to complete the security arrangements which the circumstances then required.'[19]

The following morning, Lieutenant Bottazzi saw some of those arrangements take effect:

'At the crack of dawn as a result of these arrangements, some [four] pieces of mountain artillery arrived, and these were placed at the entrance to the castle, and at other points that were deemed necessary. Soon afterwards more troops arrived.'[20]

With the castle secure, Nunziante could turn to his next task, that of accumulating evidence for the inevitable trial, or the semblance of one. Murat had, after all, landed and, with weapons in his hands, had seemingly sought to provoke an insurrection. Of course, nobody in Ferdinand's government could view him as innocent, even if he had washed up as an unarmed castaway. But armed rebellion would justify a trial, and its inevitable outcome, although Murat might have failed – and might deny that he had ever tried – insurrection would be the carefully arranged noose they would use to hang him. Lesser acts had fallen foul of Bourbon wrath and lesser men had been brought before its executioners, but Murat had

---

19. Archivio Borbone, Fascio 623, f 128–129.
20. Archivio Borbone, Carton 656.

been a king, and with both Naples and Europe watching, even the Bourbons knew that it was wise to proceed carefully and follow the letter of the law.

This unusual concern for procedural details meant that any evidence of Murat's treason would be welcome, even if the outcome was never really in doubt. With the documents implicating him having been misplaced, the emphasis switched to collecting eyewitness testimony that might provide all that was needed to show the world Murat's crime. This task also fell to General Nunziante, and he would perform it as thoroughly and conscientiously as though someone's life depended upon it.

Accompanied by just one assistant – the procurator from Monteleone, Giovanni La Camera – Nunziante began his long series of interrogations. He would interview everyone, from general to valet, fisherman to count, but he naturally began with his chief suspect, the king himself. The interview began well enough, according to General Franceschetti, who says the Bourbon general 'greeted him [Murat] respectfully, bemoaned the conduct of the inhabitants of Pizzo but also had to add that he was obliged to keep him and his followers in the same cell until tomorrow as the populace still posed a risk to his safety'.[21]

This was a courteous start and Murat seems to have repaid this courtesy in kind, apparently asking the general where he was from, for he might know the man's family. But the officer replied that while he was from Salerno, he had left the province when young and had no family there. Murat's charm faltered, but he had sufficient presence of mind to ask Nunziante to have his papers returned, most likely thinking he could make use of the safe conducts in among them, and also raised the thorny question of the jewels, adding that the diamonds belonged to him personally and were not the property of the crown.

However, General Nunziante's record of this first exchange differs markedly from that remembered by Franceschetti. Nunziante's report states:

'Murat was brought before the general and the procurator who were sat at a table. At first he was very confused. They wished to go ahead with his interrogation but he refused saying "It is not worthy of my dignity to be interrogated; tell me what you wish to know and I shall reply in writing." They asked seven questions:

---

21. Archivio Borbone, Carton 623.

'1. How is it that you find yourself detained in the fort at Pizzo?

'2. What was your purpose in coming here?

'3. Who was with you and what did you have with you?

'4. Were those with you armed or not?

'5. From where, and on what day, did you leave?

'6. What documents and other objects did you have with you?

'7. Before coming here did you communicate with anyone in the kingdom?'[22]

Following this inquisition and Murat's promise to send back his written response came a respite and food, as Nunziante's aide, Bottazzi, tells us:

'On the 9th Murat, the two generals Natale and Franceschetti, and some other officers were treated to lunch by General Nunziante, and I was among the diners invited. Murat spoke little during the luncheon, and ate sparingly. The whole thing was most decent, and as far as the local circumstances permitted.'[23]

While the officers talked, or sulked, a doctor arrived to treat the wounded. Giovanni Felice Perretti was the most severe case, and was so weak that he could not be interrogated; Galvani, whose wound was also serious, was taken from the cell and placed in a private house at the gates of the fort, guarded by two sentries. Murat, too, was on the move. His officers were finally separated from the soldiers and Murat was also moved to his own quarters, a small and scruffy room to the right of the castle staircase, quarters he would share with Franceschetti, Natali and the valet Armand. The room had a bed for Murat, while there were two mattresses infected with lice and fleas for his two generals. Poor Armand slept on the floor. The room also had a table and two chairs and there was a window that gave some light. Once he had settled in and writing materials had been provided, Murat began to compose his written statement answering Nunziante's questions:

'The dignity of my station does not permit me to reply to the questions you put to me and the way in which you are bound to act. However,

22. Archivio Nunziante, Storia della famiglia: Arresto e processo del generale Gioacchino Murat, 02.075. Trascrizione delle domande fatte dal generale Vito Nunziante al generale Murat.

23. Pasquale Bottazzi, in Archivio Borbone, Carton 623, f. 170.

I have no objection to declaring that, bearing a passport provided by the Allied Powers, signed by Metternich and the Ambassador of Great Britain, Lord Stuart, I left Corsica in order to rejoin my family at Trieste. Being unable to procure suitable vessels at Ajaccio, and having braved dangers between Corsica and here, I decided to put in at Pizzo, the sole harbour in Calabria where a larger vessel might be obtained so that I might continue on to my destination. I even had the intention of asking the general commanding in Calabria permission to go on to Cotrone for such a boat as I was sorely fatigued by the sea and all the other woes I had endured since being separated from my family. No sooner had I disembarked, and without having had the time to make any requests, I saw the people had taken up arms and they fired on me and on my escort. I ordered my men not to fire and not a shot was fired from our side. We were seized by the populace and we would no doubt have been victims of their fury had not some honest citizens intervened and saved us and we were then thrown into the prisons of this fort. Monsieur le General, that is how I find myself here. My escort was armed because I know one cannot be otherwise in Calabria without running grave risks.[24] As for your question concerning the documents I had upon me, I mentioned above the passport from the Allied powers. I add that the other documents which were forcibly taken from me, included two original letters from Lord Stuart, English ambassador at Paris; a letter from the secretary of the Austrian embassy at Paris to the Duke d'Otranto; and several letters from Lieutenant Colonel Maceroni sent from Paris to bring me the passport from Prince Metternich, and a note in response to the same Maceroni confirming reception of the passport; and, finally, a credit note from the Falconet bank. As for printed matter, and the draft of a decree, they had been produced at a time when I could no longer remain in France without running the risk of being murdered and, still not having received those passports I was long demanding, I therefore went over to Corsica to there [a]wait the outcome of the negotiations between the Duke d'Otranto and the Allied sovereigns. There I determined that, should these negotiations fail, then I should

---

24. Pasqualini says, more plausibly, that they were armed because they had had to protect themselves from the Turks, i.e. the Barbary corsairs, then plaguing the Italian coast.

determine to reconquer my kingdom. However, I must add that none of those documents were authorised by me and I defy you to find any other example in the kingdom or elsewhere other than the one found on me and which I had kept hidden so as to prevent them becoming public. How can anyone who is familiar with my style and the nobility of my sentiments think me capable of something such as that printed document? So those, Monsieur le General, are the documents that were taken from me. I say at once that, no sooner had I received my passports that I immediately gave up any attempt on the kingdom of Naples and that I therefore left Corsica determined to go to Trieste. All I had with me were the 22 diamonds, all the funds remaining to me and which I would have need of to charter the boat. Had I really had designs on the kingdom, I would have said so. I had the right to attempt such a reconquest, for I had never renounced my rights to the crown of Naples, a crown I was recognised as possessing by all the Allied powers. Monsieur le General, I hope that the contents of this letter be brought to the attention not only of King Ferdinand but also those Allied sovereigns. I pray God keeps you in his holy and worthy care, Joachim Napoleon. PS I cannot insist enough that you request your government return to me my passports so I might continue on to Trieste to rejoin my family.'[25]

It was naïve of Murat to expect he would be allowed to continue on to Trieste, but in the circumstances he had to try for he knew he had been caught by a regime not noted for its clemency and that the wheels of Bourbon justice would roll over him rather than carry him away to Austria. Not much could be expected of Murat's gaolers, perhaps, but the Allies might, again, be persuaded to intervene and settle his fate. The Spaniard had proved helpful, but Murat was keen to know whether there were any Austrian or British representatives locally who might be enlisted in his cause. This is how Antonio Perri, the British consul, and the only Allied representative to hand, came to find himself a reluctant participant in Murat's final days. For once Murat had professed his innocence to Nunziante, he began this quest for Allied support. One of his first questions, says Perri, was

25. Valente, p. 411. This letter was sent to Ferdinand.

'whether there were then there any Austrian or English vice-consuls and being informed there was an English one, I was immediately sent for and they came telling me that Murat was asking for me. They then came again, repeating this, so I went and I presented myself at the prison gates and then saw Murat. "Are you the English vice-consul?" he asked and I replied I was and asked him "and you, sir, are you General Murat?" He replied "Mister Consul, do you not know me?" I said that, no, I did not, to which Murat then replied "I am King Gioacchino and have the right to be treated as King of Naples." He then added "I possess a passport from the Allied powers permitting me to travel to Trieste in order to rejoin my family. Ask the officials to show it to you." I was not able to see it for the officials would not bring it, but he told me that the passport had been sent from Paris and had been signed by Prince Metternich and by Lord Stuard [sic], the English minister at Paris, and that it was made out in the name of Count Liponai [sic; Lipona] and he added that he was placing himself under my protection and, he added, that they had asked him when he had been arrested for what purpose he had landed in this port. He said he had told them that his only aim was to find a boat large enough to carry him to Trieste. "They asked," he said, "where had I come from and I replied Corsica, more specifically Ajaccio, from where I had sailed on 28 September. They asked how I came to be in Corsica as the French were there and I told them that it was true, but that the King of France had never raised his hand against me nor had he ever issued any orders to have me arrested and this is how it is I have managed to survive thus far."[26]

Perri judiciously avoided commenting on Murat's pronouncement that he had placed himself under British protection, and Murat's attention may have been distracted by the wrangling the pair then had over his guilt:

'He then told me "I have conquered all of Europe and now they keep me in a pigsty." I told him "you have come to ruin us for why else,

26. British Library ADD MS41537. Murat requested to see the consul again on 12 October and sent this note to Nunziante: 'Monsieur le Marechal de camp Nunziante, having need to talk to you in the presence of the English vice-consul, I beg you to therefore invite him to come and attend you.'

why, would you shout long live King Gioacchino, long live Murat!"
He answered that "I did not do that, it was my followers" and then
one of those who was standing by the gates came over and said the
following to his face: "That is wrong, you were shouting long live
King Gioacchino and now you deny it." Murat asked me for a little
water and this was soon brought for him but one of the ruffians on
guard then said the following: "By God, I had rather give him vinegar
than that."[27]

Nunziante, too, was weighing the king's guilt. He worked late into the
evening, first sending off a telegraph and then drafting a detailed report
to Prince Leopold that he finished the next morning, summarizing
Murat's crime:

'A xebec and another boat, like a bove, brought General Murat and
those who accompanied him to the beach. A launch ferried them
across to the shore where they, meaning those individuals listed in
Note 1, landed without opposition. They proceeded to the piazza.
They say that General Murat accosted the people saying "I am your
King Giacchino [sic] Murat, you must recognise me!" The population
took up arms and followed them. They took the road to Monteleone
but they were chased down the slopes to the beach where the people
fired at them; they tried to make off in a boat but it was stranded and
they were not successful. One of Murat's followers, Captain Pernice,
was killed and eight were wounded. In this encounter Murat and his
men made use of their weapons, that is their swords and pistols, but
they were overwhelmed and then subject to mistreatment, not least
Murat himself, being beaten and punched, before being arrested and
brought to this fort.'[28]

Nunziante's short text emphasizes the central, determining point: that
Murat had behaved like a brigand, leading armed supporters against the
state, and that weapons had been used against the forces of law and order.
Nunziante's opening salvo was aimed at Murat, but the general then turned

27. British Library ADD MS41537.
28. *Rivista di fanteria*, XII, p. 938.

his guns on the hero of the hour, poor Trentacapilli. Nunziante probably found him personally disagreeable, and not a little unprofessional; after all, the official had been away from his post on the day in question. But his particular grudge against the gendarme centred on the idea that he may have compromised the entire case against Murat by sending away those vital, incriminating documents. Consequently, Nunziante could not prevent the bile from showing in his letter:

'A captain of the Royal Gendarmerie, called Don Gregorio Trentacapilli, who says he has been appointed commander of the gendarmerie in Calabria Citra, claims that he was the one to arrest Murat, which remains to be proven as everyone wishes to claim some of the glory and, indeed, it seems to have been a collective effort. Perhaps animated by excess zeal, or for personal gain, he seized Murat's documents and, without making copies, or even looking at them, says he then sent them off to His Majesty. This is an unforgivable error and they probably contain information as to who he [Murat] had been corresponding with in the kingdom. He also seems to have taken the cockade from Murat's hat which they say contained 12 diamonds which he says he also sent to Naples. But Murat assures me that there were 22 each with a value of 100 Louis. A flag of the previous regime has come into my possession.'[29]

The general also made sure that another prince of royal blood, Francesco, heir and Duke of Calabria, was made aware of the following:

'[H]ad Don Gregorio Trentacapilli been content to limit himself to seizing the booty he had taken from the prisoners, and, according to his duty, handed over the documents confiscated from them, I would have been able to get to the root of the plot. It is this captain's fault that the proof which might have assured permanent tranquillity for the kingdom is missing. He says he has sent everything directly to His Majesty, both the papers and diamonds taken from Murat. I cannot guarantee the truth of this especially regarding the diamonds. Murat insists there were 22 and he pretends otherwise. As for the weapons,

---

29. *Rivista di fanteria*, XII, p. 938.

he says nothing and he probably has the sword and perhaps the pistols from the prisoner. I do not wish to suggest to Your Excellency how criminal this conduct is, but would only say that I am troubled by not being able, on account of this captain, to present to His Majesty the watertight indictment so necessary for the good of the state.'[30]

As Nunziante sent off report after report, Murat continued to make use of his writing materials to pursue the hope that the Allies would intervene in his fate. He would compose four letters in the coming hours: one to his wife, one to the British ambassador, another to the Austrian governor in Naples and the Austrian Emperor in Vienna; and a final one to his nemesis, Ferdinand in Naples.[31] That to his wife was very optimistic:

'Having finally obtained a passport for Austria, [and] hoping to be reunited with my unfortunate family later this month, I was, however, forced to put in at Pizzo so I could obtain a larger boat and here I and the officers escorting me were arrested. I hope for justice from Naples and that my passports are returned to me so I can continue my journey.'[32]

The letters to the Allied representatives were dignified diplomatic protests that he had been merely on his way to rejoin his family in Trieste, for which he had a valid passport, and that he had been unlawfully apprehended. To each he repeated the idea he had first broached to Perri, that he wished to be placed under the protection of the Allied powers. The final letter, the one to Ferdinand, was strangely impudent, addressed as it was to 'Monsieur mon frère', and while it too requested the return of the passports, Murat also asked that the Bourbon monarch furnish him with a boat so he could continue on to his destination. He closed with the almost brazen

30. *Rivista di fanteria*, XII, p. 939. Nunziante laboured this point. For example, he also told Tommasi, the Minister of the Interior in Naples, that this man 'of low birth and obscure connections' had, by sending away the evidence, committed 'an unpardonable fault as such documents would probably have allowed me to see which inhabitants of the kingdom had been in correspondence with Murat and allowed me to take precautionary measures'.
31. Baron Koller, who had escorted Napoleon to Elba before joining the Austrian occupation of Naples as an intendant, says the letters to the Austrian emperor, his wife and Ferdinand were kept back by Ferdinand.
32. Archivio Borbone, Fascio 623, f 109.

'I leave the punishment of the guilty who grievously insulted me to your majesty' before signing the note '*Le bon frère*' followed by his royal title of Joachim Napoleon.

Exhausted, perhaps, by such audacity, he then set down his pen and, with Natali reading out the libretto of Temistocle by Pietro Metastasio, he promptly fell asleep.[33]

Early on the morning of the following day, 10 October, Nunziante's work on gathering evidence for the inevitable trial continued. He methodically collected depositions and witness statements from Murat's entourage; these were centred on the same questions he had asked Murat the day before, probing for evidence of guilt, intent and use of violence. Each of Murat's followers was questioned, from the senior officers to the servants. The information of most interest to the authorities can be gauged from the records of the interrogations of Murat's former servant, Salvatore Pugi, and his current valet, Armand:

'On this day, 10 October 1815, at one in the afternoon, in the castle of Pizzo, the undersigned, then being detained, were brought before General Nunziante, commander of the 5th Military Division, and the civil commissioner representing the judiciary, with the following interrogation taking place:

Q. What is your name, first name, origin and status?
A. I am Salvatore Pugi of Portoferraio [Elba] and I am currently employed in the service of General Murat.
Q. How is it you find yourself detained in this castle?
A. I was arrested in Pizzo the other morning having disembarked with my master and others who had come from Ajaccio.
Q. How long had you been in his service?
A. For around a month when he was in the commune of Vescovado [*sic*; Vescovato] in Corsica.
Q. On what day did you leave Ajaccio?

---

33. Murat had requested books from Alcalà y Cebrian. The Spaniard replied that he only had a French dictionary, the fables of Pignotti, Metastasio, the *History of Tom Jones* and Montaigne's letters. He sent them but added he was sorry he did not have more for the rest of his library had been dispersed when his property, as well as that of all other Spaniards, had been seized in 1808 – by Murat!

A. Around the end of September last but I don't recollect the exact date.

Q. What was your destination and why?

A. We were bound for Trieste for he had received a passport from the Allied powers to join his family.

Q. How was it that you came to land here?

A. A storm damaged the boat and it was nearly swamped, and we were running short of food. So to replenish supplies and to replace the boat we came ashore.

Q. And were you able to satisfy these needs?

A. No, because when we disembarked the people of Pizzo received us in a hostile manner, shooting at us and then capturing us.

Q. Why, in your opinion, did the people do this?

A. It was not because they recognised Gioacchino as he did not wish to make himself known, so the shouts of long live Gioacchino confused them and they took to arms.

Q. Was it General Murat's plan to march through Pizzo?

A. I am only a servant so I do not know what he intended to do.

Q. Of those that embarked in Ajaccio how many carried arms?

A. I do not know exactly, but not all had weapons.

Q. It is clear that your master planned to attempt to take the kingdom of Naples and so must have been in communication, clandestinely, with someone in Calabria.

A. I know nothing about that.

Q. What was the boat you sailed on from Ajaccio?

A. The boat and the owner were Corsican but I don't know its name, nor do I know the name of its captain.

Q. What did General Murat bring with him?

A. A trunk for linen and clothes and a bag containing money, although I don't know how much.

Q. Was there a tricolour flag?

A. No sir. The boat flew the white flag of the king of France, Louis XVIII.

Q. Where are the passport and documents of your master?

A. He had them. A captain of gendarmes from here seized them, or so it seems, along with the valuable diamonds. So I understood that he had taken the documents and diamonds from my master.

Q. What orders did General Murat give to the one commanding the ship?

A. I do not know.

Nunziante, Pugi

'At nine o'clock in the morning, French time, another prisoner was brought before the general and these questions were put to him:

Q. What is your name, first name, origin and status?

A. I am called Blanchard Armand, from Paris, a valet.

Q. How did you find yourself detained?[34]

A. I have been in the service of Gioacchino for six years and I left Naples with him last May. We were in Ischia before we went and landed in Toulon. From there I went to Paris. The English lieutenant-colonel, Maceroni, left for Toulon at the end of September in order to bring Gioacchino the passport from the Allied powers as he assumed he was still in that town. I came with him. We did not find Gioacchino in Toulon so we left for Ajaccio as we learned he had gone there. We handed him the passports at noon on 28 September and that evening he set sail with some generals and soldiers heading for Trieste. I don't know about the other boats, but this one was too small. I think my master wished to land to trade in his boat for one capable of crossing the Adriatic, but I'm not sure. What I do know is that, the other morning, we landed at Pizzo and we were surrounded by the people, who had armed themselves, and we were taken.

Q. Do you know if General Murat was in correspondence with anyone in Naples?

A. I don't know, I couldn't know, for, as I said, I only joined him on the day he was setting sail. During the voyage itself he did not mention anything of the sort.

Q. Did you have a tricolour flag on board, even if it was not flying aloft?

A. No sir.

---

34. General Franceschetti's answer to the same question gives a sense of this old soldier's character: 'I was in his entourage for I swore an oath of honour and loyalty to follow him during his good fortune and through his disgrace.' Antoine Félix Lanfranchi's reply was more straightforward: 'Because I was arrested yesterday in Pizzo.'

Q. What became of your master's effects and documents?

A. The linen is in the boat. He only took with him whatever he was wearing, some documents and 22 very valuable diamonds. All these were confiscated from him in this prison by a gendarme captain who was in charge of the guards but who did not give a receipt for the items he took.

Nunziante
Armand Blanchard, valet de chambre.'[35]

Testimony such as this, as well as the earlier interrogation of Murat, allowed Nunziante to establish the rudiments of the case that they imagined they could make against Murat. He was soon telling Prince Leopoldo:

'They left Corsica on the 28th of the last month and sailed into these waters. They sought to deny their criminal intent, saying they had landed here for they had need of food, water and to charter a better boat. But it is not difficult to imagine what their true intentions were. When they disembarked they did not announce themselves to the Health Board, or alert the regional authorities, as they should have, but did all they could to make the people rise up in their favour. Murat himself demanded of those he encountered "do you know your King Gioacchino, follow me!" and it is clear what his idea was but his revolution failed because the people remained true to their legitimate king. ... his criminal intent is also clear from his having produced decrees dated 25 and 27 September last in which he falsely assumed the title of the King of the Two Scillies and he allowed himself to award and promote those officers in his suite accordingly.'[36]

The crime was clear, and the folly was becoming ever more so:

'In addition, there was the rambling and rather long letter that had been written to him by an anonymous person and which supports the idea that it was his intention to try something desperate, for that

35. Archivio Borbone, 656.
36. *Rivista di fanteria*, XII, p. 942.

letter nurtured in him the hope of reconquering his kingdom. His faithful correspondent sought to convince him that the population was waiting for him with open arms and that a single regiment would be enough to realise his ambition. This man, his imagination more aflame than that even of his imprudent and hot-headed friend, gave rise to the illusion that such an enterprise, judged impossible even by the mad, would succeed. I sense that his insistence that he was merely on his way to Austria, where he had been authorised to travel to by the Allied powers, and that he had disembarked merely to acquire supplies, stems from the shame he no doubt feels about confessing to his real folly. From what I have seen of him I have seen what he is and his situation is risible.'[37]

Nunziante was still worrying that Trentacapilli's incompetence with the documentary evidence would deprive them all better proof, but he sent another trophy, the tricolour flag, which had supposedly been captured,[38] off to Naples with Colonel Marsiglia of the staff. This officer, accompanied by a cadet, also took Murat's letters to Ferdinand, the ambassadors and his wife, Caroline. The couriers would take two days to reach Naples, arriving there at noon on 12 October.

Word had already reached the capital that Murat had landed and been captured. The first urgent telegraph message had arrived on the evening of the 9th but it was thought better to let the king sleep, so just after nine o'clock on the morning of 10 October, as King Ferdinand was out walking at Portici with his secretary, Francesco Frilli, he was handed the good news.[39] The Minister of Police, Luigi de Medici, was immediately sent for, and he was then instructed to convene the king's ministers. Medici noted the details:

'The telegraph message saying that General Gioacchino Murat and 15 or 20 of his followers have been arrested at Pizzo arrived here

37. *Rivista di fanteria*, XII, p. 942.
38. This flag was most likely the one given by Murat to one of the soldiers in the square in the hope it would be raised above the fort. It was more likely a small regimental fanion preserved by one of Murat's officers in Corsica.
39. Ferdinand told his son: 'The first telegraph reached Naples at 17.45 on 9 October. This message was handed to the king at around five the following morning.' Archivio Borbone, Fascio 141.

this morning at 09.15. His Majesty ordered the Council of State to convene.'[40]

This special council of ministers consisted of the 77-year-old president of the council and Ferdinand's Minister of Foreign Affairs, Tommaso Maria de Somma (Marquis de Circello); the comparatively sprightly Luigi de Medici, aged 66, representing the police; and the positively youthful 53-year-old Donato Tommasi, in charge of what passed for justice in the kingdom. King Ferdinand was also there, but it was this triumvirate – the trio that effectively ran King Ferdinand's creaking state while he spent his time hunting deer or women – who put their names to Nunziante's instructions and conferred upon him the responsibility of acting as the king's alter ego for all that was to follow. The instructions began innocently enough:

'Now, being 09.15 on the morning of Tuesday on the 10th of this month, we the undersigned, gathered in council in virtue of the powers entrusted to us by His Majesty, to deliberate on the telegraphic report which informed us that General Murat had been detained at Pizzo with 15 or 20 followers and that he was being guarded by the general. We therefore resolve to send General Nunziante the following orders ...'[41]

What followed made it clear that the council had drawn up Murat's death warrant and that they had appointed Nunziante executioner, for the instructions had quickly taken a darker turn, informing Nunziante that Murat would be judged and sentenced by a court martial and that his execution would follow just as soon as the usurper had been given last rites.

The full set of instructions was instantly sent out by courier and a curtailed version summarized in a telegraph that was then hastily transmitted to Pizzo. There had been no time to ask those Allied representatives who might have voiced an opinion on Murat's fate, or intervened to amend it,

---

40. Rivista di fanteria, XII, p. 947. This was public knowledge the following day, 11 October. The diarist Carlo de Nicola made the following entry on that date: 'Great fear in Naples ... The police are most active. Rumour has it that Murat has landed in Calabria at Pizzo harbour and that he has 150 men with him and a proclamation that he has come to regain his throne. But the General Nunziante had quickly captured him.' Nicola added: 'If it is true that Murat has returned to the kingdom then he must finally have lost his mind.'
41. Valente, Angela, *Gioacchino Murat e l'Italia meridionale* (Turin, 1963).

what they thought of the government's decision. Out of all of them, the Austrian, Prince Ludwig von Jablonowski, was best placed to argue that Murat should be spared and sent to Austria. After all, Prince Metternich and the Emperor had actually pledged asylum for the entire Murat family.[42] But the ambassador had wisely absented himself from the capital, although, as can be seen from the hints and winks in his letter of 18 October to his master, Prince Metternich, even the Austrians were unwilling to help the man who had twice disturbed their peace in Italy:

'Had Your Excellency consulted all the ministers at court none would have dared give advice that the sentence against Murat be suspended pending a decision of the Allies. Fortunately for me, the ministers did not place me in what would have been an embarrassing situation, which was fortunate for two reasons. Firstly, even the most extreme partisans of Murat cannot blame me for having contributed to his death, and blame the government roundly for not having consulted with me. Secondly, the fear of disobliging me and displeasing our August Master prompted the ministers to keep me informed of developments, something I helped them with, and which, I hope merits the approbation of His Imperial Majesty.'[43]

As for the other representatives of the august Allies, little sympathy for Murat could be expected. Indeed, the British seemed to positively relish the prospect of Murat's demise. The decision to finish with Murat had already been made, but this did not prevent British ambassador William A'Court from trying to claim some of the credit:

'As an act of justice or of policy it is in my mind equally to be justified and I am not afraid to own that I gave this opinion very plainly and unequivocally to the Neapolitan government the moment I heard of

---

42. This had cooled the relationship between Naples and Austria. When Ferdinand heard that Metternich had offered Murat refuge, the king had sulked and snubbed Austria's ambassador. That ambassador, Jablonowski, only learned of the reasons for this by cornering the king's young wife, the Princess de Partanna, at the opera. She told him: 'The Emperor had offered Murat asylum in his lands and so the king was most put out.'
43. Lemmi, p. 284. Ferdinand sent a letter and justification to the Emperor on 17 October, suggesting he knew that Austria had the right to be upset even if it had the sense not to show it.

the landing. My opinion, I have reason to believe, had some weight in the business.'[44]

What A'Court's opinion might have been, and what his delight certainly was, is made clear in an account he sent to Lord Burghersh on 13 October:

'Murat himself with two of the vessels reached the coast of Calabria and immediately landed at Pizzo. He ran into the market place followed by about 16 people, all armed, and cried out to the people "Behold your king!, cry long live the king!" The people, instead of doing as they were bid, ran to arms, fired upon the party, and, after killing one and wounding three to four others, made the rest, and amongst them Murat, prisoners. Murat is at present in the castle of Pizzo. I should rather say was, for I trust that by this time he is *fusillé* [shot].'[45]

The French ambassador, Narbonne Pelet, also seemed to assume that Murat would just be taken care of, for in his letter to Talleyrand, that paragon of vice at the head of France's foreign affairs, he rather washes his hands of Murat and his fellow French citizens:

'I hasten to inform Your Excellency of the outcome of the ridiculous and mad expedition that Murat has launched against Calabria. Your Excellency will certainly have known that he left Ajaccio on the 28th of the previous month with four or five boats which transported some 150 soldiers, and 40 or so officers including some generals. A gale scattered his little flotilla and, after [they] wandered about for 10 days, he reached Pizzo, in the most distant part of Calabria, with two boats on the 8th. There he landed with some 20 men and marched for the main square crying "I am your king, Joachim, shout long live

---

44. A'Court 23 October to Lord Burghersh. There is a muddled account by General Vaudoncourt that supports this view of British bloodlust. He has it that the Spanish envoy, Aguilar, stated Murat should be shot, while the French ambassador, Raymond-Jacques-Marie de Narbonne-Pelet, abstained. The Prussian, Quiss, was indifferent, so it was only the Russian envoy (whom Vaudoncourt erroneously calls Prince Italiansky when it was Georgy Dmitrievitch Mocenigo) who would not consent to it, while the Briton William A'Court was the most bloodthirsty, declaring 'kill him, I take the responsibility'.
45. Burghersh, Lord (Fane, John), Weigall, Rachel (ed.), *Correspondence of Lord Burghersh, 1808–1840* (London, 1912).

the king!" After a short hesitation caused by surprise and disbelief, the inhabitants fell on him. He was captured, clapped in irons and locked in a fort where he was strictly guarded until orders from the government could be sent as to what to do with him. Those who landed with him put up some resistance, and one or two lost their lives, but they were soon taken and disarmed. Those who remained on the boats saw what was happening and saved themselves. I shall share with Your Excellency the consequences of these events especially regarding any decision that the government takes regarding Murat and his companions who are, it seems, all Corsicans previously in his service.'[46]

The government had taken its decision, and the Allies would quietly approve. A court martial would be convened to rubber-stamp a preordained sentence of death. No evidence had been heard at the Council of State; none was needed. Murat would be killed by decree. Nunziante was still interrogating witnesses, and the key documents that Trentacapilli had sent to Naples would not reach there before 16 October, making a mockery of the judicial process then being set in motion. But Ferdinand and his ministers wanted death, and death is what they would have.

Back in Pizzo, both captives and captors were still ignorant of the plans the Bourbon government had for Murat, although many suspected what was about to pass. Nor could Murat have known that the ambassadors of the Allied powers were busy washing their hands of him, and it seemed he was still labouring under the misapprehension that British and Austrian honour still counted for something. Indeed, his stubborn belief in British fair play, even when it came to geopolitics, was revealed once again when, on 10 October, unexpected visitors sailed into the harbour.

Word of Murat's capture had been sent to the important Anglo-Bourbon garrison across the straits at Messina, from where a small flotilla under the command of the Londoner Colonel William Robinson[47] of the Royal Marine Artillery, with some gunboats under Commodore Don Saverio Natoli of the Sicilian navy, sailed up to Pizzo. When they arrived, they told Nunziante the good news that two other barques with Murat's followers

---

46. Sassenay, p. 233.
47. Admiral Penrose called him 'a man unusually fertile in resources and clear and cool in danger'.

had also been seized off Palinuro by 'Captain Cafieri [*sic*: Caffiero]', 'with 42 Corsicans onboard belonging to Murat's new army', as the general later snidely informed his superiors.[48] While this was welcome news, Robinson's mission in Pizzo itself was not quite clear to Nunziante. Nevertheless, as Robinson was a senior British officer in Ferdinand's service, Nunziante felt obliged to present the colonel to the king. Murat, perhaps hoping that this was a sign that the Great Powers were again involving themselves in his fate, jumped at this unexpected, and perhaps final, opportunity. A report sent to Admiral Exmouth by an anonymous British officer describes the ensuing conversation and conveys a sense of Murat's increasing desperation:

'While in custody, Colonel Robinson, from whom I have these particulars, was with him several hours; he affected to believe that he had done nothing which gave a right even to declare him but at most a prisoner of war for the decision of the Allies. But he never had nor ever could resign his right to the crown of Naples. He endeavoured to keep from thinking on his situation I conclude by a constant talking. He enquired how Ferdinand served his horses, if he took care of his carriages. Boasted how well he had used him by leaving his palaces furnished and that he had expended 3 millions (I think) of his own money. He said that he knew he must leave Naples 15 days before he did and that he would have surrendered his person to an Englishman but that he had no opportunity. He left Naples in a very small boat, got a larger at Ischia and had an intention of throwing himself into Gaeta but found there two British ships of the line. He must therefore have got there after the arrival of the *Malta* [80 guns, William Charles Fahie] on the 24 May. He says the Neapolitans [were] of dear affectionate natures and warmly attached to him but that he had all to do himself, there was no making a general of one of them. It is clear that his assertion of his readiness to give up to the British was false for in the first place I am almost certain you was in the bay before he left it or at any rate he could have gone to the *Malta* and *Berwick* [74 guns, John Nash]. Captain Bastard he said was his ruin, I apprehend from his having made a simple action of contempt which would not

---

48. Those captured consisted of 'one captain, five lieutenants, an adjutant, 15 sergeants, five corporals, 10 soldiers, 21 sailors and two [sick?] soldiers', according to the original report. The two vessels were seized by five gunboats, a schooner and a barque.

allow him to accept an asylum: He would be king and only king. But the primary cause of his ruin was Lord William Bentinck which pray inform his lordship with my compliments. For, says Murat, my wishes and intentions were to keep at peace with England but that his lordship's early declaration of the breach of the armistice upset all my measures. He said he passed close to an English brig of war. This was the *Sparrowhawk*, Burgogyne taking his three vessels for part of the Tunisian squadron. He said that the Turks were aiming at something great and that Tunis was to assist with 15,000 men. He had great hopes Sir Sidney Smith would raise an army against the Barbary powers in which case he intended to have acted as general in chief! He said he had passed 6 months of misery. That he had even heard people in the next room to him at Marseille planning how to cut his throat. In short, he ran on all subjects but failed not to regret beyond all things that he was not at Waterloo!'[49]

Francesco Alcalà y Cebrian largely confirms this soldierly talk:

'During the 11th and 12th nothing much new occurred although it was said that a few officers, and particularly the English naval captain Robinson, had lunch with Murat and it seemed that the latter had forgotten the sad situation he found himself in because, in the various conversations he had he talked of little else but his own bravery, what he had done for this kingdom and gave himself the airs of a king.'[50]

It was not all small talk, however, for, on 11 October, early in the process, the king, with the airs of a king, revealed his hand. This might be his last opportunity to arrange his escape, after all. Murat made a formal request to Nunziante for permission to be embarked on Robinson's ship, and then to be at least taken to Tropea for his own safety. Armand innocently presented Murat's request as being warranted by the squalor of the prison:

'On the 11th and 12th the king begged the general to have him placed on board a ship bearing the English flag, although at that time in

---

49. British Library. ADD MSS 35651, report probably by Admiral Charles Vinicombe Penrose.
50. Archivio Borbone, Carton 656.

Ferdinand's service, on the pretext that he would be much better off on board a ship than in that insalubrious room (although the king intended it so that once he was under the protection of the English flag he would be protected from that revenge Ferdinand was certainly planning against him).'[51]

Both Nunziante and Robinson saw that Murat was again seeking to place himself under British protection, and thus elude justice. Nunziante's solution was to temporize and, according to Charles and Armand, he promised that 'if he did not receive specific orders, then he would take it upon himself to permit this and the king could go aboard the ship'. It was then left for Robinson to cut this avenue of escape, and he promptly did so by refusing to receive the king on his ship, telling Nunziante that if Murat was permitted to come on board it would clearly compromise his sovereign. General Franceschetti understood that had the British taken Murat, then he would have been saved: 'Robwisson [sic] observed to Nunziante that should His Majesty Joachim be embarked upon a ship of the fleet then he could not be held responsible for what might happen as he would cease to be a prisoner of King Ferdinand as soon as he came under the protection of the English flag.'[52]

Robinson did not take Murat, and he shortly took his leave of Pizzo, leaving just a few gunboats in the bay. Thus ended his brief appearance in Murat's story. This meant that Murat's next lunch appointment with Nunziante, that on 12 October, was a relatively sombre affair. However awkward the meal itself, worse was to come, as shortly afterwards the Bourbon general received momentous news from the capital. Bad weather had been interrupting telegraph signals up and down the coast, but now one came through from Naples, albeit one that was fragmentary and enigmatic. Nunziante was handed a message that ordered that 'General Joachim Murat shall be taken'. Rather oddly, Nunziante then decided to share this with Murat, as Armand relates:

'The general came to see the king and as he looked most perturbed, the king asked him the reason and the general replied that the telegraph

---

51. Archivio Borbone, Carton 656.
52. Franceschetti, p. 74.

had just brought him instructions to hold the king but that the weather had prevented further instructions. The king said, doubtless, they intended to order him to be held in the citadel of Messina, but the general said it was impossible for him to guess and that he would have to wait for the following day.'[53]

Perhaps Murat thought the Bourbons had made a mistake and he would be allowed to go aboard one of Robinson's vessels after all so he could be taken to Messina. While on board he could then, like a medieval felon in a church, claim sanctuary. But such dreams were soon to be dashed, for awful clarification of the message's true meaning was on its way. Lieutenant Bottazzi says it was around half past midnight when Murat's fate was made clear to all the royal officials in the castle, the courier arriving from Naples bringing the detailed instructions set down by the Council of State. The telegraph should have read: 'General Joachim Murat shall be taken before a court martial selected by the Minister of War.' The rest of the royal instructions were terse, clear and just as unequivocal. Nunziante was to:

1. Convene a council of war or court martial to judge a public enemy;
2. When the sentence [sic] is issued, you shall proceed to the execution [sic] giving a quarter of an hour for any religious ceremony;
3. As for his companions, those who are subjects of the king, whether Neapolitans or Sicilians, should be judged in the same manner and the sentence must be carried out equally after just an interval of 15 minutes. The general in command shall be in charge of carrying this out. For those who are foreigners, they shall be kept under guard until further orders.[54]

General Nunziante reacted at once, as Bottazzi relates:

'I was just then sat at the table with my general drawing up a report, which was to be sent the following morning. Everything was instantly halted, and the general turned to arranging for the

---

53. AN, 31AP/21, Dossier 361, *Relation manuscrite d'Armand.*
54. Pasquale Bottazzi in Archivio Borbone, Carton 623, f. 173.

appointment of the members of the court. That done, orders were sent to some of the officers appointed to this duty to come to Pizzo from Monteleone and other nearby places, and this began to be carried out that very night.'[55]

The following morning, Nunziante put the finishing touches to his court. It was something of a hybrid, composed as it was of local legal officials and assorted officers of the nearby garrisons, as well as from Commodore Don Saverio Natoli's Sicilian gunboats in the bay.[56]

He soon had sufficient officers assembled, although some were relatively junior. The convention at the time was for officers to be tried by their peers, but lacking generals or kings, Nunziante had to make do with those he could find at such short notice, even including two officers, Natoli and Mortellari, who were in Sicilian rather than Neapolitan service. Of those assembled, the two most senior were Nunziante's deputy, Colonel Giuseppe Fasulo – who according to Galvani was a staff officer promoted by Murat and who was then Chief of Staff of the 5th Divisional District – and the president of the court, Baron Raffaele Scalfaro from Monteleone, then a colonel in the National Guard of Calabria Ultra. Then there was Commodore Don Saverio Natoli of the fleet; Captain Don Matteo Cannilli and the gunners Captain François de Vengé and Lieutenant Francesco Mortellari, who had brought the mountain guns from Tropea to Pizzo; Major Tommaso (or Gennaro) Lanzetta of the Engineers; and the court rapporteur, Lieutenant Francesco Frojo of the 3rd Foreign Regiment. The court was managed, hawkishly, by Giovanni Lacamera, the prosecutor from Catanzaro who had, ironically, served under Murat, while Secretary Francesco Papavassi

55. Pasquale Bottazzi in Archivio Borbone, Carton 623, f. 173. Giovanni Lacamera, the prosecutor Nunziante would rely on, recalled: 'At midnight I received a letter from His Excellency General Nunziante at Pizzo requesting that I hurry to him for an urgent matter in the service of the king.'

56. Consul Antonio Perri described it thus: 'During Thursday evening, at around half past six [Italian time], a message arrived from Naples for Marshal Nunziante and that a second and similar one arrived around nine [sic], ordering him to convene a court martial to judge Murat and at the same time to gather witness statements so that events which took place since Murat's arrival in this town might be set down. Before long the court martial was established consisting of Marshal Nunziante, eight captains or lieutenant-colonels and the Procurator-General from the criminal court at Monteleone. Murat's followers were being held together in one cell whilst he was being held alone in a guarded room.'

would record proceedings.[57] All they needed now was for the accused to appear before them.

The delicate task of informing the defendant that he was to be summoned to appear before a military tribunal, with all that signified as to his likely fate, was not a popular assignment. Nunziante delegated Captain Stratti of the Foreign Regiment to take care of it, but Stratti, coming over to Murat's room to ensure Murat's companions were removed from earshot, positioned four officers at the door to serve as sentries and then told one of them, Lieutenant Pasquale Bottazzi – the most senior of the four[58] – that he should inform Murat that he was to appear. Bottazzi picks up the story:

'At about thirteen o'clock [Italian time, around 7 o'clock in the morning] we had the two generals [Franceschetti and Natali] taken to another room of the fort [and] we came into the room where Murat was detained. On entering the room we came upon his valet [Armand] who was standing by the door on duty. I, who had entered before my companions, bade him leave as we had confidential orders for his master. He replied it was his duty to remain there to serve the king, who was then dressing. I replied that he must leave at once whereupon he turned and said "Sire, Sire they want me to leave." Then Murat came to us demanding "what is it you want gentlemen officers?" I replied "we have orders to share with you, general, but not in the presence of others." "Well," he replied and, addressing the valet, said "sortie, sortie". Then I said these words to Murat: "General we have orders to announce to you that you are going to be tried by a Court Martial which is going to convene here."'[59]

Murat, who was dressed in a blue jacket and trousers and with a black silk cap on his head, promptly threw his cap to the ground and exclaimed: 'Oh, damnation, a court martial; me, a court martial? Who has ordered it, who could order it? Damn it, I know what you are at. They want to assassinate me, they want me to die. How can they, if they think I have come here to

57. Archivio Nunziante, Storia della famiglia: Arresto e processo del generale Gioacchino Murat, 02.089. Compilazione del processo di Gioacchino Murat dalla Commissione militare riunita a Pizzo.
58. The others were Ensign Giuseppe Roussel, Giuseppe Nini and Raffaele Lentini.
59. Pasquale Bottazzi in Archivio Borbone, Carton 623, f. 174.

start a rebellion, which is not the case, I would have a right to do so or at least they must treat me as a prisoner of war.'[60]

Murat then sat on his bed and spent a few minutes telling the officers how he had come to Pizzo en route for Trieste, that bad weather had driven him into Pizzo and that 'I had only come to change boats as the one I had embarked on was now useless'. He then asked the officers: 'How can one believe that I would have the idea of reconquering the kingdom by landing with so few men and in this region, which has always been hostile to me even though I was always its benefactor?'[61]

Murat, having tried to assert his innocence, and after telling the officers he would refuse to appear, then began to face his fate. After asking that he be taken 'to the island of Saint Helena to the Emperor', he then took out his watch and shed some tears over the portrait it contained of his wife.

Tears were appropriate, as his death was then being arranged a few metres from Murat's room. His judges had convened at 10 o'clock that morning in a chamber across the hallway. Captain Stratti informed them that Murat had declared he would not appear before the court, saying that it was not competent to try him.[62] The court then sent Giuseppe Starace, who had been appointed to act as Murat's counsel, to him to see if he would change his mind, but the four officers guarding him noted that 'he held firm and did not wish to submit anything in writing, nor go with the Secretary [sic] before the court'.[63] Captain Frojo confirmed Murat's response to the assembled court:

'He did not wish to be seen as General Murat but as King Gioacchino Napoleone; he did not wish to state how old he was. He declared that the Court Martial was not competent to try him and, if anything, he should be treated as a prisoner of war not having renounced any of his rights and being acknowledged as such by the Allied powers. Furthermore, he was travelling under the name Count Lipona and with passports brought by Metternich and Stuart and provided to

---

60. Bottazzi's account, Archivio Borbone, Fascio 623, f 171.
61. Pasquale Bottazzi in Archivio Borbone, Carton 623, f. 174.
62. Franceschetti, who had gone by then, changes Murat's reply to: 'Tell the president of the court that I refuse to appear before such a tribunal; men such as I have nobody to answer to but God for their actions. Let them pronounce their sentence, I have nothing more to say.'
63. Pasquale Bottazzi in Archivio Borbone, Carton 623, f. 174.

him by Maceroni. He said the passports had violently been taken from him by Trentacapilli. He asked that proceedings be halted until replies had been received to his letters to Ferdinand, the Austrian general and the British minister in Naples. He did not want a lawyer.'[64]

Murat's position was that, as he had not abdicated, the judges 'are not my judges, they are my subjects and they are not permitted to judge their sovereign. Sovereigns have no other judges than God and their people.'[65] Murat wasn't a bandit, he was a monarch, and his argument that the court was not competent to try him was actually put to the court by the dutiful Starace. The president of the court sidestepped this point and replied that as Nunziante, the king's alter ego, had ordered it to sit, then the court was clearly competent to judge the transgressor. Murat was not recognised as a king but would be tried as a French general, and nobody thought to object that a Neapolitan court was trying a French subject. The Bourbon king, and any of his alter egos, were sure they were still absolute in their rule, with all the rights they needed, and with new laws and old, to try whoever they wanted to try. The outcome was never in doubt, and although legal arguments would be made and considered, and justice would be seen to be done, the deliberations were designed to lead to an ordained conclusion. This modest court intended to find Murat, that most immodest of monarchs, guilty, rendering all the gravity of the occasion a show, all the procedure a pretence and the legal textbooks mere props to that single purpose. Once it was clear Murat would not appear, the charade could begin in a closed session that would last for four hours, with a little more time added for lunch:

'This Military Commission, assembled at 10 a.m. on the 13th day of October in the year one thousand eight hundred and fifteen in the Castle of Pizzo to judge the arrested French General Joachim Murat as a public enemy.'[66]

The President of the court then asked the first, and most significant, question arising from that bland pronouncement: "Is the French General Joachim Murat a public enemy?"

64. Archivio Borbone, fascio 656, fasc. 4.
65. Valente, Angela, *Gioacchino Murat e l'Italia meridionale* (Turin, 1963).
66. Valente, Angela, *Gioacchino Murat e l'Italia meridionale* (Turin, 1963).

There were some initial nerves, diverting the court from the state crime of French General Murat, into examining one of his more minor discretions, although one that echoes through the ages to our own times:

'At around 10.00 on the morning of Sunday 8 October there appeared before the harbour of this commune of Pizzo two boats from which some 30 persons, for the most part armed with muskets and pistols, quickly disembarked and rushed forwards in clear breach of the quarantine regulations.'

Starace, defending the absent Murat, used the awkward pause that followed to interrupt this risible line of inquiry with a more significant accusation of his own. He protested to the assembled judges that proceedings could not continue as most of the evidence designed to incriminate Murat was not before the court, having been sent to Naples, and that the court was incriminating itself because sentence had been passed by the royal council on 10 October before the court had even been established and before the incriminating evidence had even reached the council. It was a brave and earnest intervention, and had there been any justice it would have won him laurels, but the judges simply ignored him and his intervention went unanswered. Instead, the court gave a collective shrug and continued with its own narrative of the events, finishing with the capture of the Corsicans and an archaic aside that one of Murat's officers was 'killed by a shot from an harquebus'. Some eyewitness evidence was heard from Mattei, Leonardo, Malerba, Salomone and Barba, and despite Starace's earlier objection, the court referred to the contents of the absent documents. After this, the court summed up and prepared to give its learned answer to that first question of whether Murat was indeed a public enemy:

'We consider that Gioacchino Murat had, four months ago, given up his occupation of the kingdom following armed combat and had assumed the situation of being a private person and being thus subject to the laws, as is each individual, and that the legitimate sovereign had been re-established on the throne. He then landed at Pizzo in the middle of the day, on a holiday, and was in the company of armed men and then proclaimed a revolt. We consider that they claim they came here for want of supplies, and to charter a boat, but this cannot be the case for they came to this commune with force to raise revolt. He had tried to disembark at San Lucido the day before, his band of foreigners landed armed and ignored the strict sanitary rules in place, they did not request food, or a boat, and did not say they were to continue their voyage, all of which shows that, far from coming ashore peaceably, their intention was to subvert the existing order. We consider the documents Murat himself wrote in the form of decrees, written on the eve of his departure from Ajaccio, which demonstrate that he had never given up his intent towards the kingdom and he had gathered the means to carry out his plan to overturn the legitimate and stable authorities and instead promote civil war, murder and force the people to arm themselves, sacrificing through his criminal acts the security of each individual who had been peace-loving, obedient to the laws and attached to their sovereign. The court finds unanimously and declares that Gioacchino Murat is guilty of having attempted the destruction of the government, to have excited the citizens to take up arms against the king and public order and to have then intended to take this revolt from this commune of Pizzo into the rest of the kingdom. Therefore this means that Murat is guilty of crimes against the security of the state and is a public enemy.'[67]

The court then moved to consider what the penalty might be for such crimes. Lieutenant Francesco Frojo declared that it should be death. There was no debate, and Frojo even rushed ahead of himself and jumbled together both verdict and sentence:

'Considering that the crimes of which Joachim Murat has been found guilty are clearly set forth in the decree of 28 June 1815, articles 3 and 4, namely that a court martial has the competence to prosecute authors of crimes committed after 28 June last of this year and that those here are guilty of crimes set out in paragraph 2, section 2, chapter 1, part 1 of the third volume of the penal code, having been taken with arms in their hands and in flagrant breach of the laws, the decision of the assembled court is to apply this sentence against Gioacchino Murat and he has unanimously been condemned and condemned to death

---

67. *Rivista di fanteria*, XIII, p. 397.

and the confiscation of property. The present sentence to be carried out and 500 copies of it printed. Five in the afternoon, day, month and year as above.'[68]

Meanwhile, even when the court was rushing to its conclusions, Murat was still fighting a brave rearguard action against the inevitable. Consul Perri says that Murat:

'requested an interview with Signor Annunziante [*sic*] but he sent word that he was not available at that time. Murat then lost patience and sent him a note but he replied that he was not in a position to receive any documents as it would compromise the case.'[69]

Nunziante had washed his hands of him. Resignation was all that was left. He had cheated death on so many battlefields, but these long hours of waiting were taking their cruel toll. He rejected a coffee brought by his valet, but a little later his final meal was brought in. According to the officers still guarding him, 'he barely touched two spoonfuls', while Armand provides some more detail of this last supper:

'His Majesty ate his final meal at three during which he was served some bouillon, a flavourless pigeon and some meagre slices of bread. On seeing this, the king said that he had before been uncertain whether he would be killed but here, now, was the proof.'[70]

Then, as he was chatting to two of the officers – the other two being also at lunch – still reminiscing about his final campaign in Italy, the defeat that had launched his long journey to the castle of Pizzo, came the knock on

---

68. Valente, Angela, *Gioacchino Murat e l'Italia meridionale* (Turin, 1963). There was no little irony that Murat would be tried using laws Joseph Bonaparte had enshrined into Neapolitan law. The laws of 3 June 1807, and 20 May 1808, reconfirmed by the Bourbons on 28 June 1815, had been designed to stamp down on banditry and subversion, a perennial problem in the south.

69. British Library ADD MS41537. Pizzo, 15 October 1815. Murat did indeed send a note to Nunziante demanding that he ask for new orders before any final determination be made without Nunziante having had sight of the documents that had gone to Naples. Murat was, of course, unaware that a decision had been made in Naples before those documents had even reached there.

70. Armand's account in AN 31AP/21, Dossier 361.

the door that they had all been waiting for. One of his guards, Lieutenant Pasquale Bottazzi, heard it and watched Murat's reaction:

'At that he interrupted his speech and stood up hastily, saying, "Oh, here we are, let's see". This was because he had seen the rapporteur [Lieutenant Francesco Frojo] enter the room followed by a priest.'[71]

The presence of the priest was sufficient for all to divine what was to come, but Frojo did his duty regardless and walked up to Murat to tell him: 'Monsieur General, the court has sentenced you to death.'[72]

Franceschetti confirms this, adding that he was told he only had minutes to live:

'The final moments of his life were those of a hero. The approach of death, which petrifies most men redoubled his bravery. The king was continuing to talk to the four officers when the door to his room opened and the rapporteur [Frojo] came in to announce he had been sentenced to death and that this would be carried out in half an hour [*sic*; fifteen minutes].'[73]

The king was silent only for a moment, and then turned to the officers guarding him and remarked: 'I would have thought Ferdinand greater than this and more humane; I would have been more generous with him had he landed in my territory and had fate of arms lead to him falling into my power.' He then added: 'So be it, let's go. I die innocent.'[74]

Antonio Perri's version of Murat's reaction puts different words into Murat's mouth, but the supreme sense of resignation still shines through:

'It was 12 hours after the arrival of the courier on the evening of the 12th and the court was due to conclude at 22 o'clock [Italian time] on the 13th of this month. The Procurator General gave the verdict of death and this was unanimously agreed upon then and there by the

---

71. Pasquale Bottazzi in Archivio Borbone, Carton 623, f. 174
72. Archivio Nunziante, V Parte.
73. Franceschetti, Domenico Cesare, *Mémoires sur les événements qui ont précédé la mort de Joachim 1er, roi des Deux-Siciles* (Paris, 1826), p. 80.
74. Pasquale Bottazzi in Archivio Borbone, Carton 623, f. 176.

court and so the sentence was read out to Murat by one of the members of the military tribunal to which he replied with the following words: "so Ferdinand wants me dead. What have I done? I am sorry, but how violently I have been treated by the court at Naples."[75]

Mattia Nunziante, nephew to the general and close enough to his uncle to know more than most, sent a description of Murat's final hours to his friend Ciccio Maria the day after the verdict. It offers a third account of Murat's reaction to his fate:

'On Thursday night, at seven a courier arrived from Naples bringing orders for my uncle deputising him to establish a court martial to condemn Murat as a public enemy and to carry out the sentence a quarter of an hour later. The court martial convened and the court rapporteur [Lieutenant Frojo] invited Murat to appear before it but he lost his temper and told him "this court is nothing and I will never recognise it!" The defence [Giuseppe Starace] had been appointed and the appointed person was sent to Murat to see if he had something to say but Murat, after setting out a few of his arguments, then interrupted himself and said "why am I wasting my breath telling you this; you want me dead and it is no use arguing". They heard the depositions and examined the witness statements and concluded that he had landed to organise a revolt. He was not represented but it did not matter and the judges condemned him to death. The rapporteur came to him to communicate the death sentence and he said "I do not fear death; the world knows how many times I have gone out to face it, without ever finding it".'[76]

It had been ordained that Murat had just 15 minutes left in which to make his peace before going out to face his death. The guards had found the priest who would administer his last rites, and the old cleric, who had spent the day waiting – another indicator that the trial was just a formality – hovered behind Frojo while Murat sat down to write a final letter of farewell to Caroline and his children Achille, Laetitia, Lucien and Louise:

75. British Library ADD MS41537. Pizzo, 15 October 1815.
76. *La fine di un re*, p. 153.

'I leave you without a kingdom and without support in the midst of my numerous enemies. Show that you can rise above misfortune. Remember what you are and what you have been and God shall bless you. Do not curse my memory. I declare that what hurts me the most is that for these final days of my life I have been far away from my children.'[77]

Murat then cut a lock of his hair to go with the letter and asked for Captain Stratti, entrusting the letter to him and also asking that his watch cover with the carnelian cameo of his wife be sent to her. He then requested that his body be sent to his family. He wanted Armand to receive the watch itself, as 'he has served me well and I have nothing else to give him',[78] and asked that Frojo receive his sword and hat as a token of his esteem. This poignant scene saw the condemned man make his final requests, for now came the final act. It was time to load the muskets and fetch the priest.

With all corporeal matters disposed of, attention moved to Murat's soul, 70-year-old Canon Tommaso Antonio Giovanni Francesco Masdea from Mileto stepping forward to hear confession and administer the final act of contrition. The canon, who knew Murat as the king, who had, in happier times, donated 1,000 Ducats for the restoration of the church of Saint Giorgio, and ironically, 100 Ducats for the poor of Pizzo. He now had just ten minutes to carry out his duties. He recalled that he found Murat seated, and that when he approached the king turned to him and demanded: 'So I am condemned to death. I knew it. So what is it you want from me?' Only slightly disconcerted by this brusque question, the cleric replied: 'To know you shall die a good Christian.' Murat, once a disciple of Marat and the Jacobins, and formerly a soldier for an atheist republic, then confessed that he now 'recognised God and the Trinity, and all that, and had never done any harm and would die a Christian'.[79] The priest then asked him to

---

77. Vanel, Jean, 'Les derniers jours de Joachim Murat', in *Le Carnet de Cavalier et Roi*, 1 (1969).

78. AN, 31AP/21, Dossier 361, *Relation manuscrite d'Armand*.

79. Romano, G., *Ricordi murattiani. L'arresto e il supplizio di Murat. Narrazione del canonico Masdea con altri documenti* (Pavia, 1890). Franceschetti's version ran: 'I declare that I have done good as much as it has been possible for me to do so; that I have only caused harm to the ill-intentioned and that I die in the arms of the Catholic faith.' Nicola, the diarist, says that Monsignor Minutolo told a friend that Murat had spent six hours confessing his sins.

write down 'I die a Christian'. This he did,[80] after which Murat received his absolution and got up.

Antonio Perri's version of this dignified exchange is a little less generous to Murat:

'Among others the Father Confessor then entered to take him to be confessed but Murat told him that his sins were so great that only God himself could forgive them. The confessor replied saying "let us say confession, however, and be penitent". "I shall", he said, and added something which gives the lie to those who might say otherwise, saying "I have lived as a Christian, and shall die a good Christian".'[81]

The allotted time having passed, Murat was brought out into the fort's inner courtyard, just outside his quarters. It was around half past five in the evening (Franceschetti says around four) of 13 October, and as Murat came out he saw a detachment of twelve soldiers drawn up in three ranks. He turned to the officer in charge of this detail, Stratti, and asked where he should go, as he thought he would be taken out of the fort for the execution, but he was motioned to sit on a chair placed before the soldiers. Murat refused, and also declined a blindfold, but stood facing the soldiers and with his back to the sea. Then he pulled aside his shirt to show his heart.

Legend has it that he then declared 'soldiers, do your duty. Shoot at my heart, but spare the face.'[82] It was a phrase in Murat's character, and worthy of him, but the truth was that, after baring his breast and holding the portrait of his wife close to his heart, he ordered the soldiers to 'shoot here, my men, and do not miss', or the even simpler 'soldiers, fire, and do not miss'.[83]

The soldiers duly opened fire. Of the twelve shots fired, seven did not miss, six bullets striking his torso and one hitting his right cheek. Antonio Perri adds a few more macabre details as the officials made sure Murat would not trouble them again:

---

80. Lieutenant Bottazzi gives us some details: 'When asked to write this Murat picked up his pen and invited me to write it in Italian, which he would then sign. But I asked him to write and set down the words in French, and handed them to the priest.'

81. Add MS41537 (Antonio Perri's account).

82. This is an invention by Colletta, and his romanticized version later became a central part of the legend of Murat's glorious death.

83. Pasquale Bottazzi in Archivio Borbone, Carton 623.

'They came then to inform him that the place of execution would be in the prison itself and brought him out of the room with a Neapolitan officer handing him a blindfold to cover his eyes but he did not want it. He came out to the designated place and he swung round to face the soldiers and, placing a hand on his chest, he commanded "open fire!" and 12 muskets were fired at his chest. He died at once but they fired another three shots into his head when he lay on the ground.'[84]

Murat's bravery before death elevated him at once from the ridiculous to the sublime. Soon, word began to circulate among those who had caught and killed him of his fearlessness. Mattia Nunziante, continuing his description of Murat's final moments to his friend the day after the execution, expressed his admiration for his enemy's unconquerable courage:

'Two officers then came in to announce that the hour for execution had arrived. "Here I am," he said, and he followed them from the room. "Where do you want me?" They showed him the place and a chair to sit on. He refused to sit. He stood and placed his left hand, holding the portrait of his wife, over his heart whilst with his right he bared his chest and told the soldiers "here I am, shoot and do not miss!" Twelve shots rang out and he fell to the ground. My friend, I can't express with what courage, with what feeling, the man pronounced those final words. What courage! What courage!'[85]

The mutilated body of this brave soul was taken to the priest's house and put in a simple coffin, which was then carried by the twelve soldiers to the parish church, the Chiesa Matrice di San Giorgio in Pizzo, a modest sixteenth-century building twice shaken by earthquakes but much improved following Murat's generosity in 1810. Antonino Condoleo, then aged 15 and an eyewitness to the procession, later recalled:

'The bloody corpse was immediately placed in a rough pine coffin and was carried by 12 soldiers to the Chiesa Matrice. When it

---

84. Add MS41537 (Antonio Perri's account). Alexandre Dumas went further, writing that Ferdinand had Murat's head removed and that he kept it in a jar of brandy.
85. Mole, pp. 129–30. Nicola, the diarist, then in Naples, says 'he clutched the portrait to his breast with his right hand and with his left gave the signal to fire'.

was placed on the ground then the coffin, whether because of the impact or because it was badly built, fell apart at the end. Oh, the unforgettable sight of that pale face, disfigured by a bullet that had horribly disfigured his right cheek, of those dull eyes, of that half-closed mouth, which seemed to want to finish some word barely begun, that martial air that death itself could not erase from his face! Having patched up the coffin as best they could, he was promptly thrown into the mass grave.'[86]

Antonio Perri's account confirms some of these macabre details:

'His corpse was wrapped in some coarse cloth and taken to the church and there were no funeral rites, or any other religious ceremony, instead he was carried there on the shoulders of six soldiers, accompanied by a crowd of 15 or 20 people, and placed in a grave where the most common people are laid to rest in the church of Saint George. Thus he was treated in the way that the most infamous brigands were once treated. This is a true account of the miserable end of Gioacchino Murat.'[87]

It seems that Murat, wrapped in his shroud of black taffeta, was indeed thrown into a common grave under the nave by the entrance of the church of Saint George the Martyr. The church had been rebuilt a few years before, so this common grave was not yet so common; it was said it then contained perhaps just one other body, that of a man called Cimmina.[88] However, it seems that all the tombs under that part of the nave were filled with the corpses of cholera victims in late 1837 and early 1838, an act of mass burial that made it impossible to find Murat.[89]

---

86. Dufourq, A., *Murat et la question de l'unité italienne en 1815* (Rome, 1898).
87. Add MS41537 (Antonio Perri's account).
88. Nicola, then in Naples, jotted down an interesting rumour in his diary at the end of February 1816: 'The people of Pizzo, the place where Murat was tried and executed, were planning to exhume the mutilated remains of their former king with the object of then burning them.' The mayor tried to prevent them but he was overpowered and burned in the town ditch along with Murat. Rumours also circulated that the ghost of Captain Pernice was haunting the town.
89. Several attempts to find Murat's remains have been made; his granddaughter tried unsuccessfully to locate them and take them to Bologna in 1899. A more recent attempt was made by Pino Pagnotta, who requested access in 2007 and was finally granted permission in 2015.

With Murat in his tomb, his notice of death was drawn up by the Justice of the Peace, Francica, and witnessed by Girolamo Tranquillo, the mayor, along with Nicola Moschella, aged 45, a silk merchant living in the town, and Diego Galeano, also a silk merchant but from San Giovanni. The notice read:

'The aforementioned state that at 21.00 on the above date in October 1815, Giocchino Murat, detained, aged *45*, by profession *French General*, domiciled *in the castle* [my emphasis], was shot in this castle. In conformity with the law, we identified the deceased and declared him dead and signed the above act.'[90]

The deacon, Carlo Antonio Zimatore, noted the following in the church records:

ANNO DOMINI MILL.OCTING.MO DECIMO QUINTO, DIE VERO DECIMA TERTIA M. S. OCTOBRIS, PITII, JOACHIM MURAT, GALLUS, EX REX, ARMORUM G.LIS, DETENTUS IN CARCERIBUS HUIUS CIVITATIS, AETATIS SUAE ANNORUM QUADRAGINTA QUINQUE CIRCITER, SS.MO SACRAMENTO POENITENTIAE EXPIATUS, A COMMISSIONE MILITARI DAMNATUS, MORTEM OPPETIT, ET FUIT EIUS CORPUS IN HAC INS. COLL. ECCLESIA SEPULTUM, ET IN FIDEM ETC.S.TH. D. R. D. CAROLUS ANTONIUS ZIMATORE ARCHIP. R.

The following day, a requiem mass was given for the soul of the French ex-King of Naples and sovereign of Pizzo. There is no record of anyone attending.

---

90. Mole, p. 131.

Chapter 9

Legacies

Few would mourn a man who had once been victory's most ostentatious child. Caroline, his beloved but often disappointed queen, was one, and the children they raised together also lamented his loss and worried at their abrupt transformation from princes to outcasts. On 14 October, as Caroline's husband was mouldering in his common grave, she was still writing of the hope that he would soon arrive in Trieste with his passport. Then, a week later, she was lamenting to her sister and her niece that she did not know what had become of him. Bad news would soon crush any lingering doubt, however, and even as Caroline was writing, Murat's execution was common knowledge in the imperial corridors of Vienna. Unfortunately, Caroline would be one of the last to learn the truth. She knew Murat had been arrested in Calabria by 2 November, and despite all indications to the contrary, was naively hoping that the Austrian Emperor would intervene to save him. Then, almost immediately afterwards, the final blow to her hopes and fortunes was struck and she learned of her husband's abject execution. Almost at once she wrote to Napoleon's step-daughter, Hortense, declaring that 'he has died and with him is lost all hope of happiness for me and my family. We shall mourn him all our lives. My children are all I could wish for and they alone give me strength to bear the grief.'[1]

Murat also had companions from better days, and men who valued him as a friend, and to them too, the news that he had been caught and shot like a criminal came as a bitter blow. General Rossetti was in Paris, and regretting the sunshine of Naples, on 22 October 1815:

'At one in the morning I was sat by the fire in my bedchamber when the door burst open and Roccaromana rushed in, pale, dishevelled and stunned. He threw himself into an armchair but still maintained

---

1. Helfert, Joseph Alexander, Freiherr von, *Joachim Murat - Seine letzten Kämpfe, und sein Ende* (Vienna, 1878).

his silence but, just as I was about to ask him what the reason was for all this, he spoke in a voice heavy with despair, saying "Oh, my dear Rossetti, the king is dead, the king has been murdered!" The duke had spent the evening with Prince Metternich and learned that one of his couriers had brought the news that the king had disembarked at Pizzo with some 30 Corsican officers and that after a struggle with the local inhabitants he had been detained and then shot on the orders of a court martial on 13 October.'[2]

Murat's patron and brother-in-law, the great Napoleon, was also shocked by Murat's dramatic end. He had been driven into distant exile and it was there, on his rocky retreat on Saint Helena, that he heard Murat had died in a valiant – or foolish – attempt to regain his crown. General Gaspard Gourgaud saw how the former Emperor spun Murat's death into a meaningful homily on the destiny of kings:

'Wednesday, 7 [February, 1816] – The doctor brings some gazettes and informs us that Murat has been shot. I announce the fatal news to His Majesty, who maintains the same countenance and tells me that Murat must have been mad to attempt such an adventure. I assert that it pains me greatly to see perish by the hand of such people a man as brave as Murat, who had so often defied death. The Emperor exclaims that it is dreadful. I object that Ferdinand should not have put him to death like this. "That's how you are, young men, but one doesn't fool with a throne. Could he be considered as a French general? He no longer was one; as King? But he had never been recognized as such. He had him shot, just as he has had so many people hanged." Dinner is sad, no one speaks. We read the English gazettes. His Majesty, sad, preoccupied, plays mechanically with some coins during the reading. He suffers, we see it clearly.'[3]

Although Napoleon had also dismissed Murat as 'a dreaming simpleton who thinks himself a great man' and who had behaved 'like a sot', the news was still painful and Napoleon was right to be thoughtful. It was a sordid

---

2. General Rossetti's unpublished diary.
3. General Gaspard Gourgaud, *Sainte-Hélène: Journal Inedit de 1815 à 1818.*

end to a man who had once been a brother in arms, and quite possibly Napoleon also felt the painful contrast between Murat's sudden death and his own drawn-out agonies on this island of eternal regret. But his mourning for the man was rare, and among those who had once ruled or now ruled again, most felt Murat's demise was an opportunity for rejoicing. Barely muted cheering was soon emanating from all of Europe's capitals that another Bonapartist was no more. Europe put its recent past behind it and looked to a future no longer troubled by a family that had turned their world upside down. None were happier with Murat's death than the Bourbons of Naples.

On the evening of 14 October, old King Ferdinand and his young wife, having enjoyed Rossini's *The Italian Girl in Algiers* at the opera, came back to their palace of Favorita by Portici, where his spirits were lifted still further when he was presented with a telegraph announcing the best of news.[4] Medici had received this urgent message from General Nunziante at Pizzo and conveyed the highlights to the king:

'Following the orders signed on the 10th of this month at 09.15, by Your Excellency and his colleagues the Marquis de Circello and the Marquis Tommasi, I immediately convened a court martial composed of Giuseppe Fasulo, adjutant general on this division's staff; Colonel Scarfaro, Lieutenant-Colonel Natoli, Lieutenant-Colonel Lenzetta, Captain Cannilli, Captain Vonge [Vengé], Lieutenant Martellari. The judges. Lieutenant Frojo, rapporteur. La Camea, royal procurator, Papa Rossi [Papavassi], secretary. The court followed the prescribed rules and, having heard the advocate speaking in defence of Joachim Murat, declared unanimously that he was a public enemy and that, in consequence, he should suffer the death sentence and confiscation of his property. This sentence has been carried out and I duly hasten to

---

4. Ferdinand's diary entry for 14 October reads: 'Saturday 14th; Slept indifferently, got up at five, got dressed, heard Mass with Leopold and at seven went to the villa, killed 22 larks and seven quails, returned at noon, changed, held conversations, had lunch, rested, spoke a little with L and then went to church; talking with the Secretaries when a telegraphic report came saying the sentence of execution by the Military Commission had seen Murat shot; [alerted?] the Council and before eleven in bed.'

inform Your Excellency [Medici] of this, and shall send a record of this [trial] once it has been written out in the appropriate form.'[5]

It was public knowledge the next day and there was universal rejoicing, or relief, from the fickle people of the kingdom who had once loved Murat, and with cause. To celebrate, their legitimate, and only surviving, sovereign threw a ball, something he did every Sunday but which seemed especially lavish that evening. The French ambassador, Narbonne-Pelet, probably attended that party and had recovered sufficiently by the 16th to be able tell his masters:

'Orders were given that he [Murat] was to be tried by court martial and this took place. The execution followed the sentence and, according to the report received here yesterday [*sic*] via telegraph, and confirmed today by a despatch, Murat was shot on the evening of 13 October. Thus ends this rather strange affair which, far from having troubled the peace of the kingdom, has, rather, secured it.'[6]

The British were almost as delighted, glad to see Murat dead and revolution to receive another nail in its rotten coffin. A naval officer's report informed Admiral Exmouth of some of the particulars, delighting in the untrue irony that the court had been composed of Murat's officers:

'He refused to appear at or answer to the board [court] appointed to try him who were all his own officers, and wore his order of the Two Sicilies. His crime, landing with arms, ordering the colours to be struck, was clear and he was shot in a tower of the fort 15 minutes after sentence. Thus perished the greatest fool in Europe. A vain, empty coxcomb but of kind and pleasant manners possessing, however, not one of the great qualities but personal courage. He talked of his kindness to the English, asked for the Oxfords, Bedfords and many

---

5. *Rivista di fanteria*, XII. Nunziante had appeased his conscience by telling himself that, after all, the Congress of Vienna had branded Napoleon an outlaw on his return from Elba, and had decreed his death just as Murat had been sentenced to his following his attempted return from Corsica.

6. Ersilio, Michel, '*Vicende dei Corsi che seguirono* G. Murat al Pizzo, 1815–1817', in *Archivio Storico di Corsica*, V, 14 (1929).

of the upper ranks.[7] About Pizzo, he appeared most affected at his fate but must have gone directly towards Monteleone either as a place of safety or to make it one for him. You will have more particulars via Naples but I have put down these few things for your amusement.'[8]

The arch-conservative British ambassador, William A'Court, was certainly amused by all this, and relieved too, as it meant that his peace, and that of his masters, could now rest undisturbed:

'Murat was tried as a disturber of public tranquillity and for invading a country at peace with all the powers of Europe. The trial was short as the facts were undeniable.'[9]

The ambassador, a virulent reactionary who couldn't imagine a Tree of Liberty without dreaming of hanging republicans or Frenchmen from it, then added, perhaps with a tinge of a guilty conscience:

'The severity (if severity it may be called) which has been exercised towards the projector and leader of this invasion can need no apology from me. As it has been the first, so it will be the last blood spilt in the glorious restoration of King Ferdinand. Besides there is every reason to hope that the execution of Murat will prove an act of humanity in the end, for it is now alone that we can securely look forward to the enjoyment of peace and tranquillity, to the total extinction of party [factions] and to the general cooperating of all classes in cordial endeavour to heal the wounds which this unhappy country has experienced during the last twenty years of revolution.'

It seems that only the Russians were disappointed Murat had been shot,[10] while the Austrians were relieved, even glad, just not yet as prepared as the

---

7. The British ambassador alluded to these friends when, on 23 October, in a letter to Lord Burghersh, he wrote: 'I enclose the Neapolitan papers which contain the pieces justificsatives of the execution of Murat. I hear of no dissentient voices respecting the justness of his fate, except amongst some of our countrymen, his quondam friends.'
8. Add MSS 35651.
9. Burghersh, Lord (Fane, John), Weigall, Rachel (ed.), *Correspondence of Lord Burghersh, 1808–1840* (London, 1912).
10. The Russian ambassador, Count Mocenigo, had been so outspoken in urging leniency with Murat that Ferdinand stopped talking to him for some months.

British to show it. First of all, Murat's death was politically awkward for the Hapsburgs; after all, the Austrians had offered Murat asylum, which his family was currently enjoying, and through his marriage he was also one of their many relatives.[11] His execution by the Neapolitans could be seen as an embarrassing breach of faith among royals, just as the lack of any meaningful protest from the Austrians would be seen as hypocritical. Fortunately, the cunning Ambassador Jablonowski had, as soon as he had heard of Murat's capture, come up with a plan to spare his masters' blushes. He had absented himself from the capital, travelling out to Gaeta, purportedly to greet his family but in reality to allow things to blow over until Murat was buried and forgotten, as he informed Prince Metternich on 12 October:

'Tomorrow evening I shall return to Naples where news of Murat's death will surely have arrived and thus I shall have avoided any embarrassing questions from all those acquaintances seeking to know what the king's intention was in regard to Murat. I can assure Your Highness that whatever action I might have taken in his [Murat's] favour would have been pointless for in all likelihood he would have ceased to exist by the time news of his capture reached Naples and, from what I know of public opinion here I have no doubt this would produce the desired effect. On the other hand I do not wish it to seem that I knew beforehand about the decision of the government, or even more that I had provoked it, but as I was amongst the first to know the confirmed news this morning, and could leave before the Marquis de Circello communicated it to me officially, so my departure seemed to be nothing unusual.'[12]

When he was informed of Murat's death on 15 October, he promptly, and rather deviously, went to see Circello to 'express my surprise that, in an affair of such import, advice had not been sought from the Allied powers, above all that of our court, which could claim to have the right to be kept informed and to be treated with respect. I did not hide from him my fear that such a measure might produce the impression of having acted hastily and in a

---

11. Napoleon had married Marie Louise, daughter of the Austrian emperor, in 1810. Marie Louise therefore became sister-in-law to Murat and Caroline.
12. Cited in Helfert, p. 207.

way which contrasted with the moderation shown by the European powers.' Circello, probably taken aback by this surprising, albeit feigned, show of principles, assured the Austrian that 'the king felt most particularly the obligations he holds towards our [Austria's] August sovereign and does not wish to cause him the least discomfort, yet each sovereign has the right to judge and punish anyone found armed and declaring openly that he wishes to overthrow that sovereign and raise the people in revolt, so His Majesty was forced to act without consulting his illustrious allies as he could not risk a delay in punishing the aggressor as this might compromise his kingdom, that of Italy and the lives of millions of his subjects'.[13]

The Neapolitan then implied that, had Murat lived, Austria would have had most to lose, for the secret societies and other 'friends of disorder', which were then replacing Napoleon as a threat to order in the fervid imaginations of Europe's reactionaries, would sooner or later have made use of him to trouble their peace.[14] Circello ended his homily with his undiplomatically frank opinion that 'the king was therefore entitled to summarily execute a man whom he viewed as no more than a French general come to usurp his throne. For the other powers of Europe perhaps the question was more complicated.'[15]

Jablonowski, having played his part in this courtly charade,[16] therefore felt able to reassure his masters that 'no blood has been spilt other than

---

13. Helfert, Joseph Alexander, Freiherr von, *Joachim Murat - Seine letzten Kàmpfe, und sein Ende* (Vienna, 1878).

14. The Carbonari of Italy were clandestine clubs formed by those with revolutionary, or at least liberal, tendencies. Nicola, the diarist, says that those who favoured Murat sported black cravats.

15. Prince Metternich, an expert in the rule of law, and its flexibility whenever it comes up against geopolitics, agreed, later telling Jablonowski: 'The king was perfectly entitled to have had him tried and executed. Despite carrying an Austrian passport, Murat cannot be considered to have been under its protection as the passport was only sent to him to persuade him to quit Corsica and not to go to Italy, which had been paralysed by his schemes and which would have led to similar troubles, and to have him come to one of the capitals of the [Austrian] monarchy and there live as a private individual under close surveillance. From that moment which he elected to prefer the risk of an adventure designed to trouble the peace of Italy over the generosity of the Allies, he renounced all benefits accorded to him and ceased to have claim on any right to our protection.'

16. The public demonstration of concern was, to an extent, necessary in case Italy blamed the Austrians for Murat's death. There was a risk this would happen, for when word of Murat's death had been sent to Terracina on 18 October, the governor noted 'a message has come from Naples bearing news that the ex-king has been shot following orders from a German commission'.

that of a man who came weapons in hand to overthrow the throne of a legitimate monarch whom we had placed back on his throne and who was supported there by our troops'.[17]

The danger of the secret societies also served as justification for Murat's execution from the British point of view, and they get a mention in William A'Court's letter to Lord Burghersh on 9 November, as did the men who had accompanied Murat and who were still languishing in Bourbon prisons:

'His Neapolitan Majesty has determined to extend mercy to those individuals who accompanied Murat in his late ill-fated expedition. As they are for the most part subjects of His Most Christian Majesty [Louis XVIII], they will be given up to his disposal and be detained in prison only until his pleasure be known. Your lordship will, I doubt not, approve this act of clemency. We already begin to feel the beneficial effects of the wholesome severity exercised towards the leader of this expedition. Many who were wavering in their opinions, and who kept aloof from a fear of those extraordinary changes which late years have rendered familiar to us, begin now to pronounce themselves more openly, and to take a more decided part than they have hitherto done. The death of Murat, at the same time that it has destroyed their hopes, has diminished their fears, and this double consideration has contributed greatly to strengthen the loyalty of many of His Majesty's subjects. A considerable degree of bad spirit, however, now exists amongst certain classes of the Neapolitans, the continual exercises of which must, I fear, in some measure be attributed to the great leniency and supineness of the existing government. There is a point after which forbearance becomes weakness and then it can only tend to encourage faction and disorder. With a view to avoiding the horrors which accompanied the last counter-revolution in this country, the allied sovereigns very wisely insisted upon a total amnesty for the past. But it never could have been their intention that impunity should be secured to every individual engaging in conspiracies and treason for the future. One extreme is nearly as bad as the other, and equally argues an incapacity in those who govern.

---

17. Helfert, Joseph Alexander, Freiherr von, *Joachim Murat - Seine letzten Kàmpfe, und sein Ende* (Vienna, 1878).

There are now in confinement here several individuals whose guilt will admit of no doubt and yet the government still hesitates to bring them to trial. The intendant of the province of Basilicata and the commander of the National Guards are amongst the number from whom letters were intercepted about the period of Murat's invasion, exhorting secret societies known by the name of Carbonari to cancel their engagements to Ferdinand and to renew their oath of fidelity and allegiance to Murat. The circumstances of the country require that such traitors should be brought to public trial and, if found guilty, to public punishment; but, evident as this necessity is, the government cannot determine upon the measure.

'*Il est ci beau* says M de Medici to declare to Europe that Murat has no adherents here and that it was necessary to spill no blood but his. It might be so if the assertion were founded on facts, but when this is merely gratuitous the moral beauty of the proceeding is very sensibly diminished.'[18]

The British evidently favoured a degree of repression to keep Europe quiet. The Bourbons were willing to comply, having in any case traditionally governed by doling out flour and using the gallows, a darker variant of the more famous bread and circuses. In 1815, unlike in 1799, however, the gallows had hardly been needed, kept by and large in the background as an inducement to loyalty. They certainly weren't required in Calabria, where Ferdinand and his ministers had been surprised at how loyal their people had proved to be, and this unexpected trait led to them being unexpectedly generous.

A deputation from Pizzo had reached Naples on the evening of 15 October and they were granted the rare favour of a royal audience at the Favorita palace the next day. On 18 October, Pizzo was awarded an annual gift of 3,160 Ducats 'for as long as the world lasts', and was entitled to be known as 'Pizzo the Loyal' and exempted from tax, with each inhabitant gifted an annual supply of salt sufficient for their families. In addition to this feudal beneficence, Pizzo's criminals were to be amnestied, the church was to be rebuilt at royal expense and the piazza of the lucky town was to

---

18. Burghersh, Lord (Fane, John), Weigall, Rachel (ed.), *Correspondence of Lord Burghersh, 1808–1840* (London, 1912).

be graced with a statue of King Ferdinand himself.[19] Many of the loyal town's inhabitants, too, would share in this royal largesse. Although his role had really been that of glorified gaoler, Nunziante was ennobled as a marquis and obtained an equally pleasing pension of 1,500 Ducats a year for life. Poor Trentacapilli, who had actually been arrested by Nunziante for not having been at his post in Cosenza, and who had even spent a few days in a cell in the castle of Pizzo as a result, was eventually pardoned and released, promoted to colonel and also awarded 1,000 Ducats a year. His brother, Raffaele, was also rewarded, as were the mayor, justices of the peace, members of the court that had sentenced Murat and, of course, Francesco Alcalà y Cebrian. Both Alemanni and Salomone received rewards, suggesting they had led Murat astray as he marched out of Pizzo, as did many of those who led, or took part in, the final battle in the sands during which Murat was overcome and beaten.

Of those in government and far away in the capital, Medici was foremost in angling for favour and made sure he received much of the credit, even hinting that he had lured Murat to Pizzo to trap him there, although nobody seems to have asked him why he had done nothing to prepare for such an eventuality, apart from sending an unarmed and out-of-condition captain of gendarmes to fight what might have been as many as 250 rebels. Still, Medici could bask in the glow of success, whether earned or unearned, and give thanks that he had done his duty for a 'fatherly king to his people whose life shall be written in histories in gold letters' and a man who, moreover, appreciated his difficult work. Such hinting aside, the people were also glad, or so Ferdinand was informed by those same ministers, and from each and every province came reassuring noises that the death of Murat had been met with universal rejoicing. From Aquila, the Marquis di Pietracatella informed Minister Tommasi: 'The general feeling upon hearing of the capture of Gioacchino was one of joy and enthusiasm. The mayor has received the most fervent pleas from the population to allow them to express their thanks through religious celebrations, and with games and fetes.'[20]

Order had been restored. The people could play and dance again, and so could the Bourbons. Murat was a sacrifice worth paying for this, a death

---

19. It was finally erected in 1820, only to be pulled down in 1860 by Garibaldi's legionaries.
20. *Rivista di fanteria*, XIII, p. 226.

needed to reinforce the status quo and to reaffirm the supremacy of the divinely appointed over those raised up by man, or emperors. So Naples would be denied its version of the Hundred Days, and Murat – a man born humble who had galloped through the history books as a general, grand duke and king – had been dragged out and executed as a common brigand. The kingdom would therefore be left in peace, and apart from a brief and desperate grab for freedom in 1821, when a rebellion sought to impose a constitution on old Ferdinand, it stumbled on, stagnant and apathetic, with the Bourbons ruling into the nineteenth century as though it was still the seventeenth.

But there came a day when it became clear that Murat had died not once but twice. Once in reality, alone; the second time as a myth, and for Italians. When, in a distant echo of that mad adventure, another adventurer, Garibaldi, burst upon the scene and overthrew the Bourbons. He had also been accompanied by just a handful of soldiers, this time armed and uniformed in their famous red shirts, but their timing was better and they managed to tear down the House of Bourbon and build upon its ruins their version of an Italy united and free. Once they had triumphed, Murat and his last hurrah could be refashioned into something more meaningful; after all, here was a man who had nobly tried to make Italy and Italians, and who had fallen, like a martyr, victim to the vilest enemies of that ideal.

Perhaps the ghost of Murat looked on as Garibaldi and his men made real the declaration he had pinned up at Rimini in the spring of 1815. His had been the first call to arms, unanswered at the time, but just within living memory. Now that Italy had been liberated and united, the man who was raised up by one revolution now found himself hailed as a hero by another.

Postscript

Murat may eventually have emerged as a hero, but those who went with him were almost completely forgotten. He had not been alone in his bid for glory. Hundreds had set out with him and dozens were captured at or near Pizzo, while others were taken at sea. Murat had, of course, paid the ultimate price, but as he had walked out before the firing squad, it was not yet clear whether his followers would be spared his fate.

Once Murat had been done away with, those he left behind in the dungeons of Pizzo were understandably fearful for their lives. But a sepulchral silence had fallen on the castle, and when Franceschetti demanded, in his inimitable style, what he might expect, Nunziante was honest enough to inform him that he was awaiting orders, adding only that the Bourbons had ruled that, for now, only any Neapolitan citizens among them would be court martialled. There weren't any, but Nunziante's words were not as reassuring as they might have seemed. Murat had of course been tried as a French general, and this hardly boded well for the others as they too were, by and large, citizens of France. 'After all', mused Franceschetti, 'our sovereign had not been spared', so why should they be?

In the early days, their immediate fear was that they would be marched overland to Monteleone, where the local guillotine was waiting. However, on the evening of 27 October, after spending two weeks in fear of their lives, they were taken from their prison, escorted down to the harbour and embarked on a sloop. The limping Galvani assumed that they were going to be executed in Naples before that city's notoriously bloodthirsty mob, but in the event they were taken first to Capri and from there to the penal island of Ventotene.

This devilish island became the collection point and prison for all of Murat's followers, for while two boats under Ettore and Courand had returned to Corsica, everyone else had been captured.[1] In addition to those

---

1. There also seems to have been a general round-up of Corsicans in the kingdom. Those captured were not always those who had taken part in the expedition. Four Corsicans were

who had landed with Murat, two other barques had been seized at sea, so when Galvani and his companions reached Ventotene they found 'a hundred of our soldiers and officers who had been seized by the Sicilian navy in the gulf of Palinuro',[2] south of Salerno. Medici reported, more accurately, that the boats had contained forty-eight men being transported on the two barques under Louis Semidei and Dominique Mattei, which had been intercepted by Captain Cafiero's gunboats.

As the eighty or so inmates settled in to their uncertain future in the care of the governor, Captain Nicola Barone of the Royal Guard, who had been in charge of this prison since 1797, their fate was actually being decided in the salons of Europe's capitals. The French, keen to wash their hands of all Bonapartist troublemakers, viewed Corsicans with particular ill-will, so it came as no surprise that the French ambassador, Narbonne Pelet, was soon informing Paris that 'the majority are, it seems, Corsicans, but, on this occasion, they have lost the rights they should enjoy as French citizens and the protection of His Majesty'. However, it proved rather more difficult than envisaged to render them stateless, and as the Neapolitan authorities were reluctant to keep them, and pay for their upkeep, Naples pushed France to take them back and the ambassador was soon noting that 'the intention of the Neapolitan government is to place them at the disposition of His Majesty [of France]'.[3] Over in Paris, on 1 November, the Neapolitan ambassador there, Prince Castelcicala, was repeating this message to the Duc de Richelieu, informing him that '78 individuals arrested with Murat

---

detained by Captain Ignazio Valentoni at San Marco, inland near Cosenza, on 10 October. One of them was Antonio Compa, a Frenchman living in Corsica, formerly of the 22nd Light, who had been swept overboard at Diamante, near Cosenza, and who had hoped to work his way northwards. The others were Francesco Antonio Astulfi, Antonio D'Angeli and Domenico Luciani of Bastia. These implausibly said they had come from Rennes in Brittany and were seeking their bread from commune to commune, although they had two muskets with them. Some fourteen Corsican officers were captured at Campobasso, perhaps on their way to Naples in the hope Murat would succeed, perhaps innocent victims, and another at Chieti. On 21 October at Lagonegro, 200 kilometres north of Pizzo, five Corsicans – Filippo Stolfi, Francesco Simonetti, Giacinto Agostini, Robertino Casabianca and the un-Corsican sounding Giovanni Scultz – having escaped from Hungarian prisoner of war camps, found themselves arrested. However, two Corsican soldiers who had set off with Murat, Simon Pietro Gilormini and Francesco Giovanni Felice, were later arrested at Castrovillari. In addition to all these Corsicans, the king's black servant, Othello, was also arrested at Naples and brought to the island.

2. Galvani, Matthieu, *Mémoire sur les événements qui ont précédé la mort de J. Murat.* (Paris, 1850).
3. Ersilio, Michel, '*Vicende dei Corsi che seguirono* G. Murat al Pizzo, 1815–1817', in *Archivio Storico di Corsica*, V, 14 (1929).

are subjects of His Most Christian Majesty' and that 'the king, my master, could have had them judged according to the laws and rights of law but, out of regard for the king, your august sovereign, he has ordered that they be placed at his disposal, leaving it to the wisdom of His Most Christian Majesty to punish or to pardon'.[4]

The French still insisted they wanted nothing to do with such troublemakers, and stuck to their guns by stressing that the King of Naples should determine their fate as they had attempted to usurp his throne and not that of His Christian Majesty. Ferdinand certainly held their lives in the balance, and those on Ventotene knew it. They therefore appealed to him for pardon, a plea forwarded to the capital by the governor, Captain Barone. Franceschetti says they wrote:

'Sire, the undersigned have the honour to address Your Majesty and to inform him that they languish in the prison at Ventotene, suffering a thousand privations, and lacking all resource. Their only crime is to have been loyal, even in misfortune, to a prince who was their sovereign. Honour has been the only guide to their conduct and whilst they may have been mistaken, their intentions were pure and right. Deign, sire, to examine their position for they suffer in a way that can only touch Your Majesty's heart. Their confidence in Your Majesty's generosity is sincere and they dare flatter themselves that you will soon restore their liberty so they might return to their families.'[5]

It seems that it was not Ferdinand, who was rarely generous to his enemies, who now intervened to settle their question, but his more humane and Francophile minister, the Marquis Saint-Clair. He persuaded the king to

---

4. Ersilio, Michel, 'Vicende dei Corsi che seguirono G. Murat al Pizzo, 1815–1817', in Archivio Storico di Corsica, V, 14 (1929). Ferdinand had been pressured by Austria to forgive and forget and to issue a general amnesty, as Count Jablonowski states: 'I hope, therefore, that there will not be the slightest disturbance in the kingdom, and I will seize the first favourable moment to beg the king to deign to pardon those who had left the kingdom in the month of May and were still exiled, such as Pignatelli-Cerchiara, Roccaromana, S. Giuliano and others: if I succeed in obtaining this pardon, this trait of clemency will produce the best effect. Besides, Murat's catastrophe consolidates the tranquillity of this country and will contribute to calming heads throughout Italy.' This was written from a bad inn room in Gaeta on 12 October.

5. Franceschetti, Domenico Cesare, Mémoires sur les événements qui ont précédé la mort de Joachim 1er, roi des Deux-Siciles (Paris, 1826).

forget them and then asked the Marquis de Circello to tell the French that Ferdinand had decided to have these men pardoned and would be returning them at his own expense to Corsica as free men. Circello then asked Narbonne Pelet to issue the necessary instructions so they could be received in Corsica by the prefect of Bastia.

The royal pardon was finally issued that December. 'A police officer has been sent to Ventotene,' the government noted, 'where they are detained, to read out to them their letters of pardon thus avoiding the formality which would have been required had the reading been performed in a law court.'[6] The pardon took the form of a personal letter to each prisoner, signed by the king himself:

'Pardon granted by Ferdinand IV, by the grace of God, King of the Two Sicilies and Jerusalem, Infante of Spain, Duke of Parma, Piacenza and Castro, Hereditary Grand Duke of Tuscany. Preferring mercy to the rigour of the law, we declare that we accord grace to the said x and shall not carry out the punishment which his crime would have warranted unless, in future, he enters our lands again, no matter when and for what purpose, as such act shall forfeit him the benefits of this act of grace and will require him to be judged by a court martial.'[7]

Eventually, just after Christmas, a boat was chartered to take the 108 pardoned officers and men, and the sailors manning Murat's ships, to Corsica. Those named and listed for expulsion included the following:

Domenico Cesare Franceschetti, aged 40
Sebastiano Natali, 35
Matteo (Matthieu) Galvani, 36
Silvio Ottaviani,[8] 42
Antoine Félix Lanfranchi, 26
Giovanni Battista Viggiani, 36
Domenico Medori, 45
Luigi Semidei, 32

---

6. Valente, Angela, *Gioacchino Murat e l'Italia meridionale* (Turin, 1963).
7. Valente, Angela, *Gioacchino Murat e l'Italia meridionale* (Turin, 1963).
8. Ottaviani and his companion had been taken earlier but sent down to Pizzo on 13 October when it became clear from a royal report that 'Giacchino Napolione [*sic*] has been arrested'.

Giovanni Multedo, 25
Pietro Pasqualini, 33
Pietro Paolo Giacometti, 30
Simone Paolo Battestini, 36
Alessandro Graziani, 42
Domenico Mattei, 31
Nicola Costa, 32
Antonio (Marc-Antoine) Raibaldi, 32
Francesco Orsati, 33
Bartolomeo Versiti, 22
Pietro Lanfranchi, 28
Giovanni Felice Perretti, 22
Bartolomeo Romeo, 40
Antonio Martino Fieschi, 25[9]
Sebastiano Pierantoni, 32
Giovanni Luca Pellegrini, 18 (General Franceschetti's cousin)
Domenico Antoni, 24
Pietro Giudicelli, 30
Pietro Francesco Di Simone, 41
Giuseppe Cristiani, 20
Angelo Francesco Romano, 57
Alessandro Antonio Maria, 30
Gerolamo Vicenzini, 41
Orso Giacinto Innocenzi, 30
Francesco Pietrobuono, 20
Giovanni Giuseppe Albertini, 17
Paolo Angelo Viso, 19
Santo Luigi Battini, 22
Ignazio Andrei, 22
Giuseppe Grimaldi, 38
Lucca Antonio Antonini, 18
Giacomo Santo Leonardi, 17
Filippo Santucci, 18
Giacomo Domenico Lega, 21

---

9. Legend has it that Joseph Fieschi had been involved, but it is an Antonio Martino Fieschi who seems to have been on one of the other ships. In July 1835, Joseph Fieschi tried to assassinate King Louis-Philippe with the twenty-five barrel 'infernal machine'.

Antonio Perini, 23

Francesco Antonio Salvadore, 21

Filippo Maria Salvarelli, 22

Giovanni Luigi Narrelli, 37 (from Tuscany)

Filippo Maria Guglielmi, 17

Orso Giovanni Sartolini, 24

Giovanni Domenico D'Angeli, 17

Matteo Santoni, 38 (former gendarme)

Giulio Perretti, 18

Francesco Perrelli, 20

Giuseppe Santoni, 20

Sebastiano De Angeli, 30

Giuseppe Maria Varese, 16

Giovanni Vincenzo Garelli, 17 (former soldier in the 23rd Light)

Maurizio Artusi, 18

Antonio Matteo Catanej, 23

Antonio Lavezzano, 14, drummer (from the 23rd Light)

Carlino Battini, 25

Pietro Paolo Casabianca, 30

Filippo Astalfo, 46

Giacinto D'Agostino, 25

Giovanni Martino Casabianca, 30 (from the Papal States)

Francesco Simonetti, 28

Giovanni Sciulzi, 37

Giovanni Reginese, 36

Matteo Natale, 45

Francesco Giovanni De Felice, 25

Francesco Giavettini, 23

Giovanni Domenico Bastiera, 20

Francesco Antonio Astulfi, 28

Felice Antonio Suzoni, 29

Pietro Gerolmini, 44

Francesco Tartaroli, 18 (former sergeant in the 23rd Light)

Antonio D'Angeli, 22

Domenico Luciani, 20

Antonio Comba, 18 (from France)

Salvadore Pugi, 29 (from Elba, former servant of Murat)

Armand Blanchard, 30 (from Paris)
Domenico Franceschi, 23 (servant of Franceschetti)
Francesco Marchetti, 24
Luigi Ferrari, 27 (from Genoa, Murat's cook)
The black Nunzio Otello Francesco Gioacchino, 23 (from Egypt, Murat's servant)

And the sailors:

Giovanni Andrea Cauro, 40
Bartolomeo Pozzo di Borgo, 64
Luigi Armei, 39
Battista Forcine, 23
Michele Appietto, 24
Battista Sullacavo, 18
Ignazio Pastieri, 33
Vincenzo Nigretti, 26
Carlo Pozzo di Borgo, 11
Giovanni Battista Cerisoldo, 23
Maddalena Osmond, 26 (wife of sailor Carlo Mariza)
François Maschetti
François Ciavatti

A few weeks later, on 17 January 1816, these individuals were loaded on board the appropriately named *Madona delle grazie*, brought round from Baia, and then set sail for Bastia. On the way, the vessel put in at Livorno; some hoped for asylum in Tuscany, fearing the French authorities. France was indeed purging Bonapartists with some enthusiasm, so the pardoned feared being rearrested as soon as they reached Bastia. However, at Livorno they suffered the familiar indignities of quarantine before being told they would be unwelcome in Italy, so they were compelled to continue on to Corsica. At Saint Florent, the captains and crews of Murat's fleet were landed and detained before being released, all on condition they only serve as simple sailors, but the officers and soldiers were in for more of a shock. Franceschetti reported that 'a launch containing gendarmes came out and our boat was seized and we were brought on board a vessel and then, without explanation, placed in irons and thrown into the hold'.[10] They were to be escorted not to Bastia and freedom, but to Marseille for punishment.

The officers were sent to the Chateau d'If, made notorious by the Count of Monte Cristo, and infamous at the time as a place where one was sent to be forgotten, while the soldiers were shackled and brought to the fort of St Nicolas in the port. Most of the soldiers were then tried by Judge Giacomoni, and thirty-three of them were promised they would be released if they volunteered for service in the 3rd Colonial Battalion, destined for the malaria-stricken colonies of France. The officers, whose offences were seen as more serious, were kept for two more months while the authorities prepared a criminal case against them. Sensing that France was about to throw away their key, these prisoners did what they could to elicit some public sympathy and even begged to be able to petition the Duchess de Berri, one of King Ferdinand's daughters, but the governor would not allow it. They pleaded their innocence to the authorities, asserting – truthfully – that the King of Naples had pardoned them and that they had committed no crime against France. Nevertheless, France was still too vindictive, especially in the south, so Franceschetti, Natali, Ottaviani, Lanfranchi and Medori were sent to Draguignan in the Var to be tried for having attempted to raise Corsica in revolt. After many more months of imprisonment, the trial fell through on a technicality as the authorities in the Var felt they did not have jurisdiction for a case involving Corsicans in Naples. Consequently, on 16 January 1817, the officers were released and sent into internal exile under surveillance. Another month passed before the Minister of Police finally conceded defeat and sent an order permitting them to return to Corsica. They only began trickling back home in February and March 1817.

The cost of following Murat had been punishing. Already, on 30 November 1816, Ottaviani had written:

'I have been reduced to absolute nudity and plunged into the deepest abyss of despair such that, without a little courage and the consolation of a religion I revere, I would have committed the most terrible crime of robbing myself of my life.'[11]

10. Franceschetti, Domenico Cesare, *Mémoires sur les événements qui ont précédé la mort de Joachim 1er, roi des Deux-Siciles* (Paris, 1826).
11. 31AP/32 *Lettres d'anciens soldats et serviteurs du roi Murat.*

Armand, still suffering from his wound, had been released on the French mainland and walked to Paris, reaching there on 31 May 1816. He spent some time living with his father in 14 rue Chabanais, but even there he was watched by government agents and one report, sent to the prefect of police, noted that he was lamenting that 'he has lost everything and that there is no happiness left in the world for him'.[12]

The cook, Luigi Ferrari, was also destitute and spent three years imploring the Corsican authorities to intercede on his behalf. Only in February 1820 did Baron Bruny take it upon himself to write to Caroline for help, noting that 'this wretched Ferrari is completely destitute. Although living here, and a stranger to Corsica (he is from Genoa), he has determined to ask me to ask you to learn of his misery, persuaded that you will assist him. This is why I am sending you this request.'[13]

Franceschetti had been ruined by his support for Murat, the merchant Gregory reneging on the bill of exchange and pocketing the money intended to defray the funds he had spent on Murat's expedition. When he turned to Caroline to ask to be compensated, she prevaricated for months before eventually refusing in writing through her friend and future husband, General Macdonald. Franceschetti sent his wife Catherine to Caroline in April 1818 to beg for something, lamenting that 'I have nothing left with which to feed my four children. If Your Majesty does not assist me then my compatriots will be astonished at how my family can be plunged into misery after I generously risked my life and sacrificed my fortune.'

Caroline was not for turning, being sunk heavily into debt herself, and replied:

'Be assured, general, that I am aware of the situation and especially everything concerning your noble and honourable conduct towards my deceased husband and king and I shall be most unhappy if I cannot give unequivocal proof of my gratitude. I ask only that you be patient until the moment comes and I flatter myself that it will not be long now. I thank you for the news you send me concerning the sums that the faithless merchant Gregory has kept. To remedy this I shall

---

12. AN, 31AP/21, Dossier 361, *Relation manuscrite d'Armand*. The valet Charles had remained with Barbara and the boats but was later arrested in Tuscany, but he seems to have rejoined his wife in the service of Caroline Murat in Austria in 1816.
13. AN 31AP/32 (Fonds Murat).

send my intendant, the Chevalier d'Hausmenil, asking you to aid him with your advice and that of your friends in order to bring this affair to a conclusion.'[14]

The chevalier was never sent. Gregory could not be pressured into paying and it was too costly to bring him to court, so Caroline was forced to ignore Franceschetti's complaints. These rumbled on into the 1820s until he tried one last attempt at shaming her in his memoirs and then sued her for some money. His case failed and he died, impoverished, in 1835.

Whenever there is a colourful and dramatic adventure that fails, there can be found men such as Franceschetti who are brought down and broken by that failure. If the wages of loyalty are paid at all, they are paid sparingly, and a slow, aching penury is the more usual reward of being on the wrong side. Yet in among the mistakes, the missed opportunities and the regret, something noble also emerged from Murat's desperate fiasco. Jean Multedo, one of Murat's companions on the beach, knew this to be true. He was 65 years old when he sent this moving tribute to Prince Lucien Murat, recalling those sad days at Pizzo:

'My soul comes alive at his memory. I loved him and am proud to say it out loud. He loved me too and was glad when I placed my body before him to shield him from harm. He told me "I shall remember your bravery, Jean Multedo". I had the supreme honour of being condemned with His Majesty and only fate saved me from certain death. I spent two years in the Chateau d'If at Marseille and throughout that time my pride and comfort flourished in that dark prison with its woe and want. It was the cause for which I fought which kept me and the scourge I braved honoured me and honours me to this day.'[15]

Whatever history might have to say about the folly of the enterprise, for those who accompanied Murat he would always be a hero and ever more the knight without fear and beyond reproach.

---

14. Franceschetti, Domenico Cesare, *Supplément aux mémoires sur les événements qui ont précédé la mort de Joachim 1er, roi des Deux-Siciles* (Paris, 1829).

15. AN 31AP/25 (Fonds Murat).

Annex I

A Conspiracy Theory

Some seventy years after Murat's execution, French author Fernand Bernard, Marquis de Sassenay, made the bold claim that Murat had been lured to Calabria and his death by the cleverness of the Neapolitan secret police. This rather lurid tale caught the public imagination at the time, nicely absolving Murat of any naivety, and so the theory found itself repeated by historians for decades thereafter. It has never entirely disappeared.

The evidence for this claim is largely based on the correspondence of Austrian officials who formed part of the forces occupying Italy after Murat's fall. On 3 November 1815, Baron Koller, commanding the Austrian army in Naples, informed his friend, Franz von Saurau, then up in Lombardy:

'The government had won over some of Murat's friends that still remained in correspondence with him after he arrived in Corsica on the possibility of a landing and the certainty of a fortunate outcome. These affairs were managed by Baron Petroni intendant at Monteleone, and he himself had written and it was due to him that Murat had received encouragement and support from others. There was a second agent, a Corsican named Carabelli who had lived in Naples during Murat's reign but despite considerable effort had never obtained a position there, indeed he was rather spurned and ignored. He left when news that Murat had arrived in Corsica came here and he told him how happy he was that the moment had come for him to assist in restoring him to his throne and to prove his boundless attachment to Murat the king even though his enemies had tried to malign him. He said there was general discontent with the current government and, in vivid colours, painted a picture of how ripe the time was for revolution, guaranteeing on his life that it would break out as soon as his landing at Pizzo was known.'[1]

---

1. Helfert, Joseph Alexander, Freiherr von, *Joachim Murat - Seine letzten Kàmpfe, und sein Ende* (Vienna, 1878).

Saurau shared this garbled information with Baron Hager on 10 November, adding to those fictions about Carabelli information that Trentacapilli had been sent to Pizzo on purpose to prepare the people against Murat. This gave rise to a rumour, carefully stoked by the Minister of Police, Medici, that the Neapolitan authorities had been cunning as well as ruthless and had lured Murat to Calabria to trap and execute him. Saurau added some spice to his tale by informing Vienna that Trentacapilli had been promised 20,000 Ducats to kill Murat, and that Petroni would receive 10,000 for his troubles.

This first bit of court gossip was quite absurd, as we have seen, for the authorities had made every preparation they could to *prevent* Murat from sailing. The second was just as brazen, for Ignazio Carabelli had also been sent to stop Murat from embarking; there was never any suggestion he had been sent to lure Murat into a prepared trap.

Then, of course, if it was a trap, it was a very badly prepared one. Nothing had been done to bolster Pizzo's defences. Indeed, as we can see, Murat's arrival came as a surprise to everyone in any position of authority.

Notwithstanding such flaws in his material, this first note was soon followed by a second letter from Koller three weeks later:

'One of the accomplices in this affair against Joachim was Barbara, a Corsican [*sic*], charged with bringing him to Calabria. He had passports on him so as not to be detained should he, en route to Pizzo, be intercepted by any Neapolitan warship patrolling the coast. The government had paid him half the value of the boat used for the voyage and this sum, although I don't know the exact amount, was paid to him at Ajaccio. After the landing took place he was to be paid a further 12,000 Ducats.'[2]

It went on:

'Barbara managed to land Murat and 27 of his followers at Pizzo and then, true to the instructions that they had given him here, he went off to wait two miles from the shore. When Murat was caught the people tore his clothes and he had no change of linen so he asked

---

2. Helfert, Joseph Alexander, Freiherr von, *Joachim Murat - Seine letzten Kàmpfe, und sein Ende* (Vienna, 1878).

that Barbara be told that he needed a change of clothing and so he should come to him and he sent a list in pencil of the items he needed. The major of Pizzo sent two fishermen off to Barbara with this note. When he heard what had become of Murat he refused to take the note and do what was requested of him. Worse, he threatened to open fire against their boat and promptly made to sail off. When Murat was told of this, he slapped his forehead and was taken aback and shouted out that it was clear that Carabelli and Barbara had tricked him and lead him to this disaster.'

Whether Koller had his own sources, or was again being fed material by a secret police too keen to prove its own importance, matters little. Barbara had not liaised with the royal authorities, and only tried to land at Pizzo because bad weather had prevented a landing further north. Besides, following the landing, orders had been issued to catch Barbara and have him taken to Ponza, which contradicts this tale of his double-crossing of Murat. Indeed, two royal gunboats had chased Barbara to Briatico, where there had been a brief exchange of shot before the Maltese captain sailed off to the south-west.

Barbara and Charles Thillier, the valet, escaped with Murat's effects. The royal authorities wondered if this also included Murat's treasure, declaring: 'It is believed the captain of the boat, who is called Barbara, has taken the lot. This Barbara was a notorious pirate who Murat named commander but who, seeing the plan was going awry, made off with everything. That's why we do not know how much money Murat had with him.'[3]

This makes it even less likely that the Maltese commodore was a royal agent. He fled to Corsica, and then to Malta and into exile rather than into Naples for his reward.

The idea that the Bourbons lured Murat to Calabria is rather unfounded. The evidence suggests they did not, and that Murat acted entirely on his own initiative, and the idea they lured him to Pizzo is even more far-fetched. He was there by chance, having failed to land further north and been driven south by storms, and he only came ashore having almost determined to give up. That Barbara or anyone else sold him to the authorities is also unlikely. Defeat is perhaps better explained by Murat's determination to do the wrong thing at every successive opportunity. He was a knight who could, perhaps, be reproached.

---

3. Archivio Nunziante, V Parte.

Annex II

Murat's Letter to Maceroni

This is Murat's second and far more frank letter to Colonel Maceroni, written just as Murat was departing to reconquer his kingdom rather than going quietly into the night with his passports. This letter has been taken from Maceroni's own account, given in his book *Interesting Facts* (pp. 161–64):

'To Monsieur Macirone [*sic*], sent by the Allied Powers to King Joachim. My first letter sent today was dictated by the circumstances of that time. Now I owe it to myself to speak the truth and trust your frankness and good faith to hear my true intentions. I value my liberty above all else. For me, captivity is synonymous with death. What treatment could I expect from powers that have left me dangling for two months within the reach of the daggers of the assassins of Marseilles. I saved the life of the Marquis de Riviere. He had been condemned to death on a scaffold. I had him pardoned by the Emperor. It is the undeniable truth. He stirred up this scum, it was he who put a price on my head! Wandering the forests, hiding in the mountains, I owed my life solely to the generous compassion my woes stirred in the souls of three French officers. They brought me over to Corsica at great risk to their own lives.

'The wretches say that I had with me the treasure of Naples. They do not know that when I received that kingdom in exchange for my Grand Duchy of Berg, an entity assigned to me through a formal treaty, I brought with me immense riches. All those were spent on improving my kingdom of Naples. The sovereign who then came to occupy it barely recognised it. I own nothing more than that which keeps me and my family alive.

'I do not accept the conditions, Monsieur Macirone, that you are charged to offer me. I see them as being nothing short of an abdication pure and simple and all this in return for them permitting me to live, although even that in eternal captivity and subject to the arbitrary whim of the laws of a despotic government. Where is there any fairness, any justice? Is there anything here which shows consideration for an unfortunate prince formally recognised throughout Europe and who, at a critical moment, decided the campaign of 1814 in their favour. These powers now, against their own interests, weigh him down with their own persecutions.

'It is a recognised truth that I only pushed the Austrians back towards the Po because intrigue persuaded me that they were preparing to attack me without, however, counting on British support. I therefore judged it expedient to advance my defensive lines and win over the people to my side.

'Nobody knows better than you, Monsieur Macirone, not even Lord Bentinck himself, that I only began that fateful retreat when he found it necessary to declare that he would lend his support to the Austrians as this had been requested by them. You know the reasons why my beautiful army fell into disorder and deserted. Rumours had been circulated of my death, and that the English had landed at Naples; then General Pignatelli Strongoli's conduct and, also, the betrayal of some of my officers who, through perfidy, and by their example and words, sowed despair and encouraged desertion. There is not one individual in that army who does not recognise his error. I am leaving to join them. They burn with the desire to see me at their head. Their affection for me is undiminished, as is that among each class of my subjects. I never abdicated. I have the right to retake my crown and God will give me the strength and the means. They cannot fear me being on the throne of Naples, they cannot accuse me of being in communication with Napoleon who is now on St Helena. Indeed, the opposite is true and both England and Austria would gain advantages which cannot be expected from the sovereign they wish in my stead.

'I share these details with you, Monsieur Macirone, because it is you who shall read them. Your behaviour towards me, your reputation, your name, have earned you rights to my frankness and my esteem. You will not be able to prevent me from leaving, even if you wished to do so.

'By the time you have received this letter I shall already be on my way to my destination. Either I shall succeed or I shall end my troubles.

I have braved death a thousand times fighting for my country; can I not do so once again but this time for myself? I shudder only for the fate of my family.

'I shall always remember with pleasure your noble and refined behaviour as you acquitted your duty towards me. It stands in most agreeable contrast to the base and revolting way others have behaved and that despite them having neither the powers nor the consideration that you enjoy.

'I have ordered your property to be returned to you. With that, Monsieur Macirone, I ask God to keep you in his holy and worthy care.'

Bibliography

Baudus, Florence de, *Caroline Bonaparte: sœur d'empereur, reine de Naples* (Paris, 2014).

Beauchamp, Alphonse de, *Catastrophe de Murat: ou, Récit de la dernière révolution de Naples* (Paris, 1815).

Bianco, Nicolantonio, *Gli ultimi avvenimenti del regno di Gioacchino Murat* (Melfi, 1880).

Burghersh, Lord (Fane, John) (ed. by Rachel Weigall), *Correspondence of Lord Burghersh, 1808–1840* (London, 1912).

Carabelli, Ignazio, *I calunniatori smascherati* (Rome, 1826).

Cicotti, Vicenzo, 'La lettre de Camillo Borgia à Joachim Murat', in *Le Carnet de Cavalier et Roi*, 32 (2001).

Cole, Hubert, *The betrayers: Joachim and Caroline Murat* (London, 1972).

Colletta, Pietro, *Storia del reame di Napoli dal 1734 al 1825*, a cura di N. Cortese, Libreria Scientifica Editrice (Naples, 1956).

D'Armenia, Nicoletta Marini, 'Murat e il Regno di Napoli: le ultime scelte', in *Napoleone dall'Elba all'Europa* (Florence, 2017).

Davies, Catherine, *Eleven Years' Residence in the Family of Murat, King of Naples* (London, 1841).

De G., M., *Notice historique sur M. le lieutenant général Charles-Antoine Count Manhès* (Paris, 1817).

De Nicola, C., *Diario napoletano*, 3 volumes (Naples, 1906).

Desvernois, N.P.H. (ed. by A. Dufourcq), *Mémoires* (Paris, 1898).

Dito, Oreste, *La campagna murattiana della indipendenza d'Italia: secondo i rapporti del Ministro di polizia napoletana ed altri documenti officiali con un'appendice sulla morte del Murat a Pizzo* (Milan, 1911).

Dufourq, A., *Murat et la question de l'unité italienne en 1815* (Rome, 1898).

Ersilio, Michel, 'Vicende dei Corsi che seguirono G. Murat al Pizzo, 1815–1817', in *Archivio Storico di Corsica*, V, 14 (1929).

Espitalier, A., *Napoleon et le roi Murat* (Paris, 1910).

Faure, Maurice, 'Murat en Provence', in *Revue des Deux Mondes*, 12 (1960).

Fortunato, G., *La badia di Monticchio* (Trani, 1904).

Fortunato, G., 'La ultime ore di Gioacchino Murat', in *Nuova Antologia*, I, May (1925).

Fortunato, G., *L'ultimo autografo politico di re Gioacchino* (Cosenza, 1917).

Franchetti, A., *Gioacchino Murat secondo i documenti di Roma e Vienna* (Rome, 1876).

Franceschetti, Domenico Cesare, *Mémoires sur les événements qui ont précédé la mort de Joachim 1er, roi des Deux-Siciles* (Paris, 1826).

Franceschetti, Domenico Cesare, *Supplément aux mémoires sur les événements qui ont précédé la mort de Joachim 1er, roi des Deux-Siciles* (Paris, 1829).

Fusaro, Patrizia Giulia, *Le carte Murat. Inventario degli atti riguardanti l'arresto e il processo a G. Murat (1815–1817)* (Cosenza, 2002).

Galvani, Matthieu, *Mémoire sur les événements qui ont précédé la mort de J. Murat* (Paris, 1850).

Gasparri, Gaetano, *La fine di un re: Murat al Pizzo* (Monteloene, 1894).

Guardione, Francesco, *Murat in Italia* (Florence, 1916).

Haegele, Vincent, *Murat: la solitude du cavalier* (Paris, 2015).

Helfert, Joseph Alexander, Freiherr von, *Joachim Murat – Seine letzten Kàmpfe, und sein Ende* (Vienna, 1878).

Johnston, Robert M., *The Napoleonic Empire in Southern Italy and the Rise of the Secret Societies* (London, 1904).

La Rocca, Jean, *Le roi Murat et ses derniers jours* (Paris, 1868).

Lemmi, Francesco, 'La fine di Gioacchino Murat', in *Archivio Storico Italiano*, 26, 220 (1900).

Lorenzo, Renata de, *Murat* (Rome, 2011).

Lorenzo, Renata de, 'Vivere e morire da re', in L. Mascilli M. (ed.), *A passo di carica. Murat re di Napoli*, Exhibition catalogue (Naples, 2015).

Lumbroso, Alberto, *L'agonia di uno regno. Gioacchino Murat al Pizzo* (Rome, 1904).

Lumbroso, Alberto, *Muratiana* (Rome, 1898).

Maceroni (or Macirone), Francis, *A Few Specimens of the Ars Logica Copleiana or Solicitor General's Logic* (London, 1820).

Maceroni, Francis, *Interesting facts relating to the fall and death of Joachim Murat, King of Naples: the capitulation of Paris in 1815 and the second restoration of the Bourbons: original letters from King Joachim to the author, with some account of the author, and of his persecution by the French government* (London, 1817).

Maceroni, Francis, *Memoirs of the life and adventures of Colonel Maceroni* (London, 1838).

Mallardi, Giuseppe, *Durante il regno di Gioacchino Murat. Diario di un capitano dei Lancieri* (Nardo, 2017).

Manchon, Pierre-Yves, *La mort de Murat et la promotion Romanesque d'une légitimité politique nationale*, thesis (Aix-Marseille, 2016).

Masson, Frédéric, 'D'Ischia au Pizzo. Les derniers jours de Murat 19 mai – 13 octobre 1815', in *Revue des Deux Mondes*, 49, 2 (1919).

Molè, Raffaele, *Fasti e nefasti della città di Pizzo* (Pizzo, 1947).

Orefice, Antonella (ed.), 'Gli ultimi giorni di Gioacchino Murat. La cronaca da un manoscritto del 1838', in *Nuovo Monitore Napoletano* (September 2013); Testimony of Giuseppe Panella.

Palermo, Francesco, *Vita e fatti di Vito Nunziante* (Florence, 1839).

Pellegrini, Amedeo, *Il capitano Trentacapilli, a proposito dell' arresto di Gioacchino Murat* (Monteleone, 1904).

Pepe, G., *Memorie*, vol. I (Paris, 1847).

Perodi, P., *Memoirs of the reign of Murat; in which the circumstances of the confiscation of the American vessels, his last campaign and death, and the character of his generals and courtiers, are fully displayed* (Boston, 1818).

Pignatelli, Francesco, *Memorie di un generale della repubblica e dell'impero,* a cura di N. Cortese (Bari, 1927).

Pignatelli, Francesco, *Poche osservazioni sopra l'opuscolo del General Colletta intitolato 'Pochi fatti su Gioacchino Murat'* (Naples, 1820).

Pinto, Francesco (Prince d'Ischitella), *Mémoires et souvenirs de ma vie* (Paris, 1864).

Poisson, 'Les comptes de Murat', in *Revue du souvenir napoleonien,* 396 (1994).

Poli, Bernard, 'Mémoires du Commandant Bernard Poli, officier de Napoleon', in *Etudes Corses,* 1 (1955).

Poupé, Edmond, 'La Cour prévôtale du Var, 1816–1818', in *Bulletin de la Société d'études scientifiques et archéologiques de la ville de Draguignan* (1914).

Provost, Sylvie, 'Les derneiers mois de Murat en Provence et en Corse' in *Le Carnet de Cavalier et Roi,* 25 (1994).

Radowski, F., *Casi memorabili antichi e moderni del Regno di Napoli ricavati dagli auto-grafi del conte R.* (Coblenz, 1842).

Rasponi, L., *Souvenirs d'enfance de la comtesse Rasponi fille de Joachim Murat (1805–1815), publiés par le comte Spalletti* (Paris, 1929).

Romano, G., *Ricordi murattiani. L'arresto e il supplizio di Murat. Narrazione del canonico Masdea con altri documenti* (Pavia 1890).

Sarrazin, J., *Défense des Bourbons de Naples contre les panégyristes de l'usurpateur Murat* (Paris, 1815).

Sassenay, Marquis de, *Les derniers mois de Murat* (Paris, 1896).

Travali, Giuseppe, *Documenti su lo sbarco la cattura e la morte di Re Gioacchino. Murat al Pizzo* (Palermo, 1895).

Tulard, Jean, *Murat* (Paris, 1999).

Valente, Angela, *Gioacchino Murat e l'Italia meridionale* (Turin, 1963).

Vanel, Jean, 'Les derniers jours de Joachim Murat', in *Le Carnet de Cavalier et Roi,* 1 (1969).

Weil, M.H., *Joachim Murat roi de Naples. La dernière année du Règne,* 5 vol. (Paris, 1909).

Archive material
Original documents have been transcribed in Valente's work above and in a series of articles entitled 'Sullo sbarco di G. Murat al Pizzo di Calabria' in the *Rivista di fanteria,* Anno XIII, fasc 1–5 (1904).

France: La Roche-sur-Yon
Archives départementales de la Vendée La Roche-sur-Yon.
Archives militaires de la reconquête du Midi après les Cent Jours (correspondence Marquis de Rivière and Damas).

France: Paris
Archives Nationales de France.
Fonds Murat
31AP/10: 42 (Le Journal du Général Rossetti).

31AP/21 dossiers 358 (Ornano and Maceroni), 359 (Maceroni), 361 (Armand), 362 (Charles), 363 (Galvani), 368 (Poli), 515 (lettres).
31AP/32 Lettres d'anciens soldats et serviteurs du roi Murat.

Italy: Cosenza
Archivio di Stato di Cosenza. Regional archives.

Italy: Naples
Archivio di Stato di Napoli.

- Archivio Borbone, particularly cartons 141, 622 (Carte dell'arresto e condanna di Gioacchino Murat), 623 and 624 (Sull' arresto di Murat), 656 (Carte relative l'arresto e il processo di Gioacchino Murat, includes interrogations of Murat's followers).
- Archivio Nunziante, V Parte, Storia della famiglia: Arresto e processo del generale Gioacchino Murat, 02.058 seq. Mostly official reports relating to Murat's landing and arrest.

Biblioteca della Società di Storia Patria in Napoli.
Carte d'Ayala (XIV, B 2).

Biblioteca del Museo nazionale di S. Martino.
Manuscript, Dall'arresto all'esecuzione di Gioacchino Murat. Arresto del Generale Giacchino Murat seguito a 8 Ottobre 1815. Condanna di morte fatta, ed eseguita a 13 dello stesso Mese, e Anno nel Castello della città di Pizzo e contiene anche l'ultima lettera di Gioacchino a Carolina. Archivio Storico, Stipo 9, fasc. 19.

United Kingdom: London
British Library.
Add MSS 35651 (account of Colonel Robinson's interview); Add MS41537 (Antonio Perri's account); Add MS 41534 (Maceroni's papers).